osCommerce Webmaster's Guide to Selling Online

Increase your sales and profits with expert tips on SEO, marketing, design, selling strategies, etc.

Vadym Gurevych

BIRMINGHAM - MUMBAI

osCommerce Webmaster's Guide to Selling Online

First published: December 2007

Production Reference: 1071207

Published by Packt Publishing Ltd.
32 Lincoln Road
Olton
Birmingham, B27 6PA, UK.

ISBN 978-1-847192-02-8

www.packtpub.com

Cover Image by Vinayak Chittar (vinayak.chittar@gmail.com)

Credits

Author

Vadym Gurevych

Reviewer

Monika Mathé

Senior Acquisition Editor

Douglas Paterson

Development Editor

Nikhil Bangera

Technical Editor

Ajay S.

Editorial Manager

Dipali Chittar

Project Manager

Abhijeet Deobhakta

Project Coordinator

Patricia Weir

Indexer

Hemangini Bari

Proofreader

Chris Smith

Production Coordinator

Shantanu Zagade

Cover Designer

Shantanu Zagade

About the Author

Vadym Gurevych holds a Masters of Software Development degree from Kharkov National Technical University (Ukraine) and has been creating commercial software products for businesses for 10 years. His interest in learning more about the management and business side of the process led him to join DataLink UK Ltd. in 2001 as Project Manager.

Based in the UK, Datalink (which also trades as Holbi) concentrates on providing a wide range of bespoke e-commerce solutions to its local and international customers. In those days, Vadym didn't imagine managing open-source projects, but since 2002 he has been creating osCommerce-based sites and this has become Datalink's main source of revenue since 2004. Now Business Development Manager of DataLink UK Ltd., Vadym is responsible for strategy development and business decisions, and for ensuring that his team of 30 provides customers with the most efficient solutions. Since he finds it exciting and sometimes challenging, he still personally supervises major sales deals and manages major projects. He has been happily married to his wife Elena for almost eight years now, and also finds time to write/maintain a popular blog, `http://www.oscommerceblog.com`, and contribute to `http://www.datalinkuk.com` and `http://www.holbi.co.uk`.

I'd like to dedicate the book to my wife Elena who inspired me to write the book and helped me a lot along the way, and who was very patient with me being "absent" while working late evenings and weekends, and to my father Eugene who I hope will find it interesting to read it.

I'd like to thank these wonderful people who helped me a lot with the book, and without whom I would have never done it:

Vladislav Malyshev, the best business partner I've ever had, and all my colleagues at DataLink UK Ltd., and Timo Brueggemann who introduced me to the world of osCommerce. Packt Publishing team of editors whose help was of the most value, Monika Mathé and Achim Keiser for their reviews and valuable comments, Appliance World UK Ltd. team for their trust and cooperation, James Knight and Russell Brammer for hundreds of fresh ideas and inspiration they gave me.

About the Reviewer

Monika Mathé, fascinated by being able to combine logic and creativity, became a software developer and Oracle Certified Database Administrator.

Landing a position in a marketing agency and working with everything from Oracle to SQL Server and HTML, ASP, and JavaScript, she learned more about marketing campaigns, e-commerce, CMS, and CRM.

Being an active member of the osCommerce Online Community, she knows preemptively which questions will arise in new shop creation. Presently, she is creating as many customized shops for clients as time permits.

With special thanks to my family, my forum friends, and my clients all over the world. You are the spice of my life!

Table of Contents

Preface

osCommerce is an open-source e-commerce solution written in PHP and MySQL that can be set up on various platforms. More than 10,000 businesses and sole traders all around the world benefit from its features and flexibility.

The importance of the osCommerce community consisting of over 100,000 cannot be stressed enough as this is where both online merchants and web developers can communicate and find solutions. There are many "contributions"—modules for osCommerce that further extend its functionality—making it suitable for almost every business's requirements.

We will look into the practical techniques and proven strategies to increase online sales: learn from an expert! This book is for anyone administering a small/medium sized osCommerce site.

This book will help you increase your sales and profits with expert tips on SEO, marketing, design, selling strategies, etc.

What This Book Covers

Chapter 1 is a brief introduction to osCommerce, and teaches you how to calculate and monitor profits. Attracting visitors to your website is an essential task to gear the business up.

Chapter 2 reviews several ways to advertise and get visitors to your site, including: organic search, banners, pop-ups, link exchange, affiliate programs, newsletters, forums and blogs, and online directories. This chapter has extensive insights on how to track the efficiency (and other variables) of an advertising campaign.

Chapter 3 shows you how to race to the top of search engine result pages. You will learn methods, techniques, and actions to make your store easily accessible to and indexed by search engines. If you decide to keep ahead of the game and hire a professional SEO consultant, you will want to dig deeper into this chapter where we review aspects of hiring professional SEO consultants and show how to track SEO campaign results. This chapter familiarizes you with the good and bad search engines practices and helps you find which keywords work best.

Chapter 4 concentrates on solutions and practices that help authoring original dynamic content, for your users and customers to post content online. We review the benefits of using dynamic content solutions like CMS, forums, blogs, and feeds, and their integration with osCommerce.

Chapter 5 gives you insight on why it is important to build customer confidence and how to do it. We review ways to improve your online store and business model to make customers more confident about placing orders with your online store. A good design often spells the difference between failure and success.

Chapter 6 covers effective design of an online store; here you will learn to optimize design for different types of customers and customize it to match your corporate identity. We discuss common-sense approaches to developing design templates and also tackle practical issues like caching and improving page loading speed using database and PHP script optimization to ensure a smoother customer experience.

Chapter 7 takes a look at how sales can be improved in osCommerce by improving your product catalog. It concentrates on improving navigation and making customer interaction intuitive and friendly.

Chapter 8 is a discussion on how and why order values can be increased, and what effect this has on the turnover and profit figures. It shows how to increase order values by putting both the customer and the online merchant in a win-win situation. Understand the dynamics of cross-linking products, creating product bundles, configurable products, and employing the minimum order amount strategy.

Chapter 9 covers how to run a properly planned promotion campaign, while keeping an eye on operational costs. The turnover of an online store can be increased by increasing its market share—this chapter shows your how. From grabbing customers to maximizing what you get from your suppliers, running affiliate programs, and B2B programs for trade customers.

Chapter 10 shows you how important it is to monitor and constantly improve the conversion rates of online business, and analyzes how conversion rates affect profitability of the business. It shows how to improve the checkout process in osCommerce, and how to utilize individual customer accounts to increase sales.

Chapter 11 is a further exploration of monitoring of the performance of the website by creating and of course understanding various reports, and using statistical information to improve the efficiency of an osCommerce-based online business. In this chapter you will get an insider's understanding of using and extending the reporting facility of osCommerce, including: reports to plan your advertising budget, re-arrange advertising campaigns, track and forecast sale figures, find bestselling and most profitable products, manufacturers, and categories and highlight certain products by marking them as featured, locate best-buying customers and reward them, track stock and ease re-ordering of the most popular products from suppliers, track customers and use previous order history for marketing purposes, send targeted newsletters to customers, and even plan your online store's net profit figures and its profitability.

Chapter 12 will take a look at how the online store can benefit from having repeat customers, and how to convert customers into repeat customers. This chapter shows how to increase this conversion rate by providing loyal customers with additional benefits, like a loyalty points, referral bonuses, etc.

Conventions

In this book, you will find a number of styles of text that distinguish between different kinds of information. Here are some examples of these styles, and an explanation of their meaning.

Code words in text are shown as follows: "We can include other contexts through the use of the `include` directive."

A block of code will be set as follows:

```
<tr>
    <td>
        <?php echo tep_display_banner('static', $banner); ?>
    </td>
</tr>
```

New terms and **important words** are introduced in a bold-type font. Words that you see on the screen, in menus or dialog boxes for example, appear in our text like this: "clicking the **Next** button moves you to the next screen".

 Important notes appear in a box like this.

Tips and tricks appear like this.

Reader Feedback

Feedback from our readers is always welcome. Let us know what you think about this book, what you liked or may have disliked. Reader feedback is important for us to develop titles that you really get the most out of.

To send us general feedback, simply drop an email to feedback@packtpub.com, making sure to mention the book title in the subject of your message.

If there is a book that you need and would like to see us publish, please send us a note in the **SUGGEST A TITLE** form on www.packtpub.com or email suggest@packtpub.com.

If there is a topic that you have expertise in and you are interested in either writing or contributing to a book, see our author guide on www.packtpub.com/authors.

Customer Support

Now that you are the proud owner of a Packt book, we have a number of things to help you to get the most from your purchase.

Errata

Although we have taken every care to ensure the accuracy of our contents, mistakes do happen. If you find a mistake in one of our books—maybe a mistake in text or code—we would be grateful if you would report this to us. By doing this you can save other readers from frustration, and help to improve subsequent versions of this book. If you find any errata, report them by visiting http://www.packtpub.com/support, selecting your book, clicking on the **Submit Errata** link, and entering the details of your errata. Once your errata are verified, your submission will be accepted and the errata added to the list of existing errata. The existing errata can be viewed by selecting your title from http://www.packtpub.com/support.

Questions

You can contact us at questions@packtpub.com if you are having a problem with some aspect of the book, and we will do our best to address it.

1
Increasing Profits and Sales with osCommerce

I was thinking about how to start this book. There's definitely going to be a lot to tell, explain, and discuss in the further chapters, but the first one was not that obvious. So what to start it with?

Probably from: Why are you reading this book right now?

According to the U.S. Census Bureau News (dated May 18, 2006):

"The Census Bureau of the Department of Commerce announced today that the estimate of U.S. retail e-commerce sales for the first quarter of 2006…was $25.2 billion, an increase of 7 % from the fourth quarter of 2005."

This of course happens not only in the US, but also in the UK, Europe, Russia, East, Japan, Asia, Australia — literally in every place where access to the Internet has been made easy by the governmental and commercial organizations, and where there are online payment methods in use.

Selling goods and services online is in most of the cases easier and cheaper than running a brick and mortar store or mail catalog business. Of course, this doesn't work for everyone, but most small, medium, and large businesses already benefit from using e-commerce for online sales. Some businesses go 100% online, some use e-commerce supplementary to their main business. And of course a well-thought-of business idea, competitive products or services, and strong organization are the primary keys to success, as with any traditional business.

This book is first of all dedicated to the businesses that use osCommerce or osCommerce-based e-commerce solutions to drive their online sales. It is dedicated to business owners, general managers, and e-commerce and marketing managers. It will be useful to web developers and web designers who create osCommerce solutions. Knowing how to make the most of an osCommerce-based online business is a benefit not only to the business itself, but literally to everybody who's involved as supplier, developer, or consultant.

osCommerce is suitable for small, medium, and large businesses. According to www.oscommerce.com, there are over 11,000 online stores, and these are only the ones registered in the Live Stores directory. For just one of the examples that prove that the e-commerce solution is really great for businesses of any size, look at the Google Store website www.google-store.com, which is based on osCommerce. Self-employed online merchants, family businesses, small businesses, retailers of almost any size, manufacturers and distributors—they power their online businesses with osCommerce.

Why osCommerce?

Having now worked with osCommerce for more than five years, while interacting with many companies and individuals, I have never found a person who wished to switch to another solution once they had an osCommerce-based online business. Instead, I've seen quite a number of people who'd like to move to osCommerce from other, custom made or publicly available online store solutions.

It's very easy to start selling online using osCommerce. Its standard installation already contains all the features and facilities to build an online store and start online sales.

For end customers, it is easy to browse and search for products, use the shopping cart, personal account with previous order history, checkout with several shipping and payment methods, and all this in multiple languages.

For Shop Administrators and online merchants, it has first of all a manageable product catalog with a tree of categories and products, a tool for customer and order management, and sales reports—among other things.

But the real key to the success of osCommerce lies in it being an Open Source solution, and in a community of more than 100,000 members who have developed more than 3,500 useful contributions (add-ons). Taking compatibility issues aside, an osCommerce store owner can add credit modules, features, images add-ons, informational boxes, additional languages, order total modules, payment and shipping modules, reports, templates/themes, and other contributions to an osCommerce-based website. More members join and more contributions get submitted daily.

Besides the standard version of osCommerce developed by its team, there exist alternative versions. Some are free, while some need to be paid for. Alternative versions usually contain a number of contributions already pre-installed, so that the store owner gets an even more featured solution for online business.

What is the Book About?

Being familiar with osCommerce and most probably already using it for your business you (business owner, marketing manager, e-commerce manager, web master) would like to learn how to increase online sales, how to increase profits and minimize expenses, how to improve your online business.

This book gives you tips and tricks from which you will gain maximum possible mileage for your osCommerce installation. This book has a plenty of advice and explains approaches based on the real-life experiences of osCommerce store owners and osCommerce developers. Every piece of advice in this book can be applicable or not applicable to a particular business—and the final decision should always be made by the business owner or online store manager.

So, what are the main goals that we try to achieve with every business?

- Increase profits.
- Which means for online businesses: increasing of online sales, and decreasing all operational, advertising, marketing and sales costs.

Profits First

OK, now we have come to the point where we want to increase profits. But first before increasing them, it would be useful to know how to calculate profit. Is the online business profitable or not?

Your accountant would probably have an answer to that question, but let us see how it's possible to calculate and monitor profits in an easier way.

So what does profit consist of? First of all, we will need to determine a period of time for which we will calculate the profit. It can be a month, a quarter, a year, or maybe a week or even a day. Then, we will need to find out the total turnover generated by the website during this period. A little trick here is that some of your offline (phone, shop) sales will be actually generated by the website. In order to properly track the online business's profits, you will need to have a referral tracking system in place. It will be enough to ask the customer before taking a phone order, where they heard about you. If the answer is "your website"—here we have another sale generated online. And so, we write down the turnover for that period of time.

Now the less pleasant part—expenses. Here we need to firstly determine the cost of products sold for the given period of time. If you buy products and your suppliers change price as time goes by, it will make perfect sense to store the product costs from the suppliers in each order placed by your customers, so that you can see the actual profit level for any period in the past.

Then come the taxes. You may have taxable and non-taxable goods in the product catalog. Also, not all your customers pay tax, so the calculations here have to be very accurate to find out proper figures.

Then comes delivery and handling charges, which actually depend on the goods you sell; but many online businesses tend to consider the handling fee to be equal for every product or order.

> We should clearly understand the difference between the Actual Shipping Charges (i.e. the expenses paid to deliver the goods to the customers) and Customer's Shipping Charges (i.e. the amount charged to the customer in addition to the order amount to cover the delivery charges). We will deduct Actual Shipping and Handling Charges to find the profits.

One more very important line in the calculations is the advertising expenses. While sometimes it's not possible to know the exact amount spent on a certain advertising campaign per given period, it's always possible to find out an approximate amount. For example, finding an approximate daily expenditure for a certain advertising campaign and multiplying it by the number of days in the period you're calculating the profits for. Of course, we should be aware if multiple advertising campaigns were running at that time, and calculate all advertising expenses.

We should continue with deducting operational costs like service and labor expenses, which would consist of the costs of updating the website, running the office, the warehouse, the call center, paying the employees, etc. It makes sense to take an average service and labor cost of running the business for the same period and split it into two parts correspondingly to how much turnover has been generated by online and offline parts of the business.

	Online Turnover
+	Offline Turnover (referred from the website)
–	Product Costs
–	Taxes
–	Shipping Fees
–	Handling Fees

- Advertising Expenses

- Service Expenses

- Labor Expenses

= Online Profits

So for each given period of time, approximate actual profits generated by your online store would consist of Online Turnover plus a Part of the Offline Turnover generated through the websites less Product Costs, less Taxes, less Actual Shipping and Handling Fees, less Advertising Expenses, and less Service and Labor expenses.

OK, we have all those nice figures, we know how to find approximate online profits—what should we do next? We will learn how to monitor profitability of the business on daily/weekly bases. Its very important to be able to see the dynamics of how the profit level changes daily or weekly, as this is the only way to make business decisions based on facts rather than on "gut feeling".

We will play with an electronic spreadsheet and draw up a table there. MS Excel or Open Office Calc will do well. Let's put in the following columns:

- Date (or number of the week)
- Number of new customer registrations
- Number of orders placed
- Online Turnover plus the part of the Offline Turnover generated through the website
- Product Costs
- Taxes
- Actual Shipping and Handling Fees
- Advertising Expenses
- Service and Labor Expenses
- Profit
- Profit versus Online Turnover (in %)
- Comments

	A	B	C	D	E	F	G	H	I	J	K	L
1	#	Cust.	Ord.	Turnover	Prod. Costs	Taxes	Shipping	Ad costs	Srv. / labor	Profit	Profit %	Comments
2	1	14	12	$14,667.00	$10,637.00	$2,184.45	$240.00	$233.33	$1,000.00	$372.22	2.54%	
3	2	14	13	$16,603.00	$11,973.00	$2,472.79	$260.00	$233.33	$1,000.00	$663.88	4.00%	
4	3	7	8	$7,772.00	$5,661.00	$1,157.53	$160.00	$233.33	$1,000.00	-$439.87	-5.66%	
5	4	19	15	$14,355.00	$10,339.00	$2,137.98	$300.00	$233.33	$1,000.00	$344.69	2.40%	
6	5	32	26	$21,204.00	$15,128.00	$3,158.04	$520.00	$400.00	$1,000.00	$997.96	4.71%	Inc. Ad budget
7	6	40	33	$27,612.00	$20,151.00	$4,112.43	$660.00	$400.00	$1,000.00	$1,288.57	4.67%	
8	7	65	45	$39,614.00	$29,152.00	$5,899.96	$900.00	$400.00	$1,000.00	$2,262.04	5.71%	
9	8											
10	9											

By filling in the table daily or weekly, we will not only see the profits changing as time goes by we will also see, for example, how the turnover changes — and most importantly — how the relation between Profit and Turnover changes with time. Obviously, the higher the profit percentage of the Turnover, the better optimized the business model is.

Sometimes you will find that even though the turnover has increased, the profit has stayed the same — which means you're doing more work for actually the same amount of money.

Sometimes you will find that even though both the turnover and profits have increased, the figures in the last column (relation between Profit and Turnover) have worsened — this means that the business model needs optimizing as operational costs have grown too fast (and too much!) as compared to the profit.

This table, if filled in regularly, will also give a good idea of how the advertising expenses affect profits. And, assuming all major website updates and improvements are put into the Comments field, they will give an idea of how this or that feature, change, upgrade may have affected the online turnover and profit.

The Strategy to Profit

Now we know how to calculate turnover, calculate profit, and see the dynamics of profit change with time. We can now concentrate on what this book is about — reviewing various possible ways to increase profit.

There are several strategies applicable to an online business, and we will cover them all in further chapters. They are:

- Increasing the number of visitors to your website
- Increasing the conversion rate of visitors to customers
- Increasing the amount of average orders

- Increasing the number of repeat customers
- Decreasing operational costs (advertising, handling and processing, service fees, etc.)

Summary

In this chapter, we have seen a brief introduction to osCommerce, and learned how to calculate and monitor profits. We have reviewed at least one simple and straightforward method to see profit figures changing with time, and have briefly touched several business strategies that become possible with osCommerce. We will review them in more detail in further chapters of this book.

We didn't talk about how to select products for online sales, why osCommerce is the e-commerce solution of our choice, and what to do with a pet dog when it misbehaves—because this book is dedicated to those merchants who already trade online or are planning to start online trading in the nearest time, and have already chosen osCommerce as the online store solution; also, we have no idea about the latter!

This book is based on over five years of the author's continuous experience building online businesses with osCommerce. All approaches and techniques described here and further are proven to have worked well for over 600 successful osCommerce-based online businesses all around the Globe in development or improvement of which the author took active part as osCommerce developer, but mostly as project manager or online business consultant.

2

Advertising an Online Store

"Why does my website or product need to be advertised?"; if you ask yourself such a question—this chapter will most probably not answer it. Only a few, if any, websites and products are so unique that the customers will run off their feet to find a path to their web pages and place orders online. Because of the most serious competition ever, in almost every market niche, attracting visitors to your website becomes an essential task to gear the business up.

What can be Advertised?

This in fact, depends on your advertising and marketing strategy. One can say at least three types of advertisement may attract more visitors to your website.

First, the website itself can be advertised. Potential visitors should be given descriptive and attractive information about the website, and about products and services they can get there.

Secondly, new and unique products can be advertised. This will stimulate potential visitors' interest in products and services available from your website.

Finally, the advertisement may contain information about discounted prices and special offers on the products available from other online and offline stores. It will explain the benefits of buying those well known products and services from your online store.

How to Advertise

There are plenty of ways to give potential customers more information about your business, your products, and your services. From online banners and TV commercials to drawings on somebody's scalp and billboards in downtown. From short printed ads in the evening newspaper to painted vehicles and product and brand placement in blockbusters.

In this chapter, we will consider several very effective ways to advertise an online store on the Internet. An effective way to advertise is one that brings as much profit as possible i.e. one that is considerably less expensive than the turnover generated by the attracted customers; one that brings profit.

Tracking Efficiency of the Advertising Efforts

We will call an advertising campaign: all advertising efforts related to promoting either the entire business, or some products and services, or some special prices and offers to prospective customers in a certain period of time, using one or several advertising approaches.

For each ad campaign, it should be relatively easy to determine its cost by adding up all the costs of all the involved advertising efforts.

Now, how do we calculate the generated turnover? It is possible to use special tracking codes in each ad. Your prospective customers will be asked to either enter it on your website during the ordering process, or tell your sales representative when placing an order on phone.

Of course, entering the tracking code should be made beneficial to your customers as well. For example, by entering the tracking (reference) code, the customer may automatically become a participant in a lottery, where the prize is either one of the products available in your online store, or one of the popular products or services from your partner businesses that your customers may be interested in.

Tracking codes can also give customers certain discounts on the orders they place or provide them with free shipping service. It is possible to use an osCommerce contribution called Credit Class and Gift Voucher to implement proper tracking codes functionality.

By knowing the expenses and the generated turnover, it's really easy to see how effective this or that ad campaign is. Actually, we should always compare advertising expenses and generated profit! For example, a successful ad campaign would bring twice as much profit as it costs. Obviously, if profit only covers advertising costs you should re-consider either the ad campaign, or maybe even the entire business model.

Advertising in Search Engines

Advertising in search engines is probably the most effective way to promote your entire website, products, and services online, if you sell well known products and services. Nowadays, prospective customers search for such goods in search engines by entering keywords and key phrases, and search engines bring up the list of websites that best correspond to the entered terms.

How do search engines know about such sites? First of all, they use special "crawling bots"—special software that "crawls" through as many websites as possible and collects information directly from the web pages. This data then gets indexed, and is later used by the search engines to determine if the website will appear in search results in response to the customer's search request. Secondly, many search engines support online directories of websites, and allow a new website to be submitted into the corresponding part of such directory.

Some of the top search engines where a store owner may want to register their websites are Google, Yahoo!, Live Search (MSN), AOL, Lycos, and Ask. Since many search engines use the dmoz.org open directory, submitting an online store into the corresponding category on dmoz.org will help the search engines to find out about your website. Of course, if there is an opportunity to put a link to the online store on another (quite popular) website, this may speed up things as search engines will most probably spot out the link and spider through the pages of the online store sooner.

Search results that are displayed to customers usually contain the link to the website or one if its pages, site or page title, and description either extracted from the web page by the search engine automatically—or specified by the webmaster on submission of the website to the search engine's directory.

In the following screenshot, Page title is marked with 1, and page description with 2.

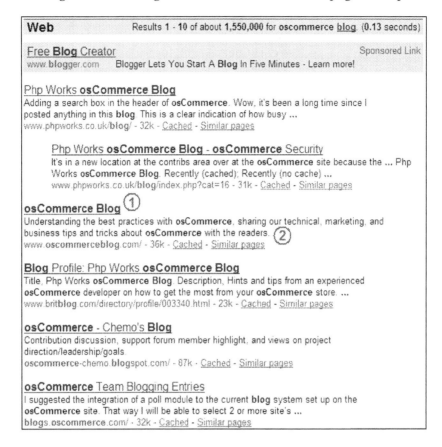

Editing page description tags (META tags) is really easy in the default installation of osCommerce. The most direct method is not so advanced as it should be, and basically requires manually editing each page script where you'd like to place proper META tags and page titles.

For example, to edit the description of the online store, the webmaster may want to edit the `index.php` file, which is located in the root folder of the installed osCommerce website. The webmaster would find the following code:

```
<head>
<meta http-equiv="Content-Type" content="text/html; charset=<?php echo
CHARSET; ?>">
<title><?php echo TITLE; ?></title>
<base href="<?php echo (($request_type == 'SSL') ? HTTPS_SERVER :
HTTP_SERVER) . DIR_WS_CATALOG; ?>">
<link rel="stylesheet" type="text/css" href="stylesheet.css">
</head>
```

and enhance it with the following inclusions:

```
<head>
<meta http-equiv="Content-Type" content="text/html; charset=<?php echo
CHARSET; ?>">
<META NAME="Description" Content="Here would go short description
of the web site, that is used by Search Engines to display web site
information in the search results listing">
<META NAME="Keywords" CONTENT="keyphrases, the most important
keywords, in multiple combinations, would be, placed here">
<title><?php echo TITLE; ?></title>
<base href="<?php echo (($request_type == 'SSL') ? HTTPS_SERVER :
HTTP_SERVER) . DIR_WS_CATALOG; ?>">
<link rel="stylesheet" type="text/css" href="stylesheet.css">
</head>
```

Page title can be set in the corresponding language file, which is usually located in the `/includes/languages/<language_name.php>` file.

For English it's usually: `/includes/languages/english.php`.

By default all osCommerce pages have one and the same title, which is equal to the name of the online store. The online store name, in its turn, is set in the Administration panel of osCommerce, Configuration section, My Store menu. Each page can be edited to have its own unique title.

Depending on how relevant the content of the website or one of its pages is to the search query, and how popular the website is, the link to the website will appear closer or farther from the beginning of the search results list.

Paid Advertisements

If you have a new website, or if there are too many competitors in your market niche, advertising through organic search may not work for your business.

In this case, you may want to consider paid advertisements in search engines. The goal of paid advertisements is to attract the customer's attention to the website or its specific sections on the search results page. Paid advertisements may allow for highlighting the website's link in the search results, bringing it to the very top of the search results list.

In early days, store owners were charged a fixed fee per each impression of their ads; now they are only charged when a user actually clicks on the ad to get to the advertised website. This is called Pay Per Click (PPC).

Due to high competition in the market, instead of a fixed fee the store owner is asked to specify the highest affordable fee per click, which affects position of the paid ad in the search results page.

Flexible enough, the paid advertisement allows for "bidding" on specific keywords or phrases that the store owner believes the target audience would use when looking for their type of products or services.

It's also possible to specify the highest affordable monthly budget and leave the search provider to decide when to display the advertisement and where on the search results page.

While many companies exist in this market space, Google AdWords and Yahoo! Search Marketing, which was formerly Overture, are the largest network operators as of 2006. MSN has started beta-testing with its own PPC services MSN adCenter. Depending on the search engine, minimum prices per click start at US$0.01 (up to US$0.50). Very popular search terms can cost much more on popular engines.

With either Google Adwords or Yahoo! Overture, it's possible to create advertising campaigns and manage them, i.e. track results—like impressions and clicks. What's also important—is that it is possible to get some sort of advice by using bid cost estimation utilities to see which search terms are more popular among the users and which search terms are more popular among other advertisers (i.e. where the cost is higher).

On the two following screenshots, we can see how a paid advertisement looks on the search results page in Google:

Web	Results 1 - 10 of about **1,580,000** for **oscommerce** books. (0.06 seconds)

osCommerce Books Announced by Packt Publishing
osCommerce Books Announced by Packt Publishing. Tuesday, November 30, 1999 |
News | Open Source Packt Publishing is pleased to announce details of two new ...
www.packtpub.com/article/oscommerce_books_announced_by_packt_publishing - 15k -
Cached - Similar pages

> Building Online Stores with **osCommerce**: Professional Edition
> As well as everything you need to get started with **osCommerce**, this book ...
> Then check out Packt's latest **book** on **osCommerce**. Deep Inside **osCommerce**:
> The ...
> www.packtpub.com/professional_oscommerce/book - 32k -
> Cached - Similar pages

osCommerce Books, Guides and Tutorials
osCommerce Books, Guides and Tutorials. The biggest problem most users have when
setting up their **osCommerce** store is the lack of documentation suitable for ...
www.oscommercebooks.com/ - 6k - Cached - Similar pages

Amazon.co.uk: Deep Inside **OsCommerce**: The Cookbook: **Books**:
Monika ...
Amazon.co.uk: Deep Inside **OsCommerce**: The Cookbook: **Books**: Monika Mathé by
Monika Mathé.
www.amazon.co.uk/Deep-Inside-OsCommerce-Monika-Mathé/dp/1847190901 - 78k -
Cached - Similar pages

> Amazon.co.uk: Building Online Stores with **OsCommerce**:
> Professional ...
> As well as everything you need to get started with **osCommerce**, this **book** goes
> onto cover how to: Increase your sales through cross-selling and up-selling ...
> www.amazon.co.uk/Building-Online-Stores-OsCommerce-
> Professional/dp/1904811140 - 69k - Cached - Similar pages

oscbooks.com - **osCommerce** Tutorials | **osCommerce** eBooks ...
Offers eBooks detailing how to make **osCommerce** site more appealing to visitors and the
Search Engines.
www.oscbooks.com/ - 6k - Cached - Similar pages

Welcome - Green **Books**, independent UK publishing company
Green **Books** is an independent publisher of **books** on a wide range of ... We are an
independent UK publishing company producing books on a wide range of...

Sponsored Links

Zen Cart eBook - Sale On
"Building An Online Store"
Get the most out of your Zen store.
www.jsweb.co.uk

Oscommerce Online Store
Bespoke Solutions
From £799, Contact Us Today
www.CE.com/OsCommerce

osCommerce templates
Large selection of **osCommerce** skins
templates and other modules
www.algozone.com

osCommerce Experts
taking **osCommerce** to the edge
Designs, Contributions, Custom Code
www.ozeworks.com

Get **osCommerce** Customized
osCommerce Design and Development
Experienced developers. $20 / hour
www.cartue.com/

osCommerce Cookbook
Extend, customize & make money from
your **osCommerce** store with new book
www.packtpub.com/inside_oscommerce

osCommerce installs
oscommerce module installs
expert custom coding
www.spireswebdesign.com

Do Not Install **osCommerce**
Until You Read This Special Notice
It Will Help You Save Time & Money

and Yahoo!:

Search Results   1 - 10 of about 3,280,000 for <u>oscommerce</u> <u>books</u> - 0.08 sec. <u>(About this page)</u>

SPONSOR RESULTS

- **Book** computer online store
  www.shop-com.co.uk - Buy **book** computer online store at SHOP.COM.
  Thousands of Brands.

1. Monika Mathé - Certified Database Professional &
   osCommerce Expert
   Author of. **osCommerce Books**. in English and German. top ... Google's #1
   osCommerce Expert. My Quality. Meet the Coder. About my Company.
   Book Projects ...
   www.oscommerce-books.com - 35k - <u>Cached</u> - <u>More from this site</u>

2. Building Online Stores with **osCommerce**: Professional Edition
   ... and immediate companion or alternative to print **books**. ... As well as
   everything you need to get started with **osCommerce**, this **book** goes onto
   cover how to: ...
   www.packtpub.com/professional_oscommerce/book - 32k - <u>Cached</u> - <u>More</u>
   <u>from this site</u>

3. Amazon.com: Building Online Stores with **osCommerce**:
   Professional ...
   ... Online Stores with **osCommerce**: Professional Edition: **Books**: David
   Mercer by David Mercer ... Explore similar items : **Books** (49) Editorial
   Reviews. **Book** Description ...
   amazon.com/Building-Online-Stores-osCommerce-Professional/dp/... - 131k -
   <u>Cached</u> - <u>More from this site</u>

4. **osCommerce** Manuals by Pithy Productions Inc.
   This **osCommerce book** is written in plain language for the non-technical
   user. ... loaded chain reaction osc max zen zencart zen-cart **oscommerce**
   books writer ...
   www.oscommercemanuals.com - 63k - <u>Cached</u> - <u>More from this site</u>

5. Do **Books** Help - **osCommerce** Community Support Forums
   ... if anyone has used a **book** such as: **osCommerce** Users Manual V. 2.0: A
   Guide ... I was wondering if this or a like **book** might help the beginner to
   osCommerce. ...
   forums.oscommerce.com/index.php?showtopic=152185 - 46k - <u>Cached</u> -
   <u>More from this site</u>

Paid advertisements can promote the online store itself, certain products—or announce certain specific offers that might be of interest to the target audience.

Based on the statistics of impressions, clicks, and purchases it is possible to calculate several important variables for each advertising campaign:

- Cost Per Click (CPC) — by dividing the amount spent on the ad campaign per a specified period of time by the number of clicks made by the prospective customers

- Revenue Per Click (RPC) — by dividing the amount of the generated turnover by the number of clicks

- Click Through Rate (CTR) — by dividing the number of impressions of the advertisement in the search results pages by the number of actual clicks

- Return on Investment (ROI) — by dividing the generated turnover less the costs of the advertising campaign by the costs

Of course, the tasks in front of every online store owner are to minimize CPC, increase RPC, CTR, and ROI, without forgetting about growth of the absolute amounts of profits generated online.

Useful Tips and Best Practices

Here are some tips that can be useful when promoting your online store via paid advertisements:

- An ad should have a call to action by itself; phrases like "see for yourself", "find exactly what you want", "browse and buy online", "contact us" and others may be used.

- Do not use just general terms, like "best", "grand", "cheapest", "all" in the ad, but rather give the prospective customer as reason to visit your online store; for example instead of "cheapest" put "we beat any prices quoted by $5", instead of "best choice of" put "over 8000 products in stock"; use the language your target audience speaks.

- Use more specific terms than general terms when entering keywords that the ad will be related to — this will ensure only your targeted audience see the ad, and also will minimize your advertising expenses; for example, selling drives and motors instead of general term "drives" it is better to use "AC drives" or "Variable Frequency AC Drives", selling kitchen appliances instead of "kitchen appliances" it is better to use "single ovens" or "Bosch single ovens", instead of "fridges" it is better to use "American Foodstore" or "Siemens Fridge Freezer".

- It's not a problem to have many ads for one advertising campaign, if they all lead customers to your online store.

- Design landing pages properly, so that the prospective customers who clicked the link are sent exactly to that part of your website that has direct relation to the paid advertisement they have just seen.

- Use "local" approach—modern day paid advertisement services allow filtering impressions of certain advertisements by locating where the user is currently situated. Therefore, if the store only delivers goods locally or nationwide—there's no sense to advertise its products or its special offers internationally. At the same time, if there are different special offers for domestic and international customers—it would make sense to run two or more corresponding advertising campaigns, each with its own ad text, landing pages, etc.

This will help to minimize the number of customers who exit your website straight away after they reach it.

Continuous monitoring of the performance of online advertisements in search engines, finding the best (i.e. attractive and informative) slogans, determining the most popular and most performing keywords and key phrases, and designing proper landing pages are the key to success and business growth.

Paid advertisements in search engines may boost up online sales, but it should be noted though that users are more likely to follow the links found in search engines in a "natural" way than paid advertisements.

Banners

Banners are yet another way to advertise a website online. Banners can be graphic or textual. It's also possible to include a movie into a banner to catch the user's attention or to give them more information about your website, products, and services. Banners can be of different sizes, and can be included into other websites and into your own site.

First of all, the banner needs to be designed. Like any advertisement, it should aim to grab attention, and contain information about what it promotes. A banner can advertise your website in general, specific products on the website, or some special offers.

Graphic and animated banners should not be made "heavy" to avoid slowing down page loading speed.

Banner Exchange

It is possible to submit a banner into a banner exchange network. It can be a paid service or, in exchange, you will be asked to build a special code into your website's pages so that you display other banners in your turn. The latter option may make sense if your website gets more visitors per a specified period of time than the number of impressions you'd like to have for your banner. Exact rates depend on the banner exchange network, but you should be ready for a 10-20% difference between the number of times your banner will be displayed on other participating websites and the number of times you will display other banners on your website.

A better idea would be to place your banner into the websites that your target audience are visiting relatively often. These can be popular forums, blogs, other portals, or other non-competitive e-commerce websites. Of course, you may be asked to display other banners on your website, or pay some fee for this advertisement.

Positioning in the Page

Where should you have your banner displayed on other websites? Its fairly simple—anywhere where the users will see it. For example, if it's possible, in the header of the web page, or on the left-side of the page, or in the middle. Sometimes, for shorter pages it's OK to have your banner put in the footer of the page, but for longer pages this may not work well as the users may not scroll down to the very bottom of the page and may not see the banner. It should be noted that the fee you pay for having your banners displayed on other websites may depend not only on the size of banner, but also on its location in the pages.

Displaying your banners on your own website helps you to attract the attention of your customers to specific products and services, making it easier for them to get to the most important web pages you want them to see. A banner can be placed on your home page, leading customers to a certain product listing page or product information page. It can advertise special price offers, special discounts, new products, and new features. A banner can be also placed on some pages of your website advertising special delivery services, or limited discounts on a part of the product range. In that case, the banner would lead the customer to a page where more description on the special offer would be displayed.

Note, that banners that do not generate sales but only provide information should not distract the customer's attention from products and services that are being sold on your website.

osCommerce Banner Managements Facilities

It's possible to manage banners in osCommerce using its built-in Banner Management facilities under the Tools menu in the Administration panel. Any number of banner groups can be created, and any number of banners can be added to a group. Clicks and impressions statistics are available in the Administration panel as well. A good improvement would be to have purchase statistics implemented in your osCommerce website for banners, so that you could see clearly which of your banners actually generates sales and brings profits.

There can be multiple banners registered in osCommerce, each belonging to one of the banner groups:

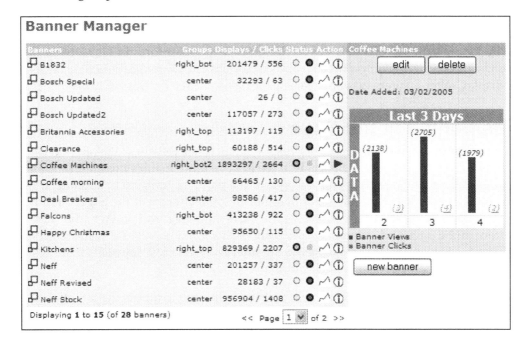

Banner groups can be easily added in the Administration panel of osCommerce when adding/editing a banner:

Banner Manager

Banner Title:	Coffee Machines	* Required
Banner URL:	http://www.mystore.co	
Banner Group:	right_bot2 ▼, or enter a new banner group below	
Image:	[ ] Browse... , or enter local file below	
	/home/html/images/	cafe.jpg
Image Target (Save To):	/home/html/images/	
HTML Text:		
Scheduled At: (dd/mm/yyyy)	▼	
Expires On: (dd/mm/yyyy)	▼ , or at	
	impressions/views.	update cancel

Depending on the parameters sent to the functions of osCommerce that display banners, a banner can be either selected randomly from a group of banners or a specific banner (if known by its ID) can be displayed on the pages of the website.

The following piece of PHP script demonstrates how a banner can be inserted as a part of an HTML table into the right-column of an osCommerce website. The script queries the database for any banner that belongs to the "right_bot2" banner group, and then displays it on the page:

```php
<?php
   if ($banner = tep_banner_exists('dynamic', 'right_bot2'))
   {
   ?>
   <tr>
       <td>
           <?php echo tep_display_banner('static', $banner); ?>
       </td>
   </tr>
   <?php
   }
?>
```

Pop Ups and Pop Unders

The so called pop ups and pop unders can be considered as a sub-class of banners that actually display new browser windows with your banners, when a user enters another website (pop ups) or when the user leaves the website (pop unders). Pop ups and pop unders can be used on your website as well.

For example, you can advertise some very new products in a pop up, or promote your free newsletter. Pop under can be used for customer survey. If the shopping basket is empty, you can ask the customers if they found the website and product information useful and prices competitive, or if they would like to suggest how to improve the website. It has to be said that most of the modern-day web browsers and protection software would block pop ups and pop unders, so one should not count on using these when advertising a website, or products and services.

Link Exchange

Link exchange is an easy and, sometimes, quite efficient way to send customers to your e-commerce website from other websites they may be visiting. It's also an important part of Search Engine Optimization.

Basically, two or more websites exchange links to each other. For example, two online stores may exchange links to each other if they sell complementary goods online. Or an online forum (or a blog) and e-commerce website may exchange links, so that customers of the online store could discuss various themes in the forum, and visitors to the forum could buy products from the e-commerce website. Web directories contain links back to various websites, and an online store may be listed in various web directories, having backward (reciprocal) links to the web directories' websites.

We will consider web directories in more detail in the next chapter of this book, which is all dedicated to Search Engine Optimization of an osCommerce website.

Though the most efficient way to exchange links is to write and post articles about each other's sites and add corresponding links to those articles, online merchants should be aware of the so called "link farms"—networks of websites that have reasonably high page ranks in search engines, but in fact that page rank is artificial and gained in an unethical manner.

Owners of link farms would often offer back links to your online store for a fee. Buying such a back link not only involves the risk of paying online to a person or a company that does not follow ethical principles in doing business, but is also to some degree, senseless, as search engines do take it very seriously, and locate new link farms sooner or later and ban them. So the back links you have paid for will disappear.

This situation is acceptable for those who run link farms as they have already been paid, but of course it's not acceptable for online merchants. It's considered to be a better practice to never use link farms to get links to your online store.

Value the Links

It should be noted that the value of the links pointing to your Ecommerce websites may vary. The value depends on:

- How popular the linking website is—it's simple mathematics—the more visitors the linking website has, the more chances that some of them will notice a link to your site and follow it.

- How their content corresponds to what you are selling to your customers— the best results can be achieved when the whole website, or at least a part of it has something in common with what your own website is about. For example, a website dedicated to digital camera buying guides will bring the most valuable customers to an online store selling cameras, MP3 players, and similar products online.

- How easy it is to find a link to your online store in the linking website—most websites would rather promote their own content and features to their visitors than links to other websites, therefore its important to have a link to your website visible, and easy to find on the linking website pages.

- How many other links exist on that website—the more links to other websites present on the page, the less prospective customers the website will send to your online store, unless your link somehow stands out from the others. It's also true for Search Engines rankings: the less links to other website present on the page—the more important they consider the links to be.

- How descriptive the link is—the main aim here is to give a prospective customer a reason to visit your website. So the link should give enough information about your online store and products you sell. Ideally, a link to your website would be located on a web page containing your website's logo, description, and of course the link itself. This would not only help the prospective customers to understand what your website is about and how they can benefit from buying your products, but also help the Search Engines to associate your website with the keywords used to describe it.

Of course, the link exchange assumes that for each link to your e-commerce site, you'll place a link back to the linking website. If you do not have many links pointing to other websites, you may want to place those in one of the columns of your osCommerce website, or in the bottom of certain pages.

osCommerce Link Exchange Facilities

If you actively exchange links with other sites and are serious about this part of your marketing strategy, a Link Manager solution built into osCommerce can be a good tool to start with.

The contribution can be downloaded from this URL `http://addons.oscommerce.com/info/1256/` and its installation process is quite straightforward.

It adds a new information box to the front end where it displays link categories. Each category leads the user to a page in the front end of osCommerce where it's possible to see corresponding links. Users can submit new links via the front end by filling in a special form. Each new link request is sent to the Administrator of the online store, and is then waiting for approval.

The Administrator can manage link categories in the back end, manage submitted links, or create new links directly from the back end. Also, the Administrator of the online store can send an email to the link owners directly from the back end.

The list of links (shown in the following screenshot) contains all links in all statuses, and the Administrator can easily filter links by status, like, for example, all pending links.

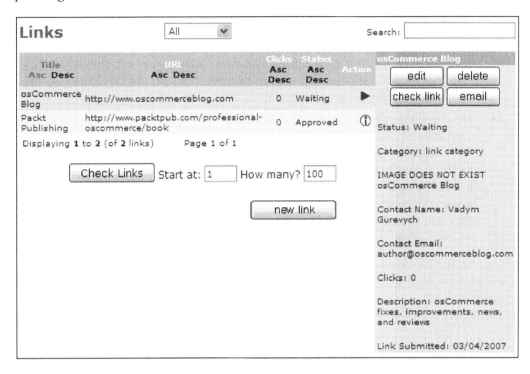

The **Check Links** button shown in the previous screenshot actually visits all specified pages with reciprocal links and validates them all, and then stores the result of whether the reciprocal link is present or not present in the database. So the Administrator of the online store can later on contact webmasters and have back links placed on the corresponding pages. Checking backward links from time to time (lets say at least once a week) is essential for maintaining a website's popularity.

The Individual Link Edit page allows for editing a link's properties (such as the link itself, the site's name, category, and description, etc.) and also has facilities to change the link's status (whether it is approved, or declined, or pending), and view the supposed reciprocal link's page.

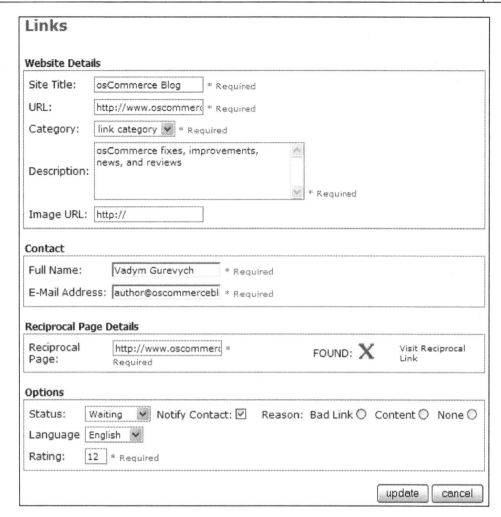

Getting Backward Links

So how can you get valuable links pointing to your website? It is possible to participate in Link Exchange networks; this may positively affect your website's ranking in Search Engines. You should be careful and always check what websites have links back to your online store.

In order to get more visitors of the targeted audience, you will need to find valuable complementary websites. You can do that by searching for websites selling or having information about products complementary to the ones you sell or containing information related to your products or to the industry you're in. Be aware of a situation when a complementary website in fact is a competitor of yours, and can simply take your customers and sales away!

If the website found contains really useful information for your customers, a good practice would be to place a link to it on your site. Add some short description and if possible a logo to let your customers know what the other website is about.

After that, it makes sense to either write to its webmaster or post a request into their automated Link Exchange system. Describe what your own e-commerce website is, and how will their visitors benefit from becoming your customers. Add a link to the page where they can see a link back to their site. In a very friendly and polite manner ask for a link back, stating what it should look like; also suggest the page on which it would be appropriate.

Don't be upset and do not delete a link to the website if you have not heard an answer—many emails get lost and caught by various email filter software nowadays. Therefore it makes sense to send a kind reminder in a couple of weeks or post a letter to the website owner.

You can also employ some companies to do this for you—to find link exchange partners based on what you can offer and what you're looking for.

Another reasonable practice is to locate the websites that contain links to your competitors' websites, and propose a link exchange. You just need to examine the websites of your competitors for reciprocal links, or find all backward links in search engines. For example, in Google it's possible to get all links pointing to a particular website by searching for:

```
link:http://www.site.com/
```

Tracking Link Efficiency

It is assumed by many website owners that link exchange is free to all participating parties. But it may not be so—sometimes a link from one website may be much more valuable than a link back to that site. So there may be some fee involved for having a link pointing to your online store from a popular, valuable website. Therefore it's essential that you have developed a method to track all online orders that are placed by customers who clicked the links to your website on other sites.

Speaking technically, you can add the "referrer" into the session variables when the customer first comes to your online store, and then add this stored "referrer" into the order when the customer actually places one. You can then run a report on how many orders have been placed by the customers who came from certain linking websites.

There are solutions, like Google Analytics, that, if they are integrated into an online store, can not only produce statistics of website visitors sorted by referring website, but also provide statistics on which linking website is responsible for generating how much turnover for a given period.

Affiliate Programs

An affiliate program can bring more customers ready to buy your products in exchange for certain rewards given to the referring websites. Actually, an affiliate program doesn't necessarily have to be limited to websites—customers can be referred from newsletters, and even from the printed media.

The main benefit of using an affiliate program is that affiliate reward is only paid for the orders placed by the end customers, and the affiliates promote your osCommerce online store and its products on their own expenses. This helps to cut down advertising expenses a bit, and have them under control—you will never pay more for a placed order than the agreed affiliate reward.

How it Works

Affiliates usually place a link to a certain page of your website (the main page, or a specific product's page) on their own website, sometimes using banners to draw the customer's attention. Each link will contain the affiliate's unique code. It is the task of the Affiliate Program to store the given affiliate code and then prepare special reports on all clicks received from the affiliate website, and all orders placed by the customers referred by that affiliate. Since each affiliate can be given a unique reward per cent, each affiliate's commission can be easily calculated.

Getting Affiliates On Board

In some sense, affiliates act as partners. Therefore they should be treated accordingly. Make it easy for a new affiliate to register on the website. All benefits of becoming a member of the affiliate program should be clearly explained.

- Obviously the first and the very main benefit is the commission that is added to the affiliate's account as soon as the affiliate's website generates sales. Therefore the commission rate should be explained in clear details on the affiliate registration pages.

- If the commission rate changes depending on the turnover generated by the affiliate's website—perspectives of increasing the commission rate should also be included into the list of benefits.

- Typical payment schedule and payment options should be clearly explained.

- Affiliates can receive notifications about forthcoming products and special offers in advance, so that they can get prepared, and get their sites prepared too.

- Affiliates can be given help in designing banners and other linking materials to be put on their websites.

- As a way to attract new affiliates, they can be given discount coupons to spend in the online store.
- Like all resellers, best-selling affiliates can be given retrospective discounts or special bonuses depending on their performance.

The registration form should be easy to find, and easy to fill in. At the same time, it should be good enough to give the store owner a complete picture of what the affiliate's business is, and how the online store will be promoted by the affiliate.

Registration forms should contain the following information about the affiliate and their business:

- Company name and address, and other details including tax IDs (if any)
- Website URL and description
- Contact person name and address
- Preferred payment method
- Affiliate program Terms and Conditions

It is essential to have new affiliates agree with the affiliate program Terms and Conditions document to avoid any issues or confusions in the future.

Once a new application is received, it's preferable to approve (or decline!) it promptly.

The affiliate program manager should provide the affiliates with complete information about the online store, and the product catalog that is on offer. Prepare banners, texts, and links for affiliates, so that they can use those ready-made materials on their own websites and in email campaigns.

osCommerce Affiliate Program Solutions

There is a contribution for osCommerce that allows for managing an affiliate program from the Administration panel of the online store.

It can be downloaded from:
`http://addons.oscommerce.com/info/158.`

The integration is seamless and allows for affiliate registration, affiliate account management, and linking materials management. It also generates click and sale reports for affiliates and the Administrator of the osCommerce website.

The contribution adds a special information box into the front end of the website, which can be integrated into either the left or right column of the layout. The box contains links to the Affiliate Information pages (affiliate program description, benefits, and preferably Terms and Conditions), Affiliate Program FAQ, and actually Affiliate Log in page.

The affiliate login page looks the same as osCommerce customer's login page. It is possible to log in using an existing affiliate's account or create a new account. Once an account is created, it still needs to be activated by the Administrator of the online store.

Correspondingly, the Administrator receives a notification about new affiliate accounts in the pending status, and can log into the back end of the online store and approve or decline an affiliate's account and set the corresponding commission per cent.

On logging into the affiliate account, the affiliate can see the following screen that contains summary of all activities, Edit Account links, links to the pages with banners and other linking information, and of course reports.

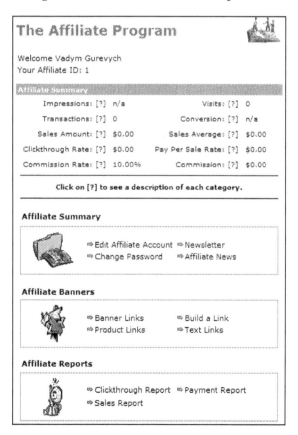

Banners are prepared in the back end by the Administrator of the online store. A banner can lead either to the whole online store, or to one of its categories only.

Product links are also built by the Administrator of the website in the back end, and lead directly to specific products. Those are especially convenient for affiliates who have some information on their websites that relates to specific products that are being sold by the online store. Another feature that is available to affiliates is the **Build a Link** option. It allows for building links to the product pages on the fly, just by knowing osCommerce product ID.

The **Text Links** feature simply lists all banners that have been earlier created by the Administrator as text links, i.e. excluding any or all images. A good use for such text links is a newsletter sent by an affiliate to subscribers, or in an email signature.

There are three reports available to affiliates:

- **Clickthrough Report** — contains information about clicks from the affiliate's website that lead to certain online store pages.

- **Sales Report** — contains information about completed sales, including dates, amounts, commission amounts earned, and sale (order) status. It is quite important to note that, should an order be canceled or refunded — the affiliate should not receive commission for that sale.

- **Payment report** — contains the list of reported payments, including payment amount, date, unpaid earnings to date and payment status.

Similar to an affiliate, the Administrator of the online store has access to the Affiliate Program summary, reports of sales, payments, and clicks. The Administrator can also access the list of affiliates and edit each affiliate's details. The Administrator can create banners (either website banners, or individual category banners, or even individual product banners) for affiliates, manage Affiliate Program news and Affiliate Newsletter, and also simply contact any or all affiliates by sending an email.

This contribution adds a new menu into the Configuration section of the Administration panel of the online store, as shown in the following screenshot:

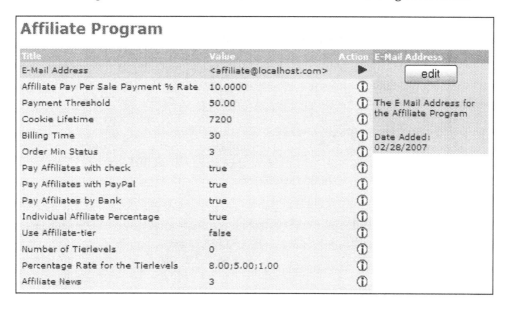

The **E-Mail Address** mentioned in the screenshot is where the emails addressed to the Affiliates will be coming from.

The Affiliate Program can have a default commission rate, which is specified in the **Affiliate Pay Per Sale Payment % Rate** option.

Payment Threshold defines the minimum amount payable to affiliates. Actually, it will very much depend on the payment methods chosen by affiliates.

Cookie Lifetime defines the time a special cookie "lives" on a customer's computer if the customer comes back to the online store. This value is set in seconds so, for example, for one week one would put 604800 as a value in that field.

Billing Time is a very important setting, and protects the online store owner from paying commission on orders that are later canceled by customers/refunded. It is set to one month (30 days) by default, and this value should remain the same if affiliates do not have any objections.

Order Min Status is also very important, and defines the minimum order status when the order starts to count, and an affiliate's commission is calculated. It supposes that in osCommerce, order statuses with higher IDs would more likely mean Processing, or Dispatched, and order statuses with lower IDs would more likely be Pending.

The Administrator of the online store can enable or disable certain affiliate payment methods.

The **Individual Affiliate Percentage** parameter enables or disables individual affiliate percentage correspondingly. If this parameter is disabled all affiliates are paid the **Affiliate Pay Per Sale Payment % Rate** on any orders generated by them.

This contribution supports a multi-tier affiliate program, so that affiliates can invite other affiliates to register, and then get commission per cent of their sales. The **Use Affiliate-tier**, **Number of Tierlevels**, and **Percentage Rate for the Tierlevels** options regulate the multiple tiers of the built-in osCommerce affiliate program.

The main benefit of a built-in affiliate program, based on the osCommerce Affiliate contribution is that it gives the Administrator of the website full control of the program, affiliates, payments, sale reports, etc.

But at the same time, this is also the main disadvantage of the built-in affiliate program—because everything is controlled by the Administration of the online store, and also because affiliates do not have access to each transaction detail, more may argue about the number of clicks or sales reported, and about amounts of payments made.

For this reason and also because of the potential reach of hundreds of affiliates, an online store owner may want to explore third-party popular affiliate solutions.

Popular Third-Party Affiliate Program Solutions

One doesn't necessarily have to go with an osCommerce integrated affiliate program. There are multiple websites where the online store owner can register to start receiving traffic and orders from other websites.

It works similar to Banner Exchange Networks, but the affiliate gets paid only for the orders placed by the referred customers.

Commission Junction

From all the available solutions, the Commission Junction is probably the biggest one. Correspondingly it provides better service and can drive more traffic to an online store. The website is located at `www.cj.com`.

Online merchants can register and receive orders or leads from its affiliates. The same as with osCommerce Affiliate contribution, affiliates only get paid for real orders, not just for referring visitors and customers to the online store. As Commission Junction says this "makes it a low-risk, high-reward environment for both parties".

The same as with the osCommerce Affiliate Program, online merchants can create links and set commissions, such as a fixed amount per lead or a percentage of a resulting sale. Affiliates can register, get access to the published links, and place those on their websites or add them into their newsletters. Online merchants pay Commission Junction a fee according to their payouts to the affiliates.

Tracking is based on cookies. Commission Junction handles all reports and all collection and processing required to ensure fair and timely commission payment for the publisher, and all of the administration and verification necessary to ensure quality sales and leads for the advertiser. Commission Junction is very well known as a premium service for affiliates, and its main benefit for affiliates is the level of trust they can put into it.

Interestingly enough, Commission Junction makes affiliates regularly generate some activity with their account to maintain an active account.

Newsletters

If you have a list of customers willing to receive updates and news from you, send them a newsletter. You can also legally buy lists of email addresses of those Internet users who have agreed to receive advertising via email and send such prospective customers a newsletter.

Tips and Best Practices

There are some tips that could be used when preparing and sending a newsletter:

- Send it only to those who really don't mind receiving it—sending a newsletter to those who never subscribed to receive it, or who never gave an agreement to receive emails from third parties like you, may upset the recipient and result in an angry Internet user reporting your newsletter as SPAM. Remember that over 80% of all emails sent and received at any moment are categorized as SPAM—do not let your newsletters to be treated that way! Note that it might even be illegal in certain countries and territories to send unsolicited emails, so it is better to check what the local law has to say before sending out a newsletter to prospective customers.

- Include unsubscribe options into each newsletter—a customer should be able to easily unsubscribe from the newsletter and all further issues of it.

- Inform the customers about new products, special prices, additional features they can find in your osCommerce website.

- Not only try to sell something to the subscribers, but also include information that may be useful to them—when selling software, describe some additional features and advanced tips on how to use it. Or when selling wine online—you can describe how to choose a bottle, which wine is good for which occasion, how to store it at home, how to better taste it. All this makes the customer interested in receiving further issues of the newsletter, and as a result, helps to convert the customer into a loyal customer.

- Customers may become interested in becoming subscribers if they can see previous issues of the newsletter and find those to be of use. A risk-free idea for both customers and online merchants is to offer customers a sample newsletter based on at least one of previous issues. A link to a special pop-up window containing at least one sample could be put onto the page where users can subscribe to receive further issues of that newsletter.

- It is better to send a newsletter in HTML format, so that the customers can actually see a very nicely designed page with information and some pictures. Make sure the HTML is tested and can be received properly by major email client software. It's better to send a newsletter in two formats—HTML and plain text.

- Make sure the subject of the newsletter tells the customer whom the newsletter is coming from and what it is about. Avoid generic phrases as anti-SPAM software may block such emails. Include the company or website name into the subject to make it easier for the customer to understand where the email has been sent from. Include information about what the newsletter is dedicated to—like some special topic, event, or special offer that will be over soon.

Designing and Sending a Newsletter

A newsletter can be sent in plain text or HTML format.

When sending an HTML newsletter to subscribers—it makes sense to use design similar to the design of the online store, to promote the brand further via newsletters. Obviously, there's no need to include all existing design elements, but a logo, color scheme, and CSS elements used in the newsletter can match the ones of the online store.

The newsletter should have a title that can be clearly seen in its header. The title can match the subject of the email, or can extend it with further details.

To make it easier for the subscribers to read the newsletter, it is suggested to add a short index of all topics included into the newsletter at the very beginning. Or if the newsletter contains only one topic—a brief summary that would help the subscriber to better understand what is it about.

An online store's newsletter can also contain links to the products or product listings that the Administrator would like to extensively advertise. In the case of sending an HTML newsletter, it is possible to include not only a product name, price, and a link to the product page, but also a product image.

Note that if you're copying links to products and categories of the online store for newsletter, it's very important to ensure those links do not contain session IDs. Sending a newsletter to customers where some of its links contain osCommerce session IDs can result in serious security issues.

Two or more customers could click the link from the newsletter at approximately the same time (with up to 15 minutes difference, depending on the configuration of the web server). They would then get access to the same user account and content of the shopping cart—depending on who clicked the link first.

Depending on the legal regulations, a newsletter might be required to contain full contact information of the company that operates the online store and also the unsubscribe options. But even if it is not required by law—it's always good to give subscribers an opportunity to unsubscribe if they do not wish to receive newsletters from that online store anymore.

There are multiple web services that can not only help in designing an HTML newsletter, but also delivering it to customers, monitoring customers' responses, and managing subscriptions.

One such service is called Campaign Monitor and is located at `http://www.campaignmonitor.com`.

There are several main features that the determine success of using such solutions when sending newsletters to customers:

- Help with designing HTML newsletters by providing access to a gallery of HTML newsletter designs; at the same time it's possible to use any custom-made design too.

- Personalized approach—user's first and last names, email addresses, etc, can be added to either the subject line of the newsletter or its content.

- Flexible schedule for already created newsletters—so that users can plan ahead and create newsletters in advance and then have those sent automatically.

- Test facilities—similar to osCommerce, it is possible to test created email campaigns by sending an email to any particular address; this also includes a facility to display previously sent newsletters on the website.

- Advanced subscriber management facilities, including subscribe and unsubscribe form generation.

- Powerful reporting tools, including bounced emails and unsubscribe requests.

Forums and Blogs

Use the power of online communities to promote your website and add more links to it. You can become a member of an online forum where its members discuss themes related to your industry, or even discuss products and services similar to the ones you sell online.

Add a descriptive and easy-to-find link back to your online store into your signature (usually you can edit a short piece of HTML called the signature, which will then be added to every post you make). Then start posting new themes and answering others posts.

Note that this may not be allowed in all forums (it is not allowed in the osCommerce support forum, for example). In that case, you can add this info normally to your forum profile page.

One should normally avoid advertising a particular website (online store, etc.) in the forum unless permitted to do so by the rules of the specific forum. If your posts are interesting, people WILL click on your profile to get to know you better…

A signature that gives other readers an idea about what your website has to offer may look like this one:

John Smith,
Online Marketing Manager
Computer hardware sold from stock, save up to 50% on today's special offers
`www.onlinestorename.com`

As a specialist in your industry, you will definitely have much to say.

One important rule is to say (write) only when you actually have something to say. All your posts should be making perfect sense, and contain information useful for other members of the forum. At the same time, it's preferable to use keywords and phrases related to your website in the posts to help the search engines build an association between the targeted keywords and a link to your online store.

It's better not to write anything negative and at the same time have a link in that post back to your site—as prospective customers and of course search engines may pick up the association and it will most definitely not result in increased profits and turnover for your online business.

Posting comments in blogs has a similar double effect—other visitors to the blog site will see your comments and a link back to your online store, and search engines will build an association between the keywords mentioned on the page and a link to your e-commerce site. So sign up to RSS feeds of several popular blogs and start posting valuable comments.

Price Comparison Directories

The last way to advertise your products that we've reviewed in this chapter is listing them in price comparison directories. There are various price comparison websites on which you may want to list your products. Some of them are free (like Google's Froogle), others are paid for (like DealTime, UBid, Kelkoo). You will be paying for the number of clicks performed by the customers during a certain period of time.

This advertising method makes the most sense for e-commerce websites that sell tangible products.

Some important tips that should be considered when advertising products in the price comparison directory:

- Watch the price—yes, that's the most important bit. A price comparison directory by its definition will help the end customer find the lowest listed price. Therefore watch what the competitors have to offer and be ready to beat their prices at least on some products Of course a product's final price consists of the product price itself and the delivery fee, so let the customer know if the price given includes delivery fee by mentioning it briefly in the short product description. Sometimes, it will be possible to include the delivery fee into the product feed as a separate column—so that price comparison engines would display it as an extra or maybe as free delivery.

- List most profitable/best selling products—since some of the price comparison directories are not free, each click made by the end customer should be used in the most efficient way. For example, it makes sense to list the most profitable products. First of all a good margin gives you flexibility to beat others' prices. Secondly, even though you will pay a certain amount for each customer referred to you by the price comparison directory, you will still have enough profit left from such sales. Listing the best selling products increases the probability of the customer actually buying those products online, not clicking links only to get more information about them.

- Provide as much detailed information as possible—not only does the price matter but also the amount and quality of information. Supply as many well prepared product details as possible to see some of the customers choosing links to your osCommerce online store.

- Update product information, price, stock levels, and shipping conditions regularly—the less precise and more out of date product information and price is in the directory, the less chances the customer will complete the order in osCommerce, because of the confusion caused and differences in product details and prices.

- Make it easy to find products in the directory—price comparison directories consist of categories, and each product should be put into the corresponding category or sub-category.

- Watch the expenses and track conversion—as with any other way of advertising, you need to watch advertising expenses, and make sure they are within the budget. Again, it's pretty important to know which products and categories are the most popular.

It is recommended that each URL leading to the e-commerce store contains a tracking code. The tracking code should be stored in the database along with the order. Following the reports provided by the price comparison directory, it is possible to calculate the conversion rate between the customers who only clicked the link, and the customers who actually bought something in the osCommerce online store.

Export Data from osCommerce to Froogle

Product data can be exported from an osCommerce online store to be later imported into a price comparison website. There are multiple contributions that can assist with exporting product catalog. To export products for Froogle (Google Base) the following contribution can be used: `http://addons.oscommerce.com/info/4513`.

Froogle is very picky about the product data it imports. Of course it expects product names, descriptions, images, and prices to match the ones displayed on the website. More than that—if a product on the website has an additional description—it makes sense to prepare it to be exported for Froogle, as otherwise the Froogle support team will most probably get in contact and ask for it anyway.

It is possible to upload products to Froogle one by one. In order to make it easier to upload multiple products, Froogle has come up with a facility to upload bulk products at one time. It is possible to upload products either from the web page when logged into a Froogle account, or to a special FTP storage where the file will be picked up by Froogle automatically. If the upload went well it will be possible to see the corresponding number of products in the Froogle account. Otherwise the account owner will be notified about problems and advised on how to fix those.

Froogle supports CSV file format; the following is an approximate list of fields, though it may be different depending on the local version of Froogle (Google Base) that the store owner wants to integrate the website into, and also on how additional attributes are configured in the Froogle account for products:

title, description, link, image_link, id, expiration_date, price, currency, manufacturer, model_number, quantity, weight, brand

It's quite obvious which osCommerce database fields would match which fields in the above list. As an "expiration_date", it's possible to put in a date one month in the future, and "brand" would be most probably equal to the content of the "manufacturer" field, unless the osCommerce online store has specific brand management facilities.

Summary

In this chapter we have reviewed several ways to advertise and promote your website and products, such as:

- Listings in search engines (both natural and paid)
- Banners
- Pop ups and Pop unders
- Link exchange
- Affiliate program
- Newsletters
- Forums and blogs
- Price comparison directories

We have learned how to track the efficiency of an advertising campaign and the most important variables of the tracking report.

In the next chapter, we will concentrate solely on SEO—Search Engine Optimization.

3
Search Engine Optimization

In the previous chapter, we reviewed several methods of getting more visitors to the website. In this chapter, we will emphasize probably one of the most important tool for an e-commerce store—Search Engine Optimization (SEO).

What is SEO? SEO is a set of methods, techniques, and actions intended to make the website (online store) easily accessible and indexed by search engines, so that the search engines list the website higher in search results on certain queries run by visitors and prospective customers.

We will discuss why SEO is actually so important, the main benefits of having the online store optimized for search engines, and of course review tips and tricks for how to optimize an osCommerce online store for search engines. We will also review aspects of performing website's SEO on your own, and hiring a professional SEO consultant.

Why SEO?

Search Engine Optimization or SEO is an important part of a marketing strategy of almost any e-commerce website. But why is that? Why SEO is so important?

There are at least two reasons for this. First of all, SEO helps to increase the number of visitors to the website by positioning the website higher in the list of matching websites produced by the search engine. It's based on how we read the web pages—from up to down, left to right. The higher the website is in the search results, the higher the chances that the users will notice it. Of course, if search results take more than one page—websites listed in the first page will receive more clicks than the websites listed on other pages, simply because the users will most probably find one or several interesting links on the first page and will not bother to check other search results on other pages. The more descriptive the title, URL, and the actual short description are—the more chances there are that the user will click the link, becoming a visitor.

And not just visitors are brought by search engines, but in most cases—visitors interested in the products and services advertised on the website, visitors who are more likely to become customers or subscribers.

It's important to note that the visitors who can find an answer to their query on the websites they are visiting will more likely become customers of those websites.

The second reason also seems obvious from the first glance—unlike paid advertisements SEO is free. Not the process of optimization of a certain website, but rather all visits made by the prospective customers do not cost a penny to the online store owner because the customers search in publicly available directories and search engines and are presented with the list of matching results sorted by relevancy to the query.

Since it usually takes quite some time to see the results brought by SEO, paid advertising may seem more effective in the beginning. SEO is really a long term perspective solution for an online store—it takes a while to pay back the initial investments, but then, once the website is optimized for search engines—it keeps working on its own and usually only requires modest upgrades and improvements from time to time.

So unless you're selling a very unique popular product or are not interested in getting more prospective customers to the website—consider SEO for your e-commerce website.

Balance between SEO and Usability

One important note to be made here is—search engines are not human beings. It seems obvious, though some store owners seem to forget about this and concentrate on making the websites best for search engines and not for the visitors and prospective customers.

We will discuss possible methods for search engine optimization further in this chapter, but it's important to remember usability of the online store should not suffer due to the SEO efforts. Otherwise, you may end up with a very popular online store with a very low visitor to customer conversion rate. An online store owner should always remember the main goal of any online store is to sell products or services. That is why after applying changes related to SEO, each time check if the customer conversion rate has stayed the same, increased, or decreased and act accordingly.

Ethical SEO

This also relates to so called "ethical SEO". Obviously, from a business point of view, it's better to have as many website visitors as possible. Though for better customer conversion, the path the visitor has used to come to the website should be straightforward, and also the user should always find what has been searched for.

A distinction between Ethical SEO techniques and methodology, and Ethical SEO firms should be made. While an SEO firm may behave ethically towards its client, it's important to ensure it uses ethical SEO techniques and methodology.

The goal of a search engine is to return documents that are most relevant for a particular search query. Ethical SEO will make your page as relevant as possible for a targeted keyword or set of keywords.

It is ethical to have the website promote and sell products and services that are advertised in search engines. It's not ethical to use some popular search terms, like for example movie titles, to get more visitors to the website that doesn't sell or advertise this kind of products.

It is ethical to sell products and services for the advertised price. It's not ethical to list low priced products in the search engines and not have them listed in the actual online store.

It is ethical to have backward links from real websites (portals, forums, blogs, directories, other online stores). It's not ethical to use specially created so called "link farms" to increase a website's page rank by having fake / "SPAM" websites linked to it.

By giving visitors the information they are looking for, you will increase the conversion rate of visitors to customers. By using unethical SEO, it is likely that you could well be losing sales to your online competition.

Not only does it distract the visitors and decrease the chances of converting a visitor into a customer, but also is bad for SEO — search engines try to fight non-ethical search engine optimizations. Un-ethical SEO may result in a drop of the page rank, and even a temporary block put on the website by the search engine.

Ethical SEO produces the most positive results and does the least harm. It should be applied so that it improves online sales and at the same time leads towards better customer satisfaction. Ethical SEO should respect products, online stores, websites of competitors, search engines, customers, and their desire to find products most suitable to address their needs.

New Site SEO

When building a new online store based on osCommerce, it makes sense to plan for search engine optimization in advance. Of course, the store owner may want to wait before investing in SEO and see if the website is picking up customers on its own, using other ways of online advertisement than in search engines. But to achieve maximum results it's recommended to start with defining SEO strategy and performing at least the technical part of search engine optimization while developing the website.

By defining the strategy for SEO we mean:

- Determining keywords and key phrases that the target audience might use to find products sold online
- Creating a list of updates to the website that are necessary to be performed to have it optimized for search engines
- Setting priorities on which updates will be performed when and in which period
- Setting up a budget for SEO and splitting it by the updates
- Listing websites you would like to get backward links from, finding webmaster contact information, creating a promotion email template for webmasters

One thing that's very important when optimizing a new website for search engines is **patience**. Even a well optimized new online store will not be listed or fully and properly indexed by search engines for a certain period of time. It makes sense to spend this time testing the online store, collecting feedback from the customers, and improving the site and product catalog.

Expected Time Frame

Once a new online store is put live a certain amount of time is required for the search engines to get to it, scan all pages, and index all keywords. During this process, search engines will also locate links pointing back to your online store and give it a so called Page Rank.

Page Rank

According to Wikipedia, Page Rank is a link analysis algorithm which assigns a numerical weighting to each element of a hyperlinked set of documents, such as the World Wide Web, with the purpose of "measuring" its relative importance within the set. In other words—the higher the Page Rank—the more important the website and higher the position in the search results it will get.

Even though PageRank itself was developed by the founders of Google Inc., other search engines use similar methods to determine how popular this or that web resource is and to sort search results.

Ageing Delay

It may take up to three or four months for a new website to become visible in search engines like Google, and to get some positive Page Rank. It may take even longer (six to eight months) to get to some relatively good positions in search results, if the web pages contain corresponding keywords and if there are a good number of good quality backward links. There's no strict definition on what actually is a "good number"—sometimes even a couple of links from pages with high Page Rank is enough to make a good number.

Good quality here means not only a high Page Rank of the linking page, but also its content, that ideally should be related to the content of your website/online store pages. Each search engine has its own schedule of updates of its page ranks. For example, Google performs such updates three or four times a year.

It should be noted that Yahoo! and MSN may not have a delay in putting your online store into search results.

A website will become visible in search engines as soon as it has been visited by special bots (web crawlers), and its pages have been indexed. But even after that it may be almost invisible in the search results until its Page Rank is calculated, and until its Page Rank is greater than zero. By almost invisible, here we mean it may still appear in the search results, but somewhere in the very end of the list. Even if the search engine comes back with 100 links in response to a certain search query, the user will most likely check the first 10 or 20. So why would a new website, your new online store, be invisible in search results? And for how long will this be happening, and is there anything to do about it?

Plan Ahead for a New Online Store

If you plan to launch your new osCommerce online store, better plan ahead publishing of some relevant pages under its domain name. Actually, the more pages with relevant content you will have published—the more chances are that the website will be reached, indexed, and ranked by search engines by the time you decide to go live with the online store.

Google "Sandbox"

There's no real proof of existence of this phenomena except for how new websites appear in Google search results. It is often noticed that a new website, even though relatively promptly indexed by Google or other search engines, may not do well in the search results for quite some time. It looks like a website is put on "probation" by the search engine, and no efforts on improving its position in the search result would make any difference at that time.

It has been also noticed that the more common, competitive keywords are used in the website — the longer it stays in this status. The more unique keywords and contents the website has — the less time it appears to be ignored by Google and other search engines and the sooner it will appear in better positions in search results.

What is a "Sandbox"?

This phenomenon was called the "sandbox" and it is assumed that all or almost all new websites are put into a "sandbox" for a certain amount of time by Google, and only then they can join other, "approved" websites in the search results.

While a website is "in the sandbox", no real attempts to improve its Page Rank will affect its position in the search results.

What is the "Sandbox" For?

It is understood that Google has come up with this idea to fight the so called "search engine spammers". Before this update had been introduced, it was relatively easy to use spam websites to affect the Page Ranks of real websites. Search Engine spammers just needed to build yet another website that, even though it would break Google policies as to the content and keywords usage, would help to increase the Page Rank of the websites to which it had hyperlinks. Once that spam website was found and blocked by search engines bots, the spammers would easily build yet another website on a different domain, with slightly different content, and would repeat the trick an indefinite number of times.

Now, with new websites getting into the "sandbox" automatically, Google runs a series of anti-spam tests against new websites and only pulls the website out of the "sandbox" after that. The whole process takes time, and Google also waits to see what is happening with the website during that time. Again, the more unique keywords are found in the website — the more chances for it to either pass the "sandbox" or get out of it sooner.

It should be understood by website owners and webmasters that the "sandbox" filter is not a punishment in any way. It's just a method that is used by Google and other search engines to prevent search engine spam and provide users with the most appropriate and accurate search results.

Once the website is out of the "sandbox" its Page Rank will soon become visible and it will start to appear in better positions in search results.

How the "Sandbox" can be Useful for Your Online Store

You can consider the time your online store spends in the "sandbox" as yet another opportunity to test the website in real life conditions but with only a few real customers, i.e. with no risk of upsetting a larger number of customers if anything goes wrong with part of the online store. You can see how the website performs, collect feedback from the first customers, and promptly update the online store accordingly.

You should also spend this time building up all SEO elements that may still be missing there, optimizing the content, product catalog, and design. You should spend this time getting more inbound links to your online store, partnering with the websites that can bring you more customers and at the same time can improve your online store's Page Rank. Once the online store is pulled out of the "sandbox" — you will see it performing quite well in the search results, if all search engine optimization has been done properly.

Finally, try to not rely solely on Google traffic. Appearance in other search engines, such as Yahoo!, MSN, and AOL can also bring you customers, and results may be visible sooner than with Google.

What can be a Reason for My Store to be "Sandboxed"?

Basically, the main reason for a website to appear in the "sandbox" is for it to look un-natural to Google.

Google seems to analyze inbound links, density of keywords in the texts, titles, META tags, and other web design and layout elements. Where it suspects anything un-natural — it will increase the chances for a website to fall into the "sandbox".

Even textual content can be analyzed for if it's created by human or if it's a specially generated content for SEO purposes.

There can be some other assumptions made, but it should be noted that even a website with unique high-quality design and content, and top inbound links may still be put into the "sandbox".

Is My Online Store in the "Sandbox"?

Here are some tips on how to determine if your online store is in the "sandbox".

First, you need to make sure the website is not banned by Google. Check HTTP access logs to see if Google bot is visiting the website. If it's not—there are high chances the website is banned. Also, try searching for your domain name in Google. If it can't be found—this either means the website has not been indexed yet (i.e. it's a very new website) or it has been banned. If your online store is well ranked in other search engines, but doesn't perform well in Google, then it may have been put in the "sandbox".

In order to get the site out of the "sandbox" the easiest and fastest way is to ... wait until Google has pulled it out of there. Eventually their aim is to index as many sites as possible and provide their users with the most appropriate valuable results based on the quality of content. If your online store offers high-quality content—your website will be out of the "sandbox" even sooner.

Google Supplemental Index

Google maintains two indexes—the so called Main and Supplemental. Since it can operate with a limited (but still huge) number of websites/pages, it has to have the most valuable websites and pages listed in the Main index, and put all the other ones into the Supplemental index.

When searching for a match to the user's query, Google first checks the Main index. If it cannot find enough information there, it will then check the Supplemental index and will display search results from both indexes.

Being in the Supplemental index should not be considered as a punishment or a penalty, though it may affect the number of visitors to one's website.

What gets an Online Store into the Supplemental Index?

The main reason for a website or one or several of its pages to be included into the Supplemental index is that Google doesn't consider them as important as other sites and pages that are included into the Main index.

Here we have prepared some tips on how you get into the Supplemental index (of course, you should try to avoid this from happening!):

- Having not enough high quality inbound links
- Having "not important" pages within the website—i.e. pages that are not linked with pages that the Search Engine considers to be important
- Having too many keywords in the title tag, META descriptions and keywords tags
- Having duplicate contents that can be also found on other websites/pages in the Web

How to Get Out of the Supplemental Index

An online store owner or a webmaster can check if some of the website pages are in the Supplemental index. In order to do this, just open Google website and type in the following search string, and then press *Enter*: `site:your-site-name-here.com`.

In the following screenshot, we can see a green "Supplemental Result" mark on some search results. This means that links have been taken from the supplemental index and brought into the search results page along with the links taken from the main index.

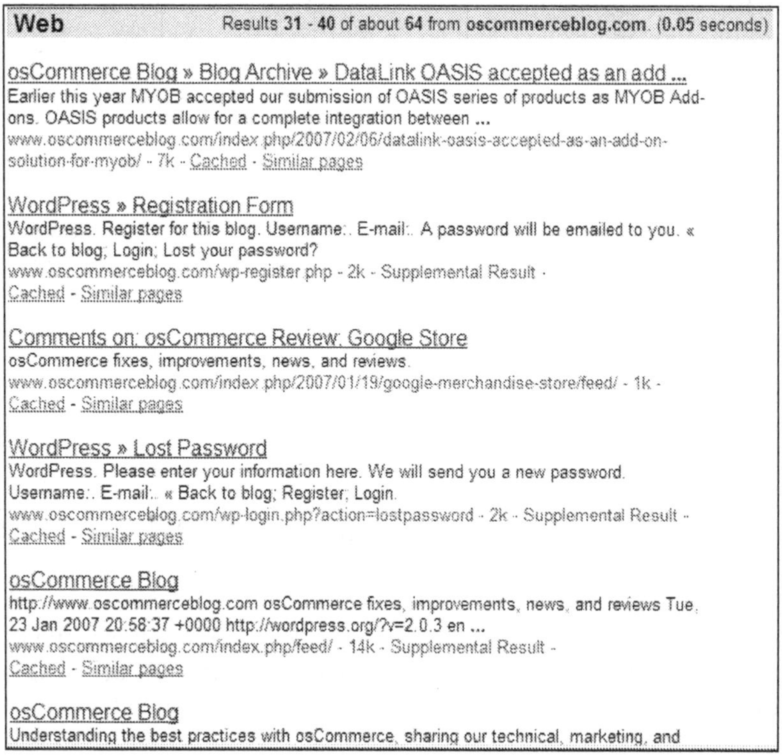

Alternatively, if the Google search result page doesn't contain links marked with "Supplemental Result", it's possible to still get the list of supplemental links by typing in the following search string, and then pressing Enter: `site:your-site-name-here.com/&.`

There is no straightforward way to get out of the Supplemental index back into the Main index. It can be said that it's all about continuing with ethical SEO efforts, building valuable inbound links to multiple pages of the website, optimizing the website, creating additional content, validating the website for errors...

Often with osCommerce, an online store, in particular a recently launched online store, that has a relatively large number of products and categories may have many links to its categories and products added to Google's Supplemental index even though a number of well ranked inbound links are pointing to its main page. In such a case, a possible solution would be to first concentrate on promoting category pages of that online store in Google. It's possible to submit a Google map containing only links to category pages using Google Webmasters tools, and not include links to products in that submission. Once category pages have been given at least some Google PageRank (even zero!), products of each category, category by a category, could be submitted too. It may take a while to see the results (several weeks), but this method can actually work! Also it's important to note that once a link to category or a product has got into the supplemental index, it may be a good idea to remove it from the online store and re-instate it again with another ID or name. If a link from the main page (most often the page with highest PageRank) of the site points to that newly reinstated category or product, it will most definitely get out of Google's supplemental index. The Search Engine needs to be shown that category or product is important.

It can also be said it's easier not to get into the Supplemental index than to get out of it, so it's better to think carefully and properly design the whole new online store link structure, and hopefully all or most of its pages will get listed in the Main index.

It's very important to ensure the online store has no duplicated pages, or at least pages with duplicated content will not be indexed by search engines (see further regarding `robots.txt` directives).

SEO When Switching to osCommerce from an Existing Website

When switching an existing e-commerce (or static brochure-like) website to an osCommerce-based online store on the same domain name, search engine optimization becomes crucial for the success of the new website, the same as its usability and advertising.

Before the actual switch, the most popular and successful (well performing in search engines) pages of the old website should be identified. They will more likely have a good page rank in Google and other search engines that rely on similar technologies. Not depending on how well the new osCommerce online store is optimized for search engines, preserving URLs of such successful pages is an essential task.

Preserving Good Page Rank

In order to preserve good page rank of certain pages, new online store based on osCommerce should do one of the following:

- Have its own pages on the same URLs as the old website
- Have special redirect rules in place to point all requests to the old URLs to the new ones

There are two main reasons why it is important to hold or implement redirects for such URLs. First, the search engines will still consider such pages existing, and having good ranks, and will give them good positions in the search results. They will also continue to parse the website from time to time to check the pages and re-index them, so it would be good to have links to older pages in place until the new pages have become known by the search engines. Secondly, as links to such pages keep appearing in search results, users will keep clicking the links and of course each such click should lead the user to the expected page.

What information can be on popular and well performing pages of the old version of the website? First of all, it could be category and product pages, it could be manufacturer information pages, buying guides, or other pages with additional information. It could also be pages with terms and conditions of trade, and other static pages.

As was said above, one of the options is to create pages with the same URLs as on the old website. But it may be difficult to maintain both old and new versions of the same pages on the same URLs. Therefore it's more reasonable to use the redirects method. The search engines, or browsers of the visitors of the new online store should be redirected to the new URLs seamlessly and without any delay.

In order to do it properly, the so called 301 redirect can be used. In this case, the web browser or a search engine bot is sent a special command to open another URL instead of the one requested. The code "301" reads as "moved permanently" and this method is considered to be the most efficient and search engine friendly method of web page redirection.

If the online store is hosted by Apache web server, and the rewrite engine is turned on, the following commands can be inserted into the `.htaccess` file to implement 301 redirects from old URLs to the new ones in the safest way for search engine positions:

```
RewriteCond %{REQUEST_FILENAME}        !-d
RewriteRule ^oldpage.html$ http://www.domain.com/newpage.html
[R=301,L]
```

or:

```
RewriteCond %{REQUEST_FILENAME}        !-d
RewriteRule ^oldpage.php$ http://www.domain.com/newpage.php [R=301,L]
```

It is also possible to use another redirection command in `.htaccess` file to redirect website visitors and search engines from old URL (the first value in the example below) to the new URL (correspondingly the second value):

```
Redirect permanent /oldpage.html http://www.domain.com/newpath/
newpage.html
```

The "permanent" parameter in the above sample is important for SEO and should not be forgotten.

The `.htaccess` file should be placed in the root folder of the website. In osCommerce you would most probably already have a `.htaccess` file there, so it will be even easier to edit the existing file and add some commands as described above (please do not forget to replace `domain.com` with your actual domain name, `newpage.html` and `newpage.php` with corresponding file names, and `newpath` with the corresponding path to the new page, if any).

If the domain name of the new website also changes, it is possible to fix this situation for search engines by adding the following code to the `.htaccess` file:

```
Options +FollowSymLinks
RewriteEngine on
RewriteRule (.*) http://www.newdomain.com/$1 [R=301,L]
```

This code above effectively redirects all requests to the files and URLs of the old domain to the same files and URLs of the new domain. It should not be forgotten to contact every backlinking website to modify their links to point to your new website or web pages.

Understanding External and Internal SEO

Search engine optimization is a complex chain of actions, approaches, and techniques that are intended to position the website and its pages higher in search engine results brought to users.

It is possible to logically split SEO into two pieces—internal and external SEO. While internal SEO makes the website and all its pages search engine friendly (i.e. as easy to index and parse as possible, rich with keywords that prospective customers would use), external SEO works on improving the website's position in search engines.

External SEO

As said above, the so called external SEO is a set of actions, approaches, and techniques intended to improve a website's positions in search engines. It looks at the website's external relationships, and tries to achieve higher results by improving the quality of such relationships with other websites and by getting involved in new relationships. It is possible to say that external SEO is working dedicatedly on making the website more popular and on increasing the number of visitors to the website.

But first, before improving it, it's important to understand the current situation with the website's positioning in search engines.

Popularity—What it is and How to Measure It

The popularity of a website can be measured by the number of websites that point back to it, and by the number of visitors it receives, directly or from other websites. Obviously, the more visitors and more backward links a website has, the more popular it is.

To measure the number of visitors, there are special software packages (like Google Analytics, Webalizer, etc.) that can be installed on a web server (or often come pre-installed with a hosting package) and provide statistics on all visits—see the *Tracking SEO Campaign Results and Web Traffic Analysis* sections of this chapter. It is possible to check the number of visitors each month or even each week and put it into a special Excel file or a database table. It will help the store owner see the trend in the change of the number of visitors over time. Another useful tip here would be to keep separate statistics for visitors that come from search engines, websites that have backward links to your online store, and the ones that entered your website's URL directly.

A website's popularity and positions in search engines depend on the number of backward links to the website. To check the number of backward links that the search engines know of, a special query should be sent into the corresponding search engines.

Google/MSN (Live Search)/AOL:

```
link:www.domain.com
```

Yahoo!:

```
linkdomain:www.domain.com or link:www.domain.com
```

Note that there's no gap allowed after the colon. The following screenshot shows a sample results page for a search of `link`:`www.oscommerce.com`.

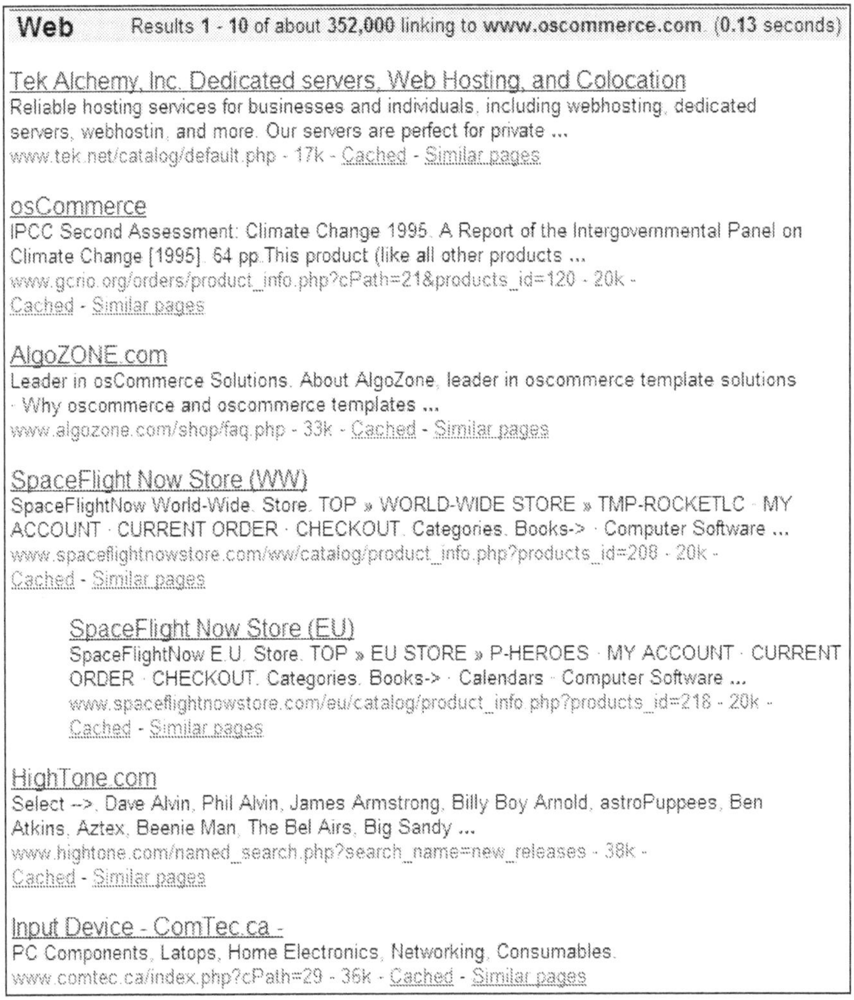

Web Results **1** - **10** of about **352,000** linking to **www.oscommerce.com**. (**0.13** seconds)

Tek Alchemy, Inc. Dedicated servers, Web Hosting, and Colocation
Reliable hosting services for businesses and individuals, including webhosting, dedicated servers, webhostin, and more. Our servers are perfect for private ...
www.tek.net/catalog/default.php - 17k - Cached - Similar pages

osCommerce
IPCC Second Assessment: Climate Change 1995. A Report of the Intergovernmental Panel on Climate Change [1995]. 64 pp.This product (like all other products ...
www.gcrio.org/orders/product_info.php?cPath=21&products_id=120 - 20k -
Cached - Similar pages

AlgoZONE.com
Leader in osCommerce Solutions. About AlgoZone, leader in oscommerce template solutions · Why oscommerce and oscommerce templates ...
www.algozone.com/shop/faq.php - 33k - Cached - Similar pages

SpaceFlight Now Store (WW)
SpaceFlightNow World-Wide. Store. TOP » WORLD-WIDE STORE » TMP-ROCKETLC · MY ACCOUNT · CURRENT ORDER · CHECKOUT. Categories. Books-> · Computer Software ...
www.spaceflightnowstore.com/ww/catalog/product_info.php?products_id=208 - 20k -
Cached - Similar pages

SpaceFlight Now Store (EU)
SpaceFlightNow E.U. Store. TOP » EU STORE » P-HEROES · MY ACCOUNT · CURRENT ORDER · CHECKOUT. Categories. Books-> · Calendars · Computer Software ...
www.spaceflightnowstore.com/eu/catalog/product_info.php?products_id=218 - 20k -
Cached - Similar pages

HighTone.com
Select -->. Dave Alvin, Phil Alvin, James Armstrong, Billy Boy Arnold, astroPuppees, Ben Atkins, Aztex, Beenie Man, The Bel Airs, Big Sandy ...
www.hightone.com/named_search.php?search_name=new_releases - 38k -
Cached - Similar pages

Input Device - ComTec.ca -
PC Components, Latops, Home Electronics, Networking, Consumables.
www.comtec.ca/index.php?cPath=29 - 36k - Cached - Similar pages

By keeping the statistics of the number of backward links, the store owner can measure its popularity in the Internet and particularly in the search engines.

Listing in Online Directories

Instead of querying search engines, some prospective customers prefer to use online directories of sites, where websites are sorted by categories and it may be easier to find a website that advertises products or services the user is looking for.

There are multiple online directories. Some of them are dedicated to a particular industry/theme only. Some of them contain links to websites of various types and categories. Also, inclusion into some directories is free of charge, and other online directories would charge the website owners a certain inclusion fee.

Listing in an online directory can bring more prospective customers to your online store. Those prospective customers would more likely be your target group of customers, as they would already be interested in the products and services that you offer on the website. This works like the Yellow Pages, and in fact Yellow Pages are available online too.

Also, listing in online directories may help to improve popularity in search engines, page ranks, and eventually positions in the search results, because online directories are parsed by search engines and backward links to the listed websites are recorded.

How should you decide which online directory is good for your online store? There could be several tips given:

- Check which online directories your well performing competitors are listed in.
- Check which online directories are popular (have good page ranks) themselves.
- Consider being listed in very specific online directories as well as in some very general ones; specific online directories where all sites are dedicated to a specific theme of content are more likely to be found by your prospective customers.
- Check how well the websites category tree is built.
- Check the information about other websites listed in the same category you would like to have your site listed in.
- Consider if your budget allows for being listed in certain paid online directories.
- Do not expect an immediate result—it may take a while for search engines to parse the online directories again and get links to your online store.

- See if listing in an online directory adds some value to the website — for example, if the directory website itself is actively advertised in the Internet, or if the editors of the online directory give reviews of the websites listed, etc.

Since many similar websites are listed in online directories, your online store should participate in a competition for winning the prospective customer's attention when the user is browsing through the directory. That is why the information about your online store should:

- Be the most accurate and correct
- Be as detailed as possible
- Be relatively short
- Contain a call to action

If it's possible — try to also give information about the company, including addresses and phone numbers to demonstrate to the prospective customers they are dealing with a real business. Also it will most probably make sense to have the website listed in multiple categories that are appropriate. For example, an online store can be listed under several categories related to its products, and also under a category related to its geographical location. Finally, for the sake of search engine optimization it makes sense to apply for inclusion of your online store into an appropriate category with the highest page rank.

To complete this section, we will review some of the most valuable online directories for websites:

`www.dmoz.org` is a free online directory that is regularly used by search engines like AOL and Google to get to know about new or updated websites. Since inclusion into Dmoz is free, there are a lot of websites being added to this online directory every day. Each inclusion request has to be approved by the moderator (Editor) of a certain category first; then it will be actually included into the online directory. There are so many of such inclusion requests received every day, that it may take a month or even more for a website to appear in the corresponding category.

`http://www.dmoz.org/add.html` describes the submission process.

A website can be submitted to the Yahoo! Search directory. There are several submission options, free and paid. More information can be found at `http://search.yahoo.com/info/submit.html`.

Google also provides a facility to submit the website to its online directory. But as its Directory is based on the Dmoz directory, the process actually repeats the one described above for Dmoz.org. It is possible to notify Google about your new online store by submitting a link to the main page of the website at `http://www.google.com/addurl.html`. It is not actually submission to a directory, but rather a way to let Google know about the newly launched website earlier than the Google bot gets to it.

In a similar way, it's possible to let MSN (now powered by Live Search of `www.live.com`) know about your new online store at `http://beta.search.msn.com/docs/submit.aspx`.

For European store owners, and also for international companies looking for a presentation of their websites in Europe, the Europages business directory (`www.europages.com`) can be an optimal choice. Inclusion is not free and the prices are quite high, but besides the inclusion into the online directory, the company also offers inclusion into the printed version of the online directory, inclusion into the national Yellow pages in several European countries, inclusion into the `www.lycos.com` directory, and many other services (like, for example, registration of several keywords associated with the website).

Backward Links

Back links play an important role in External SEO by improving a website's positions in search engines and by providing more visitors from linked websites. Those visitors are more likely to become customers as they have been referred by partner websites that advertise similar or complementary products, or provide users with information in some way related to the products of your online store.

Three key success factors for a backward linking strategy are:

- Quality of links should outweigh quantity
- Link partners must relate to your site content
- Partners should link to you from pages listing as few links as possible

The rule of thumb when starting to build the backward links profile to your online store is to check which websites have backward links to the sites of your successful competitors.

Also, it is very important to ensure the backward links are set up on websites that have a proper reputation, and not just "SPAM" websites that will disappear in the near future. In the latter case, search engines may not only ignore the links from "SPAM" websites to other pages, but also assume the linked website's participation in a "SPAM" network and somehow ban or decrease ranks of such sites.

It's always good for SEO and for getting more targeted visitors to have backward links from portals, forums, and blogs that contain information about products that are advertised on your online store.

Of course, the more non-"SPAM" websites are linked to your pages, the better it is for the business. It should be also noted that it's better to have backward links pointing not only to the main page of the online store, but to several different pages (like categories, or even individual products), so that search engines and prospective customers would be able to see exactly the information related to the pages of other websites they have been visiting just before they clicked the link to your online store. Also, try using various keywords and key phrases associated with particular pages of your site when asking other websites to place a back link to your online store.

Let's consider several types of backward links and compare the benefits of each type:

- Brochure-like, and other static and dynamic information websites — websites of other companies or websites containing information about particular products and services may be well ranked in search engines, and a backward link from such a site may well improve the position of your online store in search results with time.

- Other online stores — if an online store sells products that are complementary to the products sold online in your online store, a backward link may not only improve the position of your online store in search results, but also provide you with customers who are already interested in buying products and services similar to what you offer.

- Forums — even if you don't receive many prospective customers referred by such a website, a backward link will be quite important if the forum contains topics where the members of the forum either write about products similar to those that are offered in your online store, or discuss pros and cons of buying and/or using such products. Usually, web pages with extensive comments will be full of keywords associated in a certain way with your product catalog, which has high importance for search engines.

- This is also applicable to online blogs.

The less links to other websites located on the page, the more important the backward link to your online store. Also, it's preferable to use text phrases that contain important keywords to be linked back to your online store, so that the search engines can notice the relation between those keywords and the website. For example, a "Wide Range of Apparel" is much better for a backward link than "Visit our site now!".

Internal SEO

Internal SEO cares about optimizing the pages of the website, their content, and structure to provide the easiest way for search engines to parse the pages and to extract keywords that the store owner wants to have associated with the website.

Content and Keywords

Content is the core and the main part of internal SEO of any website. Websites get parsed by search engines and content gets extracted from the website. Then the search engines determine main keywords and key phrases and associate pages of the website with certain keywords. So when the user is searching for a certain string in the search engines, the website appears in the search results.

It is important for search engines to provide the users with the best, and the most accurate results. Therefore a website with unique content that has keywords and key phrases similar to what the user is looking for has more chances to appear in a good position in search results than a website with not much content that can be parsed by search engines (i.e. with not much textual content), or a website with non-unique content (i.e. content copied from either another website, or content from the same non-online source), even if its full of keywords and key phrases.

It's better to have natural unique descriptions for the online store, its products and categories, its manufacturers, and all other entities associated with the products. Even if product description comes from a product catalog that is shared between multiple merchants, it would do good if the store owner added some unique comments and descriptions for each product and category, so that the search engine would deal with the pages of the online store as web pages holding more or less unique content.

Actually, the best content for both search engines and end customers can be provided by the store owner. Having a very good, if not ultimate, knowledge of the industry and products that are sold online, the store owner usually can describe them in the best way, in a simple, straightforward, and keyword-rich manner. Almost any store owner can create such descriptions better than a hired writer. Here are several tips to writing SEO-friendly descriptions for products, categories, and other pages of the online store:ghg

- Write descriptions so that the target audience could understand them.
- Use professional language and terms — most of the users will find it easier to understand.
- Include details, but at the same time try to make descriptions shorter — users tend to ignore longer descriptions.

- Structure your writing well; feel free to use additional elements (images, tables, etc.) if required, but try to avoid them if possible.

- Concentrate on details (features) that would help to sell the products you offer, but do not forget to add information about other details (features) as well.

- Keep an emotional link with the content you write, write naturally, make the content of your website an additional value for your customers.

- Use paragraphs to separate parts of the descriptions; use the most important keywords and key phrases as close to the start of each new paragraph as possible.

- Feel free to highlight (with HTML header tags or bold tag, for example) certain parts of the descriptions you write — this will not only make it easier for you to make your customers concentrate on those parts, but will also show the search engines those parts are important (use this to highlight keywords and key phrases your customers will be more likely to use in search engines).

- Do not forget — almost no one knows the subject you're writing about better than you do.

Most of the search engines nowadays are able to not only index web pages, but also files and documents that are parts of websites. For example, PDF files can be indexed if they contain text content. Therefore it is possible to have a part of the web pages in the PDF format (for example, a more detailed description of certain product) and still have it indexed by search engines.

How to Define Keywords?

One of the most important tasks for an online store owner is to define keywords and key phrases the prospective customers may use to search for products and services advertised on the website.

For an osCommerce online store, the most obvious keywords to think about are the keywords and key phrases that contain:

- Product names, product attributes' names
- Category names
- Manufacturer names
- A combination of all of the above

For example, using one of the products of the demo osCommerce store (`http://demo.oscommerce.com/product_info.php?products_id=21`), we can get the following keywords and key phrases: "SWAT 3: Close Quarters Battle", "Software Stimulation", "Sierra SWAT 3: Close Quarters Battle", "Sierra Software", "Sierra Stimulation", "Sierra Software Stimulation".

Since some of the customers may be looking for cheap, or luxury options; they may add the words "cheap" or "luxury" (or similar) to their queries to the search engines. Some customers may be looking for "cheap Sierra Software".

Many customers try to refine their search queries by adding territory names. For example, a customer may be looking for "Hewlett Packard printers in Chicago".

By identifying the most popular, best selling, or most profitable manufacturers, categories of products, and products that you offer on your online store, you can refine the list of the most important keywords that are relevant for your website.

But how can you ensure the keywords and key phrases that you think or want to be popular are really popular among your prospective customers? Once the list of the keywords and key phrases is compiled, you can test it in search engines like Google or Overture using appropriate keyword suggesting tools. The good news is that these keyword selection and suggestions tools are usually free and rely on real-life data collected while the customers searched for certain keywords.

Overture's keyword selection and the suggestion tool not only gives the number of searches for a specified keyword per month, but also provides the most popular key phrases used by the customers during a certain period of time, sorted by popularity among the customers. For example, for "Hewlett Packard Printers" it suggests:

hewlett packard laser printer
hewlett packard all in one printer
hewlett packard photo printer
hewlett packard printer ink
hewlett packard printer software
hewlett packard color printer
hewlett packard printer cartridge
hewlett packard deskjet printer
hewlett packard printer software download
hewlett packard printer ink cartridge

Inclusion of all or some of suggested key phrases into the list of keywords may help to attract more customers in the future, and also cut down costs on advertising.

Overture's suggestion website is located at `http://inventory.overture.com/d/searchinventory/suggestion/`.

Google provides a free to use Keyword Tool for external users and a similar Keyword Tool for its AdWords customers. The tool is based on Google search statistics, and can generate key phrases based on the given keyword or on the given website. The tool is located at `https://adwords.google.com/select/ KeywordToolExternal`. For each suggested keyword, it gives two estimates—of advertiser competition (i.e. how many other advertisers are using the same keyword in their paid advertisements) and search volume (i.e. how popular this keyword or key phrase is among the prospective customers).

For example, for the example already used above "Hewlett Packard Printers", it suggests a list of 25 keywords. Of the following list, the following keywords can be used by the osCommerce store owner:

packard deskjet printer
all in one printers
canon printers
best printers
photo printers
inkjet printers
laser printers
scanner printers
plotter printers
deskjet printers
laserjet printers
multifunction printers
printers ink
colour printers
fax printers
color printers

Keywords in the list should be updated regularly. Those keywords should be broadly used in the content of the web pages of the online store. Also, those keywords should be used with names, news pages, and editing page properties (like titles, etc.). We will show how to utilize the identified keywords further in this chapter.

Avoiding Duplicate Product Page URLs

Search engines may get incorrect indexes when they find the same content duplicated in several pages of the same website, or in several completely different websites. Search engines strive to define the source of the content where the authentic copy is located. Once it's done, the search engines tends to ignore other pages or websites where duplicate content is present.

The main reason for this is to provide users of search engines with the most appropriate and comprehensive search results. So instead of providing users with a list of links matching the search query but containing the same or very similar content, the search engines would rather list matching but diverse authentic links.

We will call completely identical or very similar blocks of textual information on different pages of one website or different websites duplicate content.

So what does this have to do with an osCommerce online store? There are several potential issues that an osCommerce store owner should be aware of. Let us consider them and also consider how to deal with these issues.

Same Product in Multiple Categories

Quite often, one and the same product can be put in two or more categories in osCommerce. For example, a new MP3 player can be put into the `Music / MP3 Players` category and `Gift Ideas` category as well. This is correct from the marketing point of view, but may be considered wrong from the search engine's point of view. It all depends on how osCommerce generates product page URLs.

If osCommerce adds category path (cPath) into the URL, search engines will consider one and the same product included into two different categories as two different URLs, two different pages, i.e. as duplicate content.

osCommerce uses the cPath variable to extract the category path from the URL and open the category tree accordingly, and also print the so called "breadcrumbs" in the navigation part of the page, so that the customer will know what are the parent categories of the product.

There are several possible solutions when a product gets included into two and more categories in osCommerce:

- Use "301" redirects in the `.htaccess` file to redirect users, and search engine bots from all URLs of the product information page in various categories to only one chosen product information page URL. The inclusion into the `.htaccess` file may look like this:

  ```
  Redirect permanent /index.php?cPath=2_20&products_id=24 http://
  www.domain.com/index.php?cPath=3_23&products_id=24
  ```

- If you have almost all products duplicated in two or more categories, you may want to remove the cPath part from all URLs, leaving only the products_id part there. You can do it by modifying the `/catalog/includes/modules/products_listing.php` file, in the part of the code where it sets the value of the `$lc_text` variable. One has to be very careful when editing that `.php` file as the Product Listing class is used in a number of places in osCommerce (including the search results page, category listing page, etc.). In fact the `$lc_text` variable contains the complete HTML description of the product listing, so you would need to locate the place in the code where it adds category ID (cPath) to the URL that leads the customer to the product information page and comment/remove that piece of PHP script.

- Using `robots.txt`, it is possible to tell search engines not to crawl or index certain pages (product pages or category pages) of the osCommerce online store. It is possible to find more information about using `robots.txt` at `http://www.robotstxt.org/` and we also cover it in a bit more detail, later in this chapter, but here's a sample of such instructions that will prevent search engines from crawling and indexing certain product pages and category pages:

```
User-Agent: *
Disallow: /catalog/index.php?cPath=2_20&products_id=24
Disallow: /catalog/index.php?cPath=99
Disallow: /shopping_cart.php
```

Product Listing and Product Information Pages with the Same Content

Sometimes product listing pages contain complete or almost complete descriptions of products that also appear on the product information pages on the same website. Search engines may consider such pages to have duplicate content, and ignore either the product listing or product information pages.

This situation is relatively easy to fix. Instead of displaying the complete product description on the product listing page, it's better to either display a special short description there, and then have the long product description displayed exclusively on the product information page, or display only a part (let's say 100 characters or 10 words) of the product description in the listing, and display the complete description on the product information page.

If all products have very short descriptions, too short to be split between the product listing and product information pages, why is it necessary to include links to the product information pages at all? Why not leave the product listing pages only, and let the customers see complete product descriptions there and buy products directly from the product listing?

Yes, sometimes such an approach will work. But there are at least three reasons not to do it and to leave the product information pages on the website.

The first reason is SEO, keywords density in particular. It's obvious that on the product information page, keyword density will be higher for product-specific keywords than on the product listing page (because of other products listed there). The second reason is all those extra images that some or all products may have besides their main product image. Extra product images in osCommerce require additional contributions to be installed, and we will cover this in more detail in further chapters of this book. The third reason is attributes — if the online store uses attributes, the customers should be able to select certain attribute values on the product information page. Although there are certain updates for osCommerce product listing pages that allow for listing product attributes there along with the products, should products have more than one or two attributes the page will become very crowded and customers may become confused. Also, it won't be a positive improvement for search engines because of the amount of extra HTML code required to display selections of attributes.

Either way the owner of an osCommerce online store needs to make sure the usability of the website doesn't suffer from SEO improvements.

Multiple Front Ends Linked to the Same Back End, Even when Using Different Domain Names

Some higher advanced e-commerce solutions based on osCommerce may include multiple front ends linked to the same product catalog and back end. Such solutions are much easier to manage than multiple, completely separate online stores. Each front end may be on a separate sub-domain or domain name, and have different designs. Each front end may be dedicated to a certain group of products, or be optimized to address the expectations of a certain target customer group, so that the system of several front ends may be more successful in online sales than one online store with all categories and products listed under one front end.

But while improving online sales and making management of multiple front ends just as easy as management of a single online store, such e-commerce solutions may lose in SEO because of the duplicate content issue.

Then the following may be of help:

- If possible, have different product descriptions entered for and displayed in every front end. This way search engines will stop seeing duplicate content, and the customers will still be placing orders in literally one and the same online store independent of how many front ends the system has.

- If it doesn't conflict with the marketing strategy — use `robots.txt` as described earlier to tell the search engines to ignore certain parts of certain front ends.
- If there are multiple languages installed in osCommerce — make sure product description in each language is different from product description in other languages. If product description only exists in the default language — it may make sense to disable the multilingual feature on the website until the translations for all languages are ready.

osCommerce Online Stores Using Product Feed Coming from Suppliers

It is often the case that osCommerce is used as an e-commerce solution by those retailers who receive product feeds from suppliers, and as a result list products that other retailers also list on their own websites. In this situation, search engines may ignore the product pages of the osCommerce online store as they will be containing duplicate content, as well as the product pages of the websites of other retailers.

Such cases are different to the ones described above because here osCommerce store owners cannot amend the product descriptions and specifications that come from suppliers except by creating new unique content (description) for each product. Taking into account the amount of time required to do so, most online retailers would prefer to use some other method.

A possible solution would be to improve the product pages of the osCommerce online store by adding manufacturer information, category buying guides, size charts (if applicable), and other additional information based on product data. This will help to make each product page look more unique compared to the product pages of other websites that use the same product feeds.

Other Websites Using osCommerce Store's Product Feed

Finally, we will consider a situation when other websites (affiliates for example) download product information from osCommerce online stores and list it on their pages. This situation is opposite to the one described above, and here the main concern is if the search engines correctly identify the source of the content being your osCommerce online store.

First of all, it may not be a reason to worry too much. Search engines will most probably correctly identify the source of the content, and will continue to parse and index your website accordingly.

However, a link back to the corresponding page of your website from each page where your content is published may help search engines to understand that your website is the source.

If you see a website that uses your content that you think is affecting your SEO, and the website owner refuses to remove or alter the content, you may want to contact the search engines and ask for exclusion of the other website from the search results on certain keywords. For example, for Google the procedure is described at `http://www.google.com/dmca.html`.

HTML Validation and Page Structure Optimization

Since HTML formats are issued by W3C.org, a valid web page complies to the W3C. org HTML formats and recommendations.

It has almost never been the case that web browsers require the pages to be 100% correct and valid HTML. Almost any web browser allows for certain inconsistencies in HTML script that webmasters sometimes use to create impressive looking websites. Web browsers always try to find a way round such inconsistencies and compensate in different ways that merely depend on each particular browser. A web page with no inconsistencies is valid.

If this is so, and if they allow certain freedom in authoring HTML pages—does it mean the search engines ought to do the same? Actually the answer is—yes, this is how the search engines try to perform. Search engine bots try to extract as much content and textual information from websites as possible to perform the most precise analysis of the extracted data. But what if a web page is not valid HTML, but rather a freely designed HTML pages with some parts of it not being valid accordingly to the formats? In that case, search engine bots may incorrectly extract information from the website, or miss some textual information that contains important keywords.

So there are at least the following reasons to have website pages valid:

- To make web pages look the same in different browsers that support the same HTML formats
- To avoid confusion and incorrect processing by different Search Engine bots, and allow all of the important information to be properly extracted and indexed from the web pages

Even though there are certain reasons not to validate the website (valid pages may not look and work as intended originally; time and costs involved may be quite considerable), for SEO purposes it's recommended to keep your osCommerce online store valid HTML.

What should be Validated in osCommerce?

All osCommerce online stores are similar, at least in the file and website structure. Whatever the actual names of the files are, it makes sense to have the following pages/files as valid HTML:

- main (home) page
- category listing page
- advanced search page
- product information page
- shopping cart page
- information pages (like About Us, Terms and Conditions, etc.)

How do we Validate and What are the Most Common Issues?

There exist multiple validation services in the Internet, paid and free. Paid services may suggest useful tips on how to fix this or that validation error, while the free services mostly concentrate on spotting validation problems and reporting them to the customers.

The best known free HTML pages validation service is provided by W3C.org, and is available at `http://validator.w3.org`. It allows for submission of HTML scripts and also URLs and returns the list of found issues or a confirmation about the page being valid.

In order to validate an osCommerce online store, its URLs could be submitted to the W3C.org HTML Validator. You will receive a list of issues you need to tackle. The web pages should then be modified until the last reported error is gone and those pages are considered valid by this service.

There may be some situations, though, when it's better to not fix an error reported by the Validator, for the sake of desired look and feel of the web pages. There may also be situations when a reported HTML validation issue is caused by the description of a certain product that is listed on the page. In that case, the product's description should be corrected in the Administration panel of the online store.

Let us consider typical issues reported by the validation service and ways to fix them using the example of the osCommerce demo website, `http://demo.oscommerce.com/`.

The first attempt to validate the main page returns 12 errors, which is relatively few compared to over 90 issues per page reported on the main pages of some osCommerce online stores.

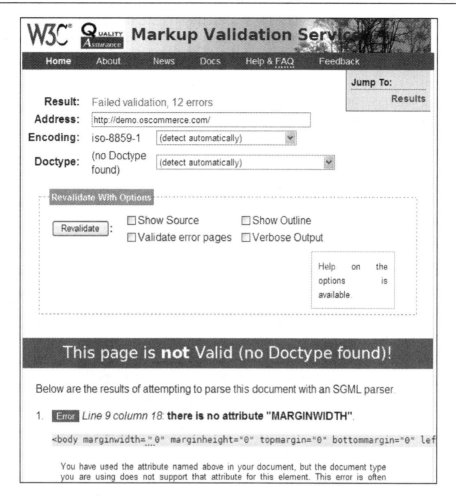

The very first error message tells us the Doctype element of HTML is missing. The strange thing about that is when we open the HTML sources of the main page of the demo osCommerce online store, we can see the doctype tag in the very first row. So what exactly is missing? It seems that the character case matters here a lot. Changing the following string:

```
<!doctype html public "-//W3C//DTD HTML 4.01 Transitional//EN">
```

to

```
<!DOCTYPE HTML PUBLIC "-//W3C//DTD HTML 4.01 Transitional//EN">
```

can solve this very first problem. Alternatively, the Validator allows overriding the doctype parameter before the validation, manually.

The following five errors are related to the `<body>` HTML tag format. They are not crucial for SEO. The easiest way to fix them would be to remove all the non-standard attributes of the `<body>` tag attributes at all (i.e. get rid of the `marginwidth`, `marginheight`, etc.).

Then until the very end of the list of errors, warnings, and advises, Validator prints occurrences of the uncoded `&` character in the page script. As suggested by the Validator itself `&` can be changed to `&amp;`, even in URLs, to fix this error.

The validator report usually contains very detailed and helpful comments and even suggestions on how to fix those reported issues. You can fix all or most of those reported issues by simply following given suggestions.

The same or very similar issues can be seen and fixed in the category product listing page, such as, for example, `http://demo.oscommerce.com/index.php?cPath=3` The W3C HTML Validator reports about 16 errors on such pages. The exact number of errors may also depend on the exact content of each individual page, and which product names or product descriptions are a part of it. The product information page contains as many as 25 errors (may depend on product description) according to the W3C.org validator.

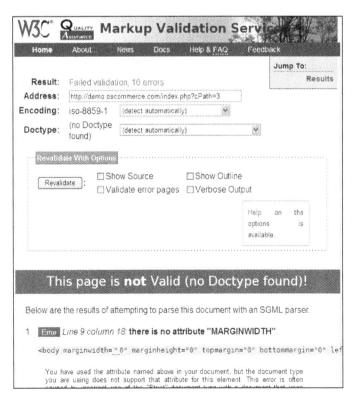

Again, it contains a number of errors related to the `<body>` HTML tag format. But first comes an issue related to the format of the `<script>` tag—it requires Type, which has not been specified in osCommerce by default. It is easy to fix this by adding: `type="text/javascript"` to `<script>`.

Then follow the issues caused by the & characters in the URLs. Those can be easily fixed by replacing & with & in URLs through the page.

Some of the errors are caused by occurrences of attributes that are not allowed in certain tags according to the HTML format (like the `border` attribute in the `<input type="image">` tag).

 It should be noted that some of the problems reported by the Validator will disappear after the original problems that caused them are fixed. For example, fixing the type issues with the `<script>` tag in the product information page will also fix an issue of the end tag for element `<a>` which is not open.

Even though validating the search results page (we searched for an "a" in product description in the demo site) results in 91 errors and multiple warnings, almost all of them can be easily fixed by fixing the & problem as already explained. The reason for that page having so many errors is in just the number of products it has found—the more products per page it shows, the more errors will be reported by the Validator.

Other pages (like the Shopping Cart page, or Privacy Notice, etc.) contain the same 12 errors according to the Validator as the main page.

It looks like the demo version of osCommerce is quite OK according to the W3C. org Validator. But each particular osCommerce online store should be validated from time to time to ensure its pages can be easily parsed by search engine bots and proper content can be extracted and used by search engines.

Optimized URLs in osCommerce

It has been a while since the search engines were not able to index pages other than .HTML or similar. With the increase of computer facilities, the search engines do not make a discretion between dynamically created pages (like .PHP) and static pages (like .HTML) anymore.

So what would be the benefits of modifying product, category, and other pages URLs in osCommerce for search engines? The main reason to change URLs in osCommerce is search engine optimization. Yes, URL matters a lot to search engines, and, should it contain keywords typed in by the user in the search engine, it increases the chances of the website (or this particular URL) to be listed higher in the search results.

A URL is optimized for SEO when it contains important keywords that are related to the content of the page, and that the potential user would type in a search engine trying to find information and/or products offered on the website. So in the case of osCommerce optimized URLs would contain all or some of the product name, category name, manufacturer name for products and category name for categories, and also page names for additional pages, like Privacy Notes, etc.

For example, instead of `http://demo.oscommerce.com/index.php?cPath=1`, an optimized URL would look like `http://demo.oscommerce.com/Hardware.html`.

And instead of `http://demo.oscommerce.com/product_info.php?cPath=1_5&products_id=27`, an optimized product URL would look like `http://demo.oscommerce.com/Hewlett-Packard-LaserJet-1100Xi.html` or like `http://demo.oscommerce.com/Hardware/Hewlett-Packard-LaserJet-1100Xi.html`.

Coming back to a demo osCommerce website, we will now look into several ways that product, category, and other pages URLs could look, and how to implement this SEO feature in osCommerce. But first we will briefly study how exactly the process works; how it is possible to receive such static-looking URLs from dynamic database-driven ones.

Of course, there is a method that allows for manual compilation of as many redirect instructions from static-looking pages to the dynamic pages as there are products and categories in the database. But we will be more interested in a solution that works automatically, once put in place. For Linux-based web servers, the method is based on mod_rewrite, which is installed as a part of the Apache web server. Following certain rewrite rules (`RewriteRule`) specified in the `.htaccess` file, the web server (Apache) can be "told" to output contents of a different page than the user's browser has requested. So if the rewrite rules are set up properly, when the user's web browser requests contents of the "static" page, the web server will actually read contents of the corresponding dynamic database-driven page.

So what can "static" URLs look like in osCommerce? Here's the list of suggested URL formats for category pages:

- `categoryname.html`
- `categoryname.id.html`

Here is the list of suggested URL formats for product information pages:

- `productname.html`
- `categoryname-productname.html`
- `categoryname/productname.html`
- `categoryname-manufacturername-productname.html`

Other combinations of parts of these URLs can be also used. Having product names, category names, and manufacturer names helps the search engines to easily understand what the website in general is about and understand its pages in particular.

Now when we know what the URLs should look like in osCommerce, let us see how to implement this feature with "static" URLs, used instead of dynamic URLs throughout the site in osCommerce. There is a free contribution called "Ultimate SEO URLs v. 2.1", which can be downloaded from the osCommerce website `http://addons.oscommerce.com/info/2823`. This contribution does its job by converting dynamic URLs into "static" looking URLs, and allows for certain flexibility in URL format. It comes with a detailed installation guide and a handful of various options. After installing it to an osCommerce website and configuring it properly, this is how the corresponding menu of the Configuration section in the Administration panel looks:

SEO URLs

Title	Value	Action	Enable SEO URLs?
Enable SEO URLs?	true	▶	edit
Add cPath to product URLs?	false	ⓘ	
Add category parent to begining of URLs?	true	ⓘ	Enable the SEO URLs? This is a global setting and will turn them off completely.
Filter Short Words	3	ⓘ	
Output W3C valid URLs (parameter string)?	true	ⓘ	
Enable SEO cache to save queries?	true	ⓘ	
Enable product cache?	true	ⓘ	Date Added: 02/28/2007
Enable categories cache?	true	ⓘ	
Enable manufacturers cache?	true	ⓘ	Last Modified: 02/28/2007
Enable articles cache?	true	ⓘ	
Enable topics cache?	true	ⓘ	
Enable information cache?	true	ⓘ	
Enable automatic redirects?	true	ⓘ	
Choose URL Rewrite Type	Rewrite	ⓘ	
Enter special character conversions		ⓘ	
Remove all non-alphanumeric characters?	false	ⓘ	
Reset SEO URLs Cache	false	ⓘ	

And this is what the improved "static" URLs look like:

category: `http://www.myonlinestore.com/hardware.html`

product:
`http://www.myonlinestore.com/hewlett-packard-laserjet-1100xi.html`

What becomes obvious is that not only product or category URLs matter, but also URLs of product images, category images, and other additional files (like .CSS or .JS). Here it makes sense to rename product and category image files according to the product and category names. It is better to use some terms related to the content of the online store when renaming additional files (`.css` or `.js`). For example, instead of the standard `stylesheet.css` the name of the `.css` file could be changed to `kitchen_appliances.css` or `silver_jewelery.css`.

Session IDs are added to the URLs by default so that the customers can log in, register, and make a purchase. But search engines do not need to log in or purchase goods online. It's a great relief as session IDs can have a negative effect on the search engine optimization. Each time a search engine bot indexes a category or product page with a session ID, it will consider that page to be a completely new one, that has never been indexed before. So instead of giving it a good page rank based on the backward links and its well indexed content, it will only give such page some low rank as if it was a very new one. The situation worsens when users find links that include session IDs in search engines. Clicking such links will automatically bring a session with the corresponding ID to live. This means that two users who have found a link to a certain page of the osCommerce online store in the search engine, and clicked that link in more or less the same time, will share one and the same session. This effectively means one user will have access to the account of the other user and vice versa!

To avoid issues with SEO and with users having access to each other's accounts, it's recommended to remove session IDs from the URLs in osCommerce for search engines.

To disable session IDs from appearing in the URLs when the website is being parsed by search engine bots, the Prevent Spider Sessions parameter should be set to TRUE in the Configuration section of the **Administration panel | Configuration | Sessions** menu item, as shown on the following screenshot:

Sessions			
Title	Value	Action	Prevent Spider Sessions
Session Directory	/tmp	ⓘ	
Force Cookie Use	False	ⓘ	edit
Check SSL Session ID	False	ⓘ	
Check User Agent	False	ⓘ	Prevent known spiders from starting a session.
Check IP Address	False	ⓘ	
Prevent Spider Sessions	True	▶	
Recreate Session	False	ⓘ	Date Added: 02/27/2007
			Last Modified: 03/07/2007

The method used by osCommerce to recognize search engine bots is based on the names of those bots. In osCommerce, the list of known bots is located in the `/catalog/includes/spiders.txt` file.

Webmasters can further extend the list of known spider bots by editing that file. Usually, this will not be required as the list supplied by default is quite comprehensive. But webmasters of online stores based on previous versions of osCommerce may find it useful to download the latest version and update the list of spider bots in their online stores.

Page Title and META Tags in osCommerce

Optimization of web page properties such as Title, and META tags is an important part of the SEO process of any website. Search Engines use page tittles and META tags to find out what the page is about along with parsing the actual content of the page.

Title and META tags are sometimes considered to be the most important for search engines, as the title is the first part of the page that the user sees in search results, and META tags can contain a special description, which is used by search engines to describe the found page.

If the page title is not specified, search engines will use the website URL instead. If the page description is not specified, search engines will try to extract a part of the page's content and display it in the search results.

Obviously, the more relevant the page title and its description are to the user's query in the search engine, the more chances there are that the user will choose to open the page. Also, the more relevant those properties are to the content of the page, the more chances there are that the search engine will list the page higher in the search results. This doesn't mean page title and META tags outweigh the value of the contents of the page. Rather proper usage of these page properties together with original keyword-rich content powers up the position of the website pages in search results.

An off-the-shelf installation of osCommerce doesn't really use titles and META tags to ensure the best visibility of the online store in search engines. By default, all pages have one and the same title "osCommerce" and no META tags for keywords and descriptions.

This is bad for SEO, as titles and META descriptions should always be unique for each page, without duplication. Also, since the title is the first thing the visitors see on a page, it should give the visitor the very description of what the page/site is about.

In the following screenshot, one can see what an osCommerce's product information page source code can look like. Page title and META tags are properly defined and describe the page, so that search engines and Internet users can easily understand what is offered on that page of an online store:

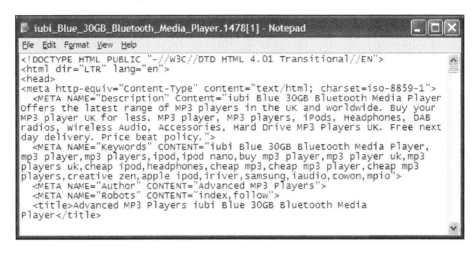

Also, in the following screenshot, one can see how the same product page is displayed in the Google search results page, and which elements of the page's header are utilized there:

Advanced MP3 Players **iubi Blue 30GB** Bluetooth Media Player
iubi Blue 30GB Bluetooth Media Player Offers the latest range of MP3 players in the UK and worldwide. Buy your MP3 player UK for less.
www.advancedmp3players.co.uk/shop/product_info.php?cPath=3&products_id=1478 - 143k -
17 Mar 2007 - Cached - Similar pages

Moreover, page title and META descriptions should be easy to read and understandable for the website visitors, and search engines should not consider them as SPAM while parsing the pages. Here are some suggestions on how to prevent giving a SPAM impression:

- Title tag—only one element per page, preferably not more than 80 characters, without comas and any other signs, preferably with 1-2 target keywords or key phrases in it.

- META description—only one tag per page, descriptive phrases with total text length up to 250 characters, at least one or more target keywords or phrases, and preferably a call to action.

- META keywords—only one tag per page, all target keywords and key phrases but preferably not more than 20 words.

In order to achieve the best results, the following pages need to be given proper page properties.

Main Page

Its title should be identical to the name of the online store, plus it's recommended to mention some of the most popular products or categories there. For example, this is a good title for a website that sells yoga and fitness products online: "Yoga Super Store - Pilates Exercise, Props, Equipment, Mats, Ball, Band Pilates, Magic circle, Pilates Ring, Roller, Reformer, Machines, Cadillac, Spine Corrector, Arc Barrel".

A rule of thumb with the page title, the same as for the rest of the SEO process, is to make a page easy to read and understandable for the online store customers, and not only optimized for SEO. Therefore the title should have up to nine words (about 80 characters or so), with no fluff and get straight to the point.

The META description tag should contain a general description of the online store, rich with keywords that prospective customers would use to find an online store like this in search engines. One can be willing to also put some location details in the META description if the marketing strategy of the online store includes advertising in the local market. This is a good sample of a META tag description taken from a website that sells drives and motors online: "Shop Drives Super Store for the best AC and DC drive selection and superior customer services. Buy Variable frequency drive or Variable speed drive backed by 12 months warranty from manufacturers such as Hitachi and Polyspede. Also get quantity discounts!".

Finally, the META keywords tag should contain all general keywords related to the contents of the website, to the products, and services it promotes. These keywords are used by search engines in addition to page contents, title, and description to better index pages and sort search results by relevancy. For the Main page of an online store, it makes sense to list keywords that are related to the whole website and product catalog, like the online store name, and the names of the best selling categories and products. As an example let's consider keywords used by a website that sells MP3 players and similar products online: "advanced mp3 players, mp3 players, portable mp3 players, cd mp3 players, mp3 accessories, dvd players, hard disk mp3 players mp3 players, mp3 player, uk mp3 players, mp3 player uk, mp3 players uk, buy, uk, portable, rio, microdrive, compact flash, wma player, compactflash, mp3/cd player, mp3 cd player, digital audio players, digital audio".

Category Listing Page

The category listing page may contain category description, featured products, and also the list of sub-categories.

Therefore its title element and META tags should mainly contain information related to the product category and its sub-categories and related categories of the product catalog.

We will use the same websites as we used in the previous sample here, and for a couple of other pages.

For example, the category listing title can look like the following for a website that sells yoga and fitness products (category Yoga): "Pilates Exercise, Props, Equipment, Mats, Ball, band Pilates, Pilates Ring - Yoga Super store Online Yoga supplier".

The category listing META description can look like the following for a website that sells drives and motors online (category AC Drives): "We specialize in Variable frequency AC drives and AC motor drives. Get the largest inventory of AC drives and Variable frequency drives online and choose the best AC drive suiting your requirements. We offer drives manufactured by Hitachi and Polyspede".

The category listing META keywords can look like the following for a website that sells MP3 players (category Portable MP3 Players): "Portable mp3 players, mp3 players, Portable Audio/Video, Electronics, MP3, Prices, Cheap".

Product Information Page

Correspondingly, all product information page titles, META descriptions, and keywords should be related to a particular product. It also makes sense to mention the category it belongs to, the manufacturer, and other properties and attributes if they are to be useful for the users of search engines.

Product page's title for a website that sells yoga and fitness products could look like (product name is Cotton Yoga Rug): "Trident Cotton Yoga Rug Yoga Mats – Yoga super store Online Yoga supplier".

The product page's META description for a website that sells drives and motors online could look like this (the product name is M3006): "M3006 Shop Drives super store for the best AC and DC drive selection and superior customer services. Buy Variable frequency drive or Variable speed drive backed by 12 months warranty from manufacturers such as Hitachi and Polyspede. Also get quantity discounts!".

The product page's META keywords tag for a website that sells MP3 and similar products could look like this (the product name Apple iPod Nano): "Apple iPod Nano - 4Gb Green, Digital Audio/Video Players (MP3/MP4) Portable Audio/Video Electronics".

How to Do It in osCommerce?

Now we know what should be put in page titles and META tags for a better performance in search engines. Let us consider ways to improve osCommerce script so that it allows the specifying of title elements and META tags manually for each particular page and for each category and product or generates them automatically.

There is a contribution that allows the editing of title element contents and META tags (keywords and descriptions) for specific osCommerce pages (like the main page, shopping cart page, category listing page, product information page, etc.) and also for specific categories and products.

It is called the "Header Tag Controller" and can be downloaded from `http://addons.oscommerce.com/info/207`.

This contribution not only allows us to specify manually default titles and META tags for pages of an osCommerce website, but also allows the use of product or category or manufacture name and/or description for each individual category, product, or manufacturer page.

It is also possible to set titles, META descriptions, and keywords for pages with New products, Special products, Product reviews, etc.

Main Page URL and Redirects

Many websites suffer from a main (home) page that has low page ranks in search engines, even though other pages are ranked well. The main reason for this is that there are multiple links to different URLs of the main page of such websites from other websites and from internal pages of the website itself.

Page rank then splits between those multiple URLs, and thus none of them usually gets high rankings. If there was only one URL to the main page of the website, it would have a higher page rank in the search engines.

This problem often appears in osCommerce online stores, when the main page can be referred to in multiple different ways. For example, the main can be referred as `http://www.mystore.com` and as `http://mystore.com` and as `http://www.mystore.com/index.php`.

Effectively the page rank that could have been given to the main page of such an osCommerce online store is split between the three URLs, as search engines consider those three URLs to be different. Moreover on this, a duplicate content issue may appear as well since all three different URLs would be pointing to one and the same page with one and the same content.

To avoid such issues in osCommerce the following can be implemented:

- First let's solve the `http://mystore.com` and `http://www.mystore.com` issue by adding the following redirect command into the `.htaccess` file, which is located in the root folder of the osCommerce website:

```
RewriteCond %{HTTP_HOST} ^mystore\.com$ [NC]
RewriteRule ^(.*)$ http://www.mystore.com/$1 [R=301,L]
```

- Secondly, in the `/includes/configure.php` file make sure the website's URLs are properly specified. Like, for example:

```
define('HTTP_SERVER', 'http://www.mystore.com');
define('HTTPS_SERVER', 'https://www.mystore.com');
```

- Finally, get rid of the `http://www.mystore.com/index.php` links and change them to `http://www.mystore.com/` by modifying the `.htaccess` file again:

```
RewriteCond %{THE_REQUEST} ^[A-Z]{3,9}\ /index\.php\ HTTP/
RewriteRule ^index\.php$ http://www.mystore.com/ [R=301,L]
```

These fixes above, assume osCommerce is running in the root folder of the website. But some store owners prefer to put osCommerce into a sub-folder, or even on a sub-domain.

Even though it may look easier to create a sub-domain with some target keywords used as a name (`http://mp3-players.mystore.com` for example) it may not be such a good idea after all. The reason is that sub-domains are considered as completely separate websites by search engines. Correspondingly, the page rank of the main website will not increase if its sub domain's page rank increases. Even worse, should there be too many links between the sub-domains or between the sub domains and the main site, the search engines may penalize the sites for improper cross linking! Also, as new sub-domains are considered like separate websites, Google may put them in the "sandbox" for some time before they start to appear in the search results.

If it's an option, get a new domain name for the online store to avoid such issues.

It's possible to use folders without any fear of being penalized for cross-linking. If the main website is well promoted in search engines, newly added folders will automatically start receiving popularity and page rating of the main site and will rank very high once they have been indexed unlike sub-domains, where each one would have to gain the same amount of popularity and page rating as the main site on its own. Using folders also increases the count of the pages of the main website, when pages belonging to sub-domains would not count as pages belonging or related to the main website.

Internal Linking between the Pages

Even though external links are considered to be more important, internal links (i.e. links from page to page of one and the same site or links within the same page) are still a good weapon in SEO arsenal.

What are internal links in osCommerce?

First of all, these are links from the main page to further pages, like category pages for example, and eventually to the individual product pages.

In order to use all features of the internal linking, it is possible to link such internal pages back to the main page of the website. Of course, there should be links to only one main page used through the website as described in the previous section.

This way search engines will know the online store's main page is related to the content of all product and category pages. This will not only improve the page rank of the whole website, but also give the search engines a better understanding of the content of the site.

The more descriptive phrases used, the more beneficial and powerful they are in the results. Using words like "read here" or "go there" is not the way to do it.

Links to the main page and also to the parent categories are implemented in standard osCommerce as "breadcrumbs" in the header section of the page. However, it's recommended to change the text of the main page's link from the standard "catalog" to either the name of the online store, or better to the most important key phrase/best selling product or category name. In order to do this, one has to edit the `/includes/languages/english.php` file, and edit the `HEADER_TITLE_CATALOG` text constant there.

Besides linking back to the main page, categories and products may be linked to similar categories and products, or to categories and products of the same level in the product catalog hierarchy. This way, if one of the categories or product pages gets ranked well in the search engines, other pages will be boosted by that one. This also helps visitors to stay on the website longer when they can browse similar/related products and categories.

Such internal links between product and category pages should use link text that is similar to or the same as certain key phrases the online store is targeting for ratings. Internal links of this type can be either added manually for each product or category, or generated automatically listing sibling products or categories correspondingly, as on the following screenshot of a category page:

and this screenshot of a product page (with links to similar/related products put in the very bottom of the page):

Electrolux American Foodstore ERL6296KK1

- Independant fridge &, freezer controls Energy consumption: 492 kWh/year Freezing capacity: 7.5 kg/24 h Fridge and freezer are side-by-side Frost free freezer Gross capacity refrigerator: 402 litres Gross capacity freezer: 218 litres Colour: Black Net capacity refrigerator: 357 litres Net capacity freezer: 165 litres Rising Time: 4.7 hours

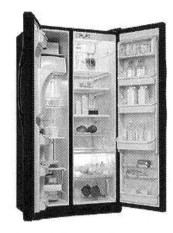

Colour: Black

Type: Free standing

 Delivery
Delivery is by our own logistics team with the exception of American Foodstores and some Falcon Appliances. Deliveries are made within 10 - 14 **working days** providing the goods are in stock at our warehouse or with the manufacturer.

Image shown is for illustration only. It may not reflect the colour or configuration of the model chosen

£996.69

Price includes VAT and delivery with the exception of American Foodstores and some Falcon Range Cookers

 Finance is available for this product!
Get to the checkout page to find out more about available options.

 Add Electrolux ERL6296KK1 to cart

We aim not to be beaten on price..
Click here if you have had a more competitive quote

Need Assistance?
Call our service team on
0870 757 2424

If you are interested in the Electrolux American Foodstore ERL6296KK1 you might also want to look at **these products**

Electrolux American Foodstore ENS5700X   Electrolux American Foodstore ERL6296SK1

An extra improvement of page rank in search engines can be given to a category or product page by placing a "direct" internal link on the main page of the website. Such "direct" links from the main page increase positioning of the linked pages in search engines, and also improve page ranks of the related (linked) pages. Of course, the main page should still look attractive and "direct" links should not look like a mess.

Besides category and product pages, pages that contain additional product information like what each option in the specification means, technology used, user manuals, installation instructions, i.e. every bit of information naturally related to the products have a great value for SEO.

It is possible to create static HTML pages or use one of the Content Management Systems developed for osCommerce (like this one for example: `http://addons.oscommerce.com/info/1026`) to add pages with such content to the website. Additional information pages containing manufacturer descriptions can be added to the shop, and linked with the corresponding products.

Good for SEO is the `<acronym>` tag, and links to the pages explaining terms from product descriptions. Acronyms are often used in technical specifications, where the language is rather reminiscent of some jargon rather than natural language.

So acronyms do not only give search engines an opportunity to read and index additional keywords-rich contents, but also help users a lot!

Finally, buying guides intended to help the customers make their choice can be prepared for each category as separate information pages and linked with corresponding products and categories, either manually when editing product description in the Administration panel, or automatically by modifying the product information page script and also the category editing routine in the Administration panel.

Site Maps

Site maps help the users to find information they are looking for on the website, and also help search engines a lot to index all pages of the website. A site map is usually represented as a tree starting from the main page. A site map is like a navigation help for visitors of online store.

osCommerce site map

A site map for an online store would include:

- Main categories
- Sub-categories of main categories
- Best selling/featured products in a separate branch of the tree
- Information pages

There is a contribution for osCommerce that generates site maps. It can be downloaded from `http://addons.oscommerce.com/info/2208` and can generate site maps automatically based on the product catalog tables:

In osCommerce, a link to the site map can be put into the footer or into the Information box.

Google and Yahoo! Site Maps

Google and other search engines have introduced their own site maps to get more precise and up-to-date information about changes in the website structure. Updates to the site maps are provided by webmasters and store owners directly.

Since the site map is submitted into the search engine directly, it is processed promptly, and the pages it consists of are indexed promptly as well. Again, any changes in the product catalog structure will be known to the search engine once the latest version of the site map is submitted. Therefore the search engine site map needs to be regenerated (preferably automatically) each time anything changes in the product catalog.

A Google site map is an XML file that should be submitted into a Google Webmaster's account. In order to become an approved webmaster for a certain website Google usually requires the webmaster to either upload a file with certain name to the website, or add a temporary META tag to the website pages. Once the ownership/editing rights are approved by Google, the webmaster can submit an XML site map of the following format for Google site map index file:

```
<?xml version="1.0" encoding="UTF-8"?>
<sitemapindex xmlns="http://www.google.com/schemas/sitemap/0.84">
    <sitemap>
        <loc>http://clients.holbi.co.uk/site1/sitemapcategories.xml</loc>
        <lastmod>2007-03-18T21:15:38</lastmod>
    </sitemap>
    <sitemap>
        <loc>http://clients.holbi.co.uk/site1/sitemapproducts.xml</loc>
        <lastmod>2007-03-18T21:15:38</lastmod>
    </sitemap>
</sitemapindex>
```

for Google site map categories file:

```
<?xml version="1.0" encoding="UTF-8"?>
<urlset xmlns="http://www.google.com/schemas/sitemap/0.84">
    <url>
        <loc>http://clients.holbi.co.uk/site1/-c-21.html</loc>
        <lastmod>2007-03-13T14:12:29</lastmod>
        <changefreq>weekly</changefreq>
        <priority>0.5</priority>
    </url>
    <url>
        <loc>http://clients.holbi.co.uk/site1/-c-1.html</loc>
        <lastmod>2007-02-27T14:05:44</lastmod>
        <changefreq>weekly</changefreq>
        <priority>0.5</priority>
    </url>
</urlset>
```

and for Google site map products file:

```
<?xml version="1.0" encoding="UTF-8"?>
<urlset xmlns="http://www.google.com/schemas/sitemap/0.84">
    <url>
        <loc>http://clients.holbi.co.uk/site1/-p-8.html</loc>
        <lastmod>2007-02-27T14:05:45</lastmod>
        <changefreq>weekly</changefreq>
        <priority>1.0</priority>
    </url>
    <url>
        <loc>http://clients.holbi.co.uk/site1/-p-27.html</loc>
        <lastmod>2007-02-27T14:05:45</lastmod>
        <changefreq>weekly</changefreq>
        <priority>0.5</priority>
    </url>
</urlset>
```

Of course, the files generated by the script can be altered if need be, in order to highlight certain products or categories that are likely to change more often than the others (the <changefreq> tag), or are far more important than the others (the <priority> tag).

A contribution is available on osCommerce that can generate site maps for Google. It is based on the product catalog. It can be downloaded from http://addons.oscommerce.com/info/3233. It's preferable to use a contribution like this than third-party site-map generation tools. Having this contribution installed, the store owner receives control over the process of site-map generation and flexibility for further modifications.

In order to submit a site map in Google, you would have to create an account with Google and then log in, enter the Webmaster Tools section, register the URL of the website there, and then verify your ownership over the website. This will not only allow for submitting the site map(s) but also for getting access to a number of useful tools and reports.

Yahoo! site map submission service is a simpler solution that only accepts plain CSV files with only one column—web page URLs. The site map file can be uploaded to https://siteexplorer.search.yahoo.com/submit.

The robots.txt and .htaccess Files

robots.txt is a special file that contains commands and directives for search engine bots and tells them how to deal with the pages of the website. Using robots.txt, it is possible to tell the search engine bots to index or not to index certain folders and individual pages.

In osCommerce, robots.txt can be used to avoid duplicate contents being parsed by search engines. For example, if one and the same product is listed in two different categories, a command can be put into the robots.txt file to let the search engine bot know it should not parse the product page that is a part of certain category.

It should be noted though that even though the search engine bots won't parse such pages, neither robots.txt nor any other method can forbid the search engines to index the pages. So even though the page won't have its title or description, it may still appear in the search results.

Additional instructions can be given to the search engine bots to avoid entering certain folders. So, for example, the /images folder can be restricted for search engine bots if the store owner doesn't want the search engines to index it.

One should be very careful with `robots.txt` — as it can prevent access to a certain part of the website, it can prevent access to the whole website too! If for some reason the website has disappeared from the search results after the `robots.txt` file has been modified, check all commands in that file in the first place!

The `.htaccess` file is used for multiple purposes, including giving directives to web server, protecting folders with passwords, or not allowing access to certain file types or whole folders, and so on.

In osCommerce, the `.htaccess` file stored in the main folder of the online store is used by default to adjust the SSL protocol settings for MS Internet Explorer browsers.

The `.htaccess` file is an essential part of osCommerce search engine optimization, as it contains all main "rewrite" directives that allow for having search-engine friendly URLs on products and categories of osCommerce. It can also be used to reduce or completely get rid of the issues related to duplicated content as we described earlier in this chapter.

Navigation gets Optimized

osCommerce navigation usually includes a clickable category tree, which links back to the main page or links to other pages (like the "about us", "contact us", "terms and conditions" and other pages). Navigation is an essential part of the site that the customers use to get to the products they are looking for. Therefore, its optimization should be done in a way that doesn't make it inconvenient for customers to use it to navigate on the website.

Since search engine bots "read" the page in the same way humans do — for example from top to bottom, from left to right (or vice versa — it depends on the locale installed in osCommerce) — it's recommended to put the navigation in the very beginning of the page if the store owner wants the search engines to process product catalog first, and in the very end of the page if the store owner wants the search engine bots to first process the content of the page and then process further pages (including category listings and product information pages). The choice here may depend on what content is displayed on the page, how important it is for customers, and how important it is to have the page indexed in search engines, or if individual product and category pages are far more important.

For example, menu-style navigation—links to the top categories—can be put in the header of the page, and also the category tree can be put in the left column as in the following picture:

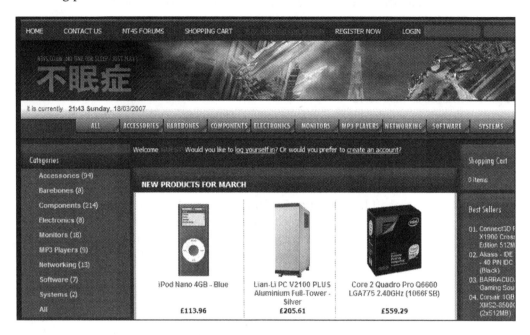

Drop-down menus in JavaScript or DHTML often look good and work well for customers, but they may be confusing for search engine bots. Therefore the amount of JavaScript should be minimized and it's recommended to use CSS-based drop-down menus as much as possible. If you decide to still use JavaScript to allow for some extra features or visual effects, it may be sensible to add plain links to menu items somewhere else to the same page (into the bottom of the page for example) so that search engines can easily find and index all those menu links.

Regardless of whether the category tree expands to show parent and child categories or if it only shows the top categories, the breadcrumbs are a must-have element of navigation for SEO. Breadcrumbs are usually put just under the header of the page, but before the actual content. The breadcrumbs categories are usually listed in the parent-child order, i.e. first comes the top category, then its sub-category, and so on. It is recommended to include a link to the main page of the osCommerce online store in the first position in the breadcrumbs for internal linking purposes. Also, such links to the main page of the online store should be named appropriately—it's recommended to use the most targeted key phrase there, so that search engines would associate that key phrase with the online store after they've indexed all the pages, as in the following sample:

Kitchen Appliances » Cookers » Freestanding Cookers » Electric Ceramic Cooker »

where the first key phrase ("Kitchen Appliances") is pointing to the main page of the online store, and all the other ones are actual links to the corresponding categories and product listings.

In osCommerce, customers can also navigate through the website by using buttons. Even though text links may be preferred by the search engines, for customer convenience and design purposes it's better to have nice looking buttons of the pages of osCommerce online store.

Therefore, it is recommended to add at least some text content to each such navigational button as `title` and `alt` properties of the HTML `<img>` tag.

For example, instead of just having "Add to cart" as title and alternative text of the "Add to Cart" button, for SEO purposes the product name can be added to the title, like this: "Add Microsoft IntelliMouse Explorer to Cart" (and do not forget leading and trailing gaps in the title, so that it looks nicer). The same goes for the "Reviews" button; its title can be changed to "Microsoft IntelliMouse Explorer Reviews". Where on the pages like "Conditions of Use" the "Continue" button's title is "Continue"—it is recommended to add the store name to the title of that button as it points back to the main page of the online store. So its title could look like, for example, "Continue to MP3 Players Super store".

This last advice is actually a part of another quite important recommendation, all pages of the online store should be linked back to the main page in this or that way. This improves internal linking and eventually, online store's positioning in search results.

Another good piece of advice is pretty simple—if it is required to put a link to an external website—better do it closer to the very end of the page. This will ensure that search engine bots first spider the content of the online store and then navigate away. Of course the minimum of external links is a suggested option.

For SEO purposes, it's recommended to put links to the most important pages underneath the page, in the bottom, where they will be found by search engine bots and also by some of the customers. Those links can point to specific categories or even products, which depend on how important certain categories and products are and how important good position of those pages in search results is. A direct link from the main page of the online store to certain category or product helps improve the page rank and popularity and is much more effective than links from parent categories to the same page.

The final recommendation in this section is about the situations when an online store runs from a sub folder. In this case, the sub folder should be used as a benefit for SEO. The sub folder should be renamed into the most targeted key phrase related to the online store. By default osCommerce runs in the "catalog" sub folder. For a website that sells Celtic jewelry, the obvious choice would be to rename "catalog" into "celtic-jewelry". Then all URLs of the online store will contain the most important key phrase "Celtic jewelry" by default.

It is a good point for those merchants who do not own a domain name yet to make a decision about it; so that the domain name itself should contain the most important keyword(s).

Contexts

The context is the most important part of the website for modern-day search engines. Search engines use algorithms that assign relevancy rankings based upon the context within a page's title and body. Proper placement of keywords on all your pages is essential for good listing.

How to Write Context that Works

The context that works best for customers is usually the best context for search engines. The texts should be original, keyword rich, and explain the exact benefits and features of products and services sold online.

If the task to write product description is given to an expert in a certain industry that text, created even by a non-professional writer, will usually be best for search engines as it will be full of professional terms (keywords) and definitions that search engines relate to. With more context come links, and with quality contexts come even more links!

Of course, some work on such text should be performed further to make it look right from the marketing point of view. It may make sense to hire a professional marketing writer to make sure that your website is conveying the message you want, in verbiage that your visitors will understand. Assuming a fine writer is chosen, you will not only have a well-written site but will also gain the advantage of having an outsider, who is more likely to write for people who aren't experts, creating your content.

Ideal context will both grab visitors' attention and at the same time, make them want what the online store has to offer. To test how good it is, the best way is to ask somebody who belongs to the target audience to read and comment on it. The more comments you get, the more extra money the online store will eventually bring.

Each product and category description should contain an answer to what the target audience want to find. It should contain descriptions of the main features and, which is more important, how those features address the customers' needs. Even though the main purpose of the online store is to sell products, additional contexts that contain answers to the customers' questions and can "help" rather than just "sell" would be appreciated by customers and well indexed by search engines. This is covered in depth in the next chapter of this book.

There can be no harm in adding new contexts and improving existing texts. If the online store changes contexts often, on its own it doesn't guarantee better positions in search results, but gives an advantage since search engine bots will visit such websites more often, and important changes in the contexts and structure will be recognized faster by search engines.

osCommerce Contexts Authoring

There exist several contributions for osCommerce that allow for advanced contexts authoring within the Administration panel of the online shop.

One called Information Pages Unlimited can be downloaded from the osCommerce Contributions website at `http://addons.oscommerce.com/info/1026`. Its installation is pretty easy and it allows for authoring pages that will be later listed in the Information Box of osCommerce.

In the Administration panel, it allows for context pages authoring. A page can have a parent page—it becomes really easy to group similar pages together, or to publish contexts in several pages all related to the same topic.

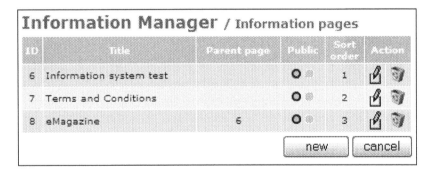

The contribution not only allows for context page authoring, but also simplifies the process of editing certain osCommerce greeting and heading texts:

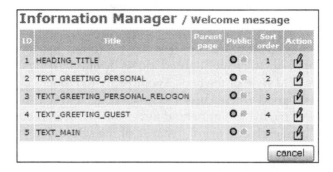

Another solution called FAQDesk allows for creating series of questions and answers for customers. It can be used for sales support and technical support, and also to explain to customers how to use specific features of the advertised products. The contribution can be downloaded from `http://addons.oscommerce.com/info/1106`.

Yet another contribution that allows for article authoring is NewsDesk. The administrator of an osCommerce store can create any number of category levels and post news and articles into each news category. The link to the news categories tree appears on the main page of osCommerce. A relatively simple bit of osCommerce programming can create a new box for either left or right columns where the latest news will be displayed. The contribution can be downloaded from `http://addons.oscommerce.com/info/934`.

SEO for Contexts

There are several tips and tricks that can be utilized to improve visibility of the online store in search engines:

- Keywords and key phrases—put them close to the beginning of each new page or paragraph (`<p>`) within the page. This way it will be easier for search engines to find the keywords, and also more importantly such keywords will look for search engines

- Use header tags (`<H1>`, `<H2>`, etc.) within the pages where appropriate. For example, the product information page will benefit from the product name being enclosed in `<H1>` tag, and also it is possible to use the `<H2>` tags to print the names of the related products and categories on the same page. Header tags are important to search engines. Note that only one `<H1>` should be placed per each page; several `<H2>` tags will also look appropriate. If some part of the text needs to be highlighted, use some other methods to do it rather than re-using the `<H1>` tag.

Using CSS to hide `<H>` tags is unethical SEO practice and a website that does this can be banned from search engines.

- Special/highlighted text—if a part of the text (often just several words or a phrase) needs to be highlighted, do so by either using quotes, bigger font size, or bold style of the text. Avoid using too much highlighting as it does not look good when a user reads the page, and it also can lower the importance of the main highlighted keywords for search engines. There's no need to bold each and every instance of the selected keywords in the text of the page—common sense should guide the context's author in establishing what should and what should not be marked as special text. To provide the maximum effect, the highlighting should be achieved by using corresponding tags in the text content of the page, so that search engines can understand it. Using CSS will not really help to "explain" which part of the text is highlighted to search engines.

  Only use highlighting when appropriate for both users and search engines.

- Keyword density is in other words the number of keyword occurrences per page compared to total size of the content of that page. Different SEO consultants suggest different "optimal" keyword density levels, though on the average it's recommended to use keywords and key phrases as from 3% to 10% of the page content. It seems reasonable to aim to achieve 5% keyword density on product pages and additional article pages.

  The best advice that could be given is to place keywords in the context as often as possible keeping in mind the text is created for customers in the first place and only in the second place for search engines. So it should be readable, understandable and look natural. Use variants and synonyms too; search engines will understand this. Do not be afraid to see the keywords and key phrases stand out, as it's what the customers were searching for and seeing the terms they searched for on the page will improve their confidence in the page having exactly what they need.

  In order to improve keyword density, it is recommended to minimize the size of the non-textual part of the page as much as possible. For example, all JavaScript additions, if any, should be put into `.js` files and linked to the page as external files. The same should be done with CSS entries; fortunately in osCommerce CSS classes are already gathered in one file.

Hiring an SEO Specialist

A store owner may want to outsource search engine optimization of the online store to concentrate on other aspects of the business, or maybe because there's no SEO specialist among the staff.

Choosing an SEO specialist can be a real problem considering the number of offers on the market.

But first, it should be decided what will be outsourced to the SEO specialist, and what will still be done in-house. SEO is often critical to the success of an online business, so it's essential to have the most important processes in control.

So what can an SEO specialist do for an osCommerce-based online store?

- Develop online marketing strategy in search engines, including both paid advertisement and natural searches

- Manage paid advertisement campaigns, editing the keywords, marketing pitches, assigning maximum CPCs on keywords

- Optimize the website for search engines

- Write contents for the website in general, and individual products in particular

- Create and publish press releases

- Continuously monitor the success of the online store in search engines and continuously improve it to win the competition with other players in the same market

Two major problems have to be solved by the owner of online store when choosing an SEO specialist company — the problem of choice and the problem of false promises. Google.com gives over 38 million results when searching for "Search Engine Optimization". How can you know which SEO company is the right one for you?

First of all, define your SEO budget. This is the total amount of money you're ready to invest during the year into SEO optimization and marketing.

Secondly, define the goals you are aiming to achieve within a month, 6 months, a year. Also describe your target audience, and work out a preliminary list of keywords you want to be found in search engines.

Then, find several SEO companies and ask them to quote on improving your positions in search results within a certain time frame, taking into account your target audience and the keywords you've prepared.

You may want to come up with some of the following questions and ask them to answer in detail:

- How many years in the industry does the company have?
- Will you sign a contract indemnifying my company from brand damage in case of unethical SEO?
- Is there any minimum term on the contact?
- What technical and marketing expertise do you have? In particular related to online stores and osCommerce?
- Can I see what monitoring reports look like?
- Can you train me to do some of SEO work in the future?
- Can we meet in your offices to discuss details of the deal?
- Will you be outsourcing any part of work on my online store?
- I have other services providers working on my online store, will it affect your work in any way and how do you plan to resolve this issue?
- Can you offer copywriting services for SEO? Press releases?
- Is SEO your main source of profits?
- Will I be able to get contact details of some of your clients?

When comparing the quotes, make sure you compare identical services. Sometimes some companies just would not be able to provide proper paid advertisement management or copywriting and will not include those services into their quotes.

Ask the SEO company of your choice what kind of control you will have over the optimization process, and what kind of reporting and monitoring tools you will have access to. A really good SEO company would not like to hide any information about the performance of your online store in search engines.

Once you've chosen a handful of the best quotes, check what customers of those SEO companies have to say about the services they've received. Prepare a list of their questions and make some phone calls—it's not a big time waste anyway, and especially when choosing a consultant that would be dealing with your online store, and on whom improvement of online sales will depend.

A good idea would be to read success stories carefully and check if the mentioned websites can be still found in the top positions in search engines.

One should be very well aware that search engine optimization is a time-consuming continuous process, which is unlikely to be substituted by a cheap software product or cheap services that some companies tend to promote on their websites. Very cheap services will be most likely based on illegal or unethical practices and will only harm the positions of the online store in search engines. So double-check the cheapest options to ensure your online store will only get the best service.

Tracking SEO Campaign Results

A successful SEO campaign will result in increase of the turnover, which is obviously easy to notice. But how is it possible to measure the success of an SEO campaign more precisely? Also, how can we identify weaknesses of an SEO campaign to improve it accordingly?

An online store owner will require the help of certain tools to monitor the following parameters of an SEO campaign:

- Overall website popularity in search engines
- Positions and dynamics of position changes on specific keywords
- Statistics of clicks and orders by search engines and referring websites
- Users to customers conversion for all users and for users referred by search engines

Positions in search engines on specific keywords affect popularity of the website and its individual pages. Therefore those positions should be monitored and changes should be tracked in order to make a decision about if the SEO campaign is successful or not and if it requires any tweaking.

When hiring an SEO specialist, one of the requirements should be to provide access to either a real-time statistics of exposure in search engines, or reports that can demonstrate changes in the search engine exposure over a certain period of time.

There are several software packages that allow for this kind of functionality.

One of the free tools available in the Internet is WatchRank from `www.rankquest.com`. The software (less than 1 MB) can be downloaded from `http://www.rankquest.com/watchrank/download.php` and is very easy to install. Once installed, it asks to specify a web page that it will be monitoring and then proposes to either extract keywords from that page or type them manually. Once the keywords have been specified, the tool is ready to query the search engines for the specified keywords. As soon as it finds a link to the previously specified page in the search results, it adds a record to its history database. It can display the dynamics of changes from a certain time until now.

Based on the overall dynamics of position changes during the specified period, WatchRank displays the overall page performance to date.

Google Analytics (formerly known as Urchin) is a free tool that can be easily integrated into osCommerce and provides probably the most comprehensive and detailed statistics on website popularity, e-commerce performance, success of marketing campaigns, conversion rates, best performing keywords and pages, etc.

It can be accessed at `http://www.google.com/analytics/`. In order to have Google Analytics integrated with osCommerce, one has to first register for an account with Google Analytics, and then create a "Website Profile". Google Analytics will then generate a special tracking code that should be integrated into each and every page of osCommerce. e-commerce statistics should be enabled for a website profile.

Using an osCommerce contribution that can be downloaded from `http://addons.oscommerce.com/info/3756` the tracking code can be integrated into osCommerce. It's integrated to monitor web traffic and purchase statistics. Purchase statistics integration requires certain modifications in the checkout pages. After Google Analytics is installed, it's possible to get various marketing reports on how the website performs in search engines, how many users and customers are referred by search engines, where the users and customers are coming from, which search engines generate more customers than others, what are the most popular keywords typed by the users to find the online store in search engines, and what are the keywords that convert more users into customers.

Google Webmaster Tools is yet another freely available solution that allows webmasters to access brief but still useful information on how Google indexes the website, how it "sees" its pages, if there are any errors that the webmaster should check and fix, and so on. Using Google Webmaster Tools, a webmaster can also submit a site map to Google, and exclude certain URLs of the website from the Google index.

In order to get access to Google Webmaster Tools one just needs a Google account. Several websites could be associated with one and the same webmaster's account in Google. Each website has to be verified to prove the webmaster really has authorized access to the site. The verification is pretty straightforward and is about either uploading an empty page of a certain name to the website, or adding a certain META tag to the site's pages. If your osCommerce online store uses SEO-friendly URLs of products and categories, it's recommended to use the META tag-based verification method.

Using monitoring and tracking tools should not slow down the site. If the site opens slower than before, the installed monitoring and tracking tools should be turned off one by one until the reason of the poor performance is located and that tool is removed from the website.

By combining solutions like WebRank and Google Analytics, it's possible to monitor how the wesite performs in search engines, track SEO campaign results, and also perform web traffic analysis.

Web Traffic Analysis

Web traffic generated by search engines or referral websites can be measured. It will include not only clicks performed by real humans, but also clicks and page views performed by the search engine bots. For better and more accurate web traffic analysis such clicks and page views performed by bots should not be considered. Therefore when measuring web traffic the traffic figures per certain period of time with and without search engines bots should be calculated.

Also, taking into account that search engine bots usually follow certain schedule, it is possible to find out when they visit your website in order to prepare and publish updates before the next time your website will be searched, parsed, and indexed.

There exist many solutions for analysis of web traffic. Such as, for example, WebTrends Analytics, Google Analytics, and many others. Some of them are available for free, others would require a payment. A solution like Google Analytics provides online merchants with all essential figures and extensive reports, and costs absolutely nothing to use!

Web traffic analysis can give reports on:

- What customers are looking for in search engines that bring them to your online store:

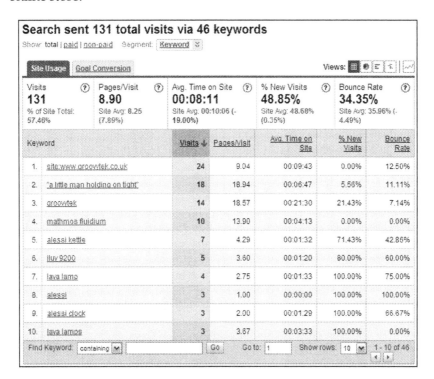

- Which of the websites with backward links to your online store provide the largest number of visitors:

- Which of the websites with backward links to your online store provide the largest number of customers
- Conversion from visitors to customers is better for which search engine, which website, which keyword
- How many pages an average customer views on your website, how many pages an average referred customer views on your website and how many pages are usually viewed before the customer is ready to place an order

Summary

Search engine optimization is an important process that helps online stores and other websites achieve better positions in search results in search engines. SEO is used to cut down the costs of paid advertising and convert more users into customers as users prefer natural search listings to paid advertising.

There can be ethical and unethical SEO; unethical SEO should be avoided. External SEO is responsible for popularity and ranks in search engines, when internal SEO is responsible for web page optimization, proper content, structure, keyword density.

We have reviewed various methods of both external and internal SEO. They should always be used in combination to achieve maximum results.

We have also reviewed tips and tricks on how to hire an SEO specialist and track SEO campaign results.

In the next chapter, we will concentrate on solutions and practices that help authoring original content, and also allow users and customers of an online shop to post content online. We will review benefits of using dynamic content solutions like CMS, forums, blogs, RSS feeds, and their integration with osCommerce.

4
Dynamic Content to Improve Sales

Most of the websites that sell products online try to create detailed product descriptions and publish extensive product information. They are concentrated on products and obviously pay much attention to having all product names, model numbers, descriptions, images, and (what's more important) prices correct.

So when a user comes to the website, and then comes back again some time later—the only noticeable change would be seeing new products and updated prices. It isn't that bad and it will work well for many online stores, but there are ways to improve the situation, increase user's interest in coming back to the website more often, and so improve online sales.

In this chapter, we will review various ways of using dynamic content in osCommerce to make users come back to the website more often, to stimulate their interest in the website and products it sells, convert visitors into customers, and eventually into repeat customers.

We will also consider ways to attract readers and writers more actively with read and write dynamic content.

Dynamic Content: What and Why?

What do we actually mean when we call it "dynamic"? Does it mean the content itself changes while the customer is browsing through the website? Here, we mean that the content of the whole website changes as time goes by, and more and more content is added. At this stage, it doesn't really matter who or what adds the content—whether it's the Administrator of the osCommerce website, or the website's visitors, or customers, or if the content is downloaded from another source (another website).

Why is dynamic content important for osCommerce? It's not only important for osCommerce, but for any website that is supposed to generate traffic and has goals to attract more visitors. The more professional, detailed, and interesting the content of the site is, the more customers will find it potentially useful to visit the website again and read newly posted materials. If the content of the website changes quite often, it will keep constantly growing with the flow of visitors.

For online stores, including osCommerce dynamic content is especially important.

First of all, it attracts more visitors who are interested in reading new and updated content to the website. It attracts more target audience visitors, who are likely to become customers and existing customers who are likely to become return customers. And all this without any advertising expenses involved!

Then, well prepared content increases the visitor's confidence and helps to increase the "visitor to customer" conversion rates.

Finally, keyword-rich content is well indexed by search engine crawlers, and search engines are more likely to put a website that constantly updates higher in search results than a website that doesn't.

So publishing dynamic content on an osCommerce site may increase the number of visitors, make the website more noticeable in search engines, and also increase the number of sales.

How Can We Make Users Participate?

By inviting not only readers but also writers it is possible to publish even more articles, news, reviews, etc. Such an approach may also help a lot in attracting users and converting them into customers, as they will know your osCommerce online store as a place in the Internet where they can both buy goods online and read what other customers have to say, express their thoughts, and participate in discussions, etc.

Here are several ways to invite users and customers of the website to participate in creating dynamic content:

- First and most important, is to make customers and website users aware of a possibility to participate and post content or just comments on other posts.
- Give them technical means to participate.
- Ask them to describe their own experience or opinion on a product or service.
- Ask them how you could improve your services and product range.

Even though it's extremely important to get feedback and content from users and customers of an online store, the Administrator of such a site should be ready to fight SPAM, fraudulent posts and content, copyright violations, and content that harasses, abuses, or threatens other users or customers.

Different Types of Dynamic Content in osCommerce

There can be multiple types of dynamic content present in osCommerce. There are osCommerce contributions and website authoring and building techniques and methods that allow for dynamic content to be added to an osCommerce online store.

We will start with product reviews and customer testimonials—the most obvious dynamic content that can be added to an osCommerce online store.

Reviews

Reviews are a part of standard osCommerce functionality. A customer can log into their osCommerce account and write a review on any product. Along with the review it's possible to vote for product rating.

It's important to note that reviews and testimonials are created by customers of the osCommerce online store, and not only by its Administrator. Even though reviews and testimonials should not be edited by the Administrator before they get published (while they are within the guidelines), customers should be clearly told there is neither guarantee nor a promise the Administration of the online store will use the feedback given as a review or testimonial.

Once approved, those reviews are then displayed in osCommerce by default, along with the products they are related to.

An osCommerce store owner should prevent fake reviews from being submitted and published on the website. It's fairly important to let only real customers write reviews—this way it's possible to ensure the customer had actually had a chance to review and test the product bought earlier.

A review approval system can be of assistance to fight hacks and fake reviews. Once a customer writes a review, the Administrator of the online shop is notified via email. If approved by the Administrator the review then appears published on the website.

There is a contribution available for free download, which is called "Review Approval System", that helps the Administrator of the online store approve only decent reviews, submitted by real customers who ordered such products from the online store in the past. The contribution can be downloaded from `http://addons.oscommerce.com/info/76`.

Once installed, it adds a new menu item "Reviews" into the "Catalog" section of the Administration panel. All reviews submitted by customers are listed there, and the Administrator has got a chance to check the database of orders and only accept (activate) real customers' reviews.

Product reviews are useful for visitors and Administrators of the online store:

- Users who are looking for certain products would be willing to read what other customers think about the products they consider buying. Reading a real person's positive review makes an effect on the user that is similar to hearing a recommendation from a good friend.

- Administrators of the online store can see what customers think about the store in general and products in particular. Administrators can act according to the comments made by the customers in order to improve the product range and services, and make online store more user-friendly. Also, Administrators should read feedback on products and make notes on if they want to order more products like the ones reviewed or not.

- Finally, since reviews are usually rich with keywords, it makes sense to display reviews on the Product Information page to increase keyword density in osCommerce.

By default, osCommerce product reviews are displayed on a separate page, other than the product details page. This is not the best approach because it makes the user make yet another click to reach the page with product reviews.

Usability of osCommerce can be improved by putting all product reviews (or at least some of them) directly on the product page. This way the visitors to the website will not only see information about the products on the product detail pages, but also reviews posted by real customers who bought such products earlier.

Putting detailed reviews on the product information page also improves the page in terms of search engine optimization, as in most cases, it the increases keyword density of the page.

Sometimes, product reviews can be added to the product information page on another information tab, to make the page shorter and easier to read.

Product reviews in osCommerce go into one text field. To make it easier for customers to write reviews, and for other customers and visitors to read them, and also for the Administrators to manage and approve reviews a split into several fields is recommended. The number of fields and titles for each field depend on the nature of the business and the products the website sells online. For example, for a website that sells bakery online, the following questions/sections may help the customers to sort out their thoughts and write detailed and useful product reviews:

- Are you happy with our delivery service?
- Was the product fresh when you got it?
- Did it look similar to how it looks on our website?
- Did you like the wrapping?
- Did you invite somebody to share the product with you?
- Tell us how you enjoyed the product you've bought
- What about value for money?
- Will you buy from us again and would you recommend our services to your friends?

It should be noted that the list of questions/review sections may differ from one online store to another, and even from one type of products to another within the same online store.

For example, an online store that features high-class coffee making machines has the following fields filled in for its reviews:

- Looks
- Usability and Performance
- Value for money
- Pros
- Cons

An online store that sells mobile phones uses only these three fields for customer reviews:

- Design
- Usability
- Features

In order to make it easier to post reviews for customers, and manage reviews for online store owners, one can use the so called "Complete Reviews System" that can be downloaded from `http://addons.oscommerce.com/info/4397`.

In addition to the standard features of the osCommerce reviews system, this contribution allows the Administrator to approve, edit, or reject customer reviews, notifies (via email) the Administrator of the online store once a new review is placed, allows for the Administrator to enter reviews, for example, when a product gets reviews in some media, and adds several more improvements to the standard functionality.

Third-Party Reviews Solutions

Since an ideal product review would be written by a customer who purchased the product, used it for a while, and took some time to write a detailed review on its features, not every online store would be able to provide its new customers with appropriate reviews on the products it sells. This is especially true for online stores that have only just started trading online.

At the same time, there are plenty of established businesses that actually sell similar products, receiving them from the same suppliers or directly from the same manufacturers.

Hence a product review doesn't necessarily need to be written by a customer of a particular online shop anymore. A detailed and helpful review can be given by the customer of any online shop, and then used by other shops to provide their own visitors and customers with information on a real customer's experience with the product, or at least an expert's review.

There are some solutions in the market that collect reviews from real customers on products sold online, and then share the collected review information with other shops. This approach requires all product models to be the same across several online shops, but since many online shops sell the same products, it doesn't look like a big problem. There are services that specialize in general or industry-specific reviews.

A product review provided by such third-party services should not have any mention of the services the customer had been provided with, or any feedback on other aspects of the online trade. It should only be concentrated on the characteristics and features of the product being reviewed, and contain enough information to help the new customers to make their choice.

The following screenshot, powered by an independent reviews provider
www.reevoo.com , demonstrates how several independent reviewers rate an LCD
TV set. The most important aspect is that all the reviewers could have bought the
product from different online stores, but nevertheless their reviews have been
gathered together to be presented to the customers of all participating online stores
where that product is being sold online.

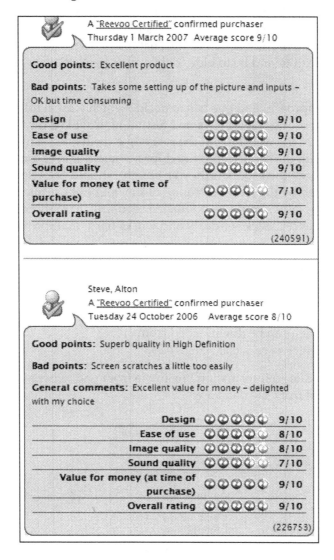

Testimonials

Customer testimonials are very similar to product reviews, except that testimonials contain customer feedback on the services provided, and the customer's general impression about the online store. Customer testimonials can be put into pages like About Us, Shopping Cart, and also into the main page, in one of the side columns.

Positive feedback should be made visible to help convert more visitors into customers. Obviously, first of all, no osCommerce store owner would like displaying any negative feedback from the customers. So the first and the very "easy" thought in one's head would be to hide/delete such feedbacks at once, as if they were never there.

There is another approach, and one has to decide which way to follow. This approach still supposes some reviews and testimonials will be disabled/deleted by the Administrator of the website. But the rest of the feedbacks, where the customers were not happy with the services provided for no particular reason, or the customers were not happy about the products they've bought, should be collected and commented in detail by the Administration of the online shop. Such responses to questions and complains should be published regularly, to demonstrate the online shop takes customer feedback seriously and works hard on improving products and services.

There is a contribution for osCommerce that is similar to product reviews: it helps customers submit their website reviews, and helps the Administrator of the online shop manage those testimonials and publish them on the website.

The contribution itself can be downloaded from `http://addons.oscommerce.com/info/839`.

Once installed, it adds an information box to the front end, where it picks up one random testimonial from the database:

In osCommerce Administration panel it adds a **"Testimonial Manager"** menu item under the **"Tools"** section. There the Administrator can approve or decline testimonials given to the online store, and also manually add new testimonials, which is convenient in case the online store gets reviewed somewhere else.

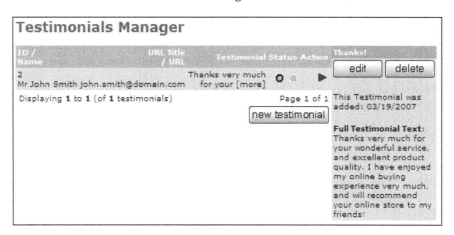

Attracting Customers to Read and Write Reviews and Testimonials

Attracting customers to read reviews and testimonials is usually not required, since the customers are interested in knowing more about products and the online store itself. They will be glad to find this information on the website, and will be interested in reading it through. Yet again we'd like to stress that only real reviews and testimonials can make up the customer's mind on buying products from an online store.

A customer who's satisfied with the purchase would not mind leaving a review on the product bought. Yet to attract more customers to write their product reviews, an online store can do the following:

- Run a contest on the best and most detailed review, where a prize would be either a gift voucher for a certain amount or a discount on all or certain products of the online store during a period of time. Of course, it's important to demonstrate to the customer the contest is real, and that the customer can really win the prize.

- Run a lottery with similar prizes and put every customer's review or testimonial into the draw.

- Remind customers some time after a purchase to write a review if the customer liked/didn't like the product. Reminders can be sent automatically via email.

Information about currently running contests and lotteries should be advertised on the website and also on the checkout pages of the osCommerce online store, so that the customer can not miss it when buying a product.

It is a good idea to send an automatic reminder to the customer some time after the purchase is complete, and suggest writing a review on the product(s) bought and/or a testimonial on the service provided and participate in the contest and/or lottery.

Polls and Lotteries (Surveys)

Polls and lotteries (surveys) are probably one of the best ways to ask the end customers questions and get answers already processed and sorted.

Such polls can be open to the public or only to registered customers.

In the former case, the questions asked would be more about the reasons why a website's visitor would become a customer, i.e. why a visitor would buy this or that product online.

In the latter case, the questions asked would be more about the customer's experience with the shop and products bought earlier, and about the products the customer would like to buy in the future.

As it was said above, the content of polls may depend on the circumstances, such as, for example, if the customer is logged into their customer account or not, if the customer bought certain products in the past or not, or if the customer has participated in polls before or not.

The customer should be told why and how participating in the polls will help the online store to better serve its customers by constantly improving the product range and service.

For correct statistical figures, each customer should be allowed to vote only once during the poll's life time. Also, the customer should be given easy access to the total vote results after participating in the polls.

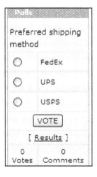

Individual and more detailed are customer/product/service surveys. These contain more questions, often with more variants, and more questions where the answer should be added as free text.

Such surveys may not be open to the public, but only to certain customers, depending on their previous order history.

To get more customers to submit their thoughts and comments in the surveys, a link to the survey can be sent automatically to the customer some days after a purchase.

Lotteries are a "subsidiary" of surveys, where by answering certain questions the customer enters a draw to win certain prize(s). It may be beneficial for attracting more customers to participate in the lottery to publish photos and short text about previous winners.

Polls, surveys, and lotteries give the store owner an opportunity to interview customers, and give customers the unique opportunity to be heard. They also demonstrate to the customers that the online store takes customers seriously, and cares about their needs being addressed and their opinion being considered, whether it's about existing or new products, or it's about the service provided.

The Polls contribution for osCommerce can be downloaded from `http://addons.oscommerce.com/info/20`.

The front end of the online store gets enhanced by yet another information box, where either the latest, or the most popular, or a random active poll is displayed. It is also possible to see vote results and comments left by other users of the website. It is possible to run several polls at a time if they are all set to be picked up randomly, or if the Administrator of the online store manually enables and disables active polls daily.

The Administration panel is also updated with a new section "Polls" with "Poll Configuration":

and "Poll Manager":

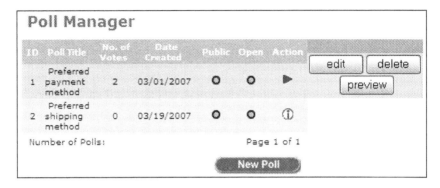

menu items.

Attracting Customers to Vote in Polls and Participate in the Surveys

The easiest way to encourage customers to vote in polls and participate in the surveys would be again to run lotteries where each customer who either votes in polls or answers survey questions becomes a participant.

Information about previous winners should be made available. Also banners or texts promoting possible winnings should be put on the website.

It's important to ensure the customers see that by answering questions or voting in polls, they actually provide the store management team with information that helps to improve services and/or expand product range. Then the customers will be more willing to participate in this improvement process.

News and Newsletter Archives

News is an important part of today's life. Everything around us is changing so quickly, that sometimes the amount of news that an average person receives daily is even too much to handle. In this situation, it's especially important for the store owner to provide customers with a comprehensive, dynamic, and reliable source of information.

The online store can publish various sorts of news:

- Industry news—news received from different sources, all related to the specific industry that the online store specializes in. If an online store sells products related to similar but still different industries (like, for example digital cameras and TV sets)—news categorization could be introduced for further customer convenience.

- Online store news and announcements—this type of news would be telling the customers about new arrivals to the online store, price drops and special offers, new shop features, and about all possible events and exciting news in any way related to the online store.

- Product news—new product releases, upgrades, and additional features announced by manufacturers will drop into this news category.

The most important note about the news is that each and every news post should be read and approved by the authorized staff in order to avoid unwanted information being automatically published on the online store website.

Newsletters

News posts can be grouped into newsletters. A newsletter is an email that is sent to customers who are subscribed (willing) to receive it. Newsletter support is enabled in osCommerce by default.

Newsletters should ONLY be sent to the subscribed customers if they do not contain negative or critical matter.

By sending out newsletters regularly, the shop owner informs subscribed customers about new product arrivals, special offers, industry news, and includes any other marketing information that can be of interest to customers. It makes perfect sense to include the latest news of each category into the newsletter that is sent to subscribers.

Subscribers will only consider a newsletter useful if it contains information that can be of real interest to them, and does not just advertise plenty of new arrivals and encourages to buy more products. A newsletter that besides advertising new products and special offers also educates and helps will always receive more positive feedback and eventually result in more online orders.

It may be required by law to include instructions on how to unsubscribe from the newsletter in each of its issues.

Once a newsletter is sent to the subscribers, it can be put into a special newsletter archive. Newsletter archives serve two main goals:

- First of all, having a newsletter archive on a website helps in indexing this website in search engines as well, since the newsletter archive will be full of proper keywords, all related in some way to the website's product catalog.

- Secondly, newsletter archive can help newcomers decide if they want to subscribe to a newsletter to receive news and updates similar to the already published materials.

Text versus HTML

By default, osCommerce supports sending newsletters in plain text and in HTML format, depending on the Configuration settings. The settings can be changed under the **"E-mail Options"** menu of the **"Configuration"** section in the Administration panel of osCommerce.

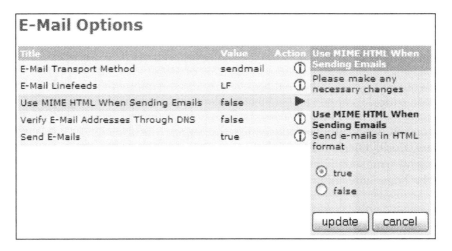

Of course, a newsletter (or any other email) has to be properly designed to be sent and received without any damage to its look, feel, and functionality.

In the following sample screenshots, one can see the difference between HTML and plain text emails:

Sunday 10 September, 2006

SPECIALS
Sweet Orange Lip Balm

only $4.10

Pregnancy Box

only $15.75

Dear Ms. Johnes,

We welcome you to **Purely Natural Online**.

You can now take part in the **various services** we have to offer you. Some of these services include:

- **Permanent Cart** - Any products added to your online cart remain there until you remove them, or check them out.
- **Address Book** - We can now deliver your products to another address other than yours! This is perfect to send birthday gifts direct to the birthday-person themselves.
- **Order History** - View your history of purchases that you have made with us.
- **Products Reviews** - Share your opinions on products with our other customers.

For help with any of our online services, please email the store-owner: store.owner@yahoo.com.

Note: This email address was given to us by one of our customers. If you did not signup to be a member, please send an email to store.owner@yahoo.com.

Copyright @ 2006 Purely Natural Online

```
Dear Ms. Johnes,

We welcome you to Purely Natural Online.

You can now take part in the various services we have to offer you.
Some of these services include:

Permanent Cart - Any products added to your online cart remain there
until you remove them, or check them out.
Address Book - We can now deliver your products to another address
other than yours! This is perfect to send birthday gifts direct to
the birthday-person themselves.
Order History - View your history of purchases that you have made
with us.
Products Reviews - Share your opinions on products with our other
customers.

For help with any of our online services, please email the store-
owner: store.owner@yahoo.com.

Note: This email address was given to us by one of our customers. If
you did not signup to be a member, please send an email to
store.owner@yahoo.com.
```

Sending a newsletter and other emails as HTML has several advantages compared to sending plain text email messages:

- It is possible to use website's color scheme and logo to promote the brand of the site in the newsletters.
- It is possible to include product images and related photos that will make it easier for subscribers to read and understand the information.
- It is possible to link any part of HTML back to the online store to make it easier for the subscriber to navigate there and eventually make a purchase.

So if the situation allows, HTML newsletters are more preferable from the marketing point of view.

Attracting Customers to Subscribe and Read Newsletters

Obviously, if a newsletter contains original and interesting information, more customers would be willing to subscribe. Content is THE most important part of success in attracting customers to receive and read newsletters.

What is also important is new announcements that are only made in the newsletters. For example, monthly special offers can be only published in the newsletters. The customers should be made aware of the fact that if they want to receive an update on monthly special offers, they have to subscribe to the newsletter as the information about all products on special offer is not otherwise available.

Also, the online store can advertise special discount coupons that are only available to the subscribers of the newsletter, and are included into each issue (if a newsletter archive is available on the site, the discount coupon code should not appear there to keep customers interested in receiving newsletters into their mail boxes).

Finally, the online store may run a monthly, quarterly, semi-annual, or annual draw for the newsletter subscribers with any prizes that the target newsletter audience would be interested in (not necessarily products available in the online store).

CMS, Blogs, and Online Magazines

Article marketing means that you will write articles about your field of interest and distribute them for publication on other websites, blogs, and ezines with a link back to your site. Each time your article is published on a website you get a one-way link to your site. As with most good things, this method has been pounced upon by Internet marketers and the net is flooded with a lot of low-quality articles. However, if you produce meaningful articles, you can still get a lot of benefit by distributing your articles.

By publishing articles in your own online store, you not only get better indexed by search engines, but what's more important provide useful information to your customers who may be seeking for it.

What can the articles be about?

- Articles can be about products or series of products available for purchase online.

- Articles can be about specific features of products and help customers to choose the product they want based on the detailed explanation of what this or that feature actually means. This sort of articles are called "buying guides". Also, in the articles, authors can compare features of several products and provide comprehensive information on what is the best choice for what needs.

- Articles can contain information on the best practice, tips, and tricks for using certain products advertised in the online store. Such articles help customers imagine how they would use this or that product, which increases chances for customers to buy the product online.

- Articles can be about some interesting facts related to the products sold online (similar to how Starbucks write in their brochures about water supplies in dry regions where their coffee grows).

- Articles can be about tendencies in certain industries, related to the products available in the online store.

Actually blog posts would not be that different to the articles, except that an article is supposed to be more detailed and informative than a blog post. Also, in the blog posts the author often can ask the readers to comment on certain questions/topics to make the discussion live and initiate opinion exchange.

When running a business blog, it makes sense to create several categories where the articles could be sorted. This way the customers will be able to find previous posts more easily, and also the blog author(s) will have certain goals, like, for example, to write to each category regularly.

Online magazines would contain articles grouped by certain theme and would be issued/updated regularly.

With both articles and blog posts, a facility to leave a comment is important to make the customers participate in discussion.

For search engine optimization purposes and for better user (reader)-to-customer conversion, links to the related products advertised on the online store can be added to each article or blog post, or be published alongside it.

Besides a facility to publish articles in other websites and online magazines, there are a number of content management solutions that can be integrated into the online store.

But first, we will consider a very effective and free way to publish content on the Internet. Open encyclopedia Wikipedia.org allows for publishing content. Of course the content needs to be properly prepared and be very detailed and to the point. But if you have anything to say about the products advertised in the online store, the technology that stands behind those products, or e-commerce approach that stands behind the online store, that qualifies to become an article in the electronic encyclopedia—a post in Wikipedia would be one of the most effective ways to promote your online store, its technology, and products.

Existing Content Management Solutions

There are a number of open-source solutions available to an osCommerce store owner that could be used to publish content directly on the website. We will consider several of the most popular ones, and also general integration practices with osCommerce.

osCommerce Information System and News Desk

osCommerce Information system is a publicly available contribution that can be downloaded from the osCommerce Contributions website at `http://addons.oscommerce.com/info/1709`.

It allows managing content of pages like Terms and Conditions, Privacy Policy, etc.

osCommerce Newsdesk contribution allows for creating multi-level categories of articles and actually posting articles into the categories. It has support for multiple languages and each article can be posted in several languages. It also has built-in support for the so called WYSIWYG HTML editor, so that the Administrator of the online store can create nice-looking HTML content directly in the Administration panel of the osCommerce online store, with no use of any additional HTML authoring tools.

Articles Configuration

Title	Value	Action	Display New Articles Link
Display New Articles Link	true	▶	
Number of Days Display New Articles	30	①	edit
Maximum New Articles Per Page	10	①	
Display All Articles Link	true	①	Display a link to New Articles in the Articles box?
Maximum Articles Per Page	10	①	
Maximum Display Upcoming Articles	5	①	
Enable Article Reviews	true	①	Date Added: 02/27/2007
Enable Tell a Friend About Article	true	①	Last Modified: 02/27/2007
Minimum Number Cross-Sell Products	1	①	
Maximum Number Cross-Sell Products	3	①	
Show Article Counts	true	①	
Maximum Length of Author Name	20	①	
Authors List Style	1	①	
Authors Select Box Size	1	①	
Display Author in Article Listing	true	①	
Display Topic in Article Listing	true	①	
Display Abstract in Article Listing	true	①	
Display Date Added in Article Listing	true	①	
Maximum Article Abstract Length	300	①	
Display Topic/Author Filter	true	①	
Location of Prev/Next Navigation Bar	both	①	
Display Box Authors ?	true	①	
Display Box Articles ?	true	①	
USE FCKeditor ? Need exist	false	①	

Left navigation menu:
- Configuration
- Catalog
- **Article Manager**
  - Topics/Articles Configuration
  - Authors
  - Reviews
  - Cross-Sell Articles
- Modules
- Customers
- Locations / Taxes
- Localization
- Reports
- Tools

Posted articles can be added to the front end of the online store, either into an information box in one of the side columns, or displayed on one page, grouped by categories.

Posting an article is really easy. In the Administration panel, one has to fill in the article name, abstract, content, and may also want to fill in page title and keywords for the sake of SEO. Articles can be posted in different topics (categories), and the system allows for a multi-level tree of categories to be built in the Administration panel of the site. When posting an article, one can also select author from the drop-down list. Authors are managed separately.

It becomes possible to add the Tell a Friend box on the Article page, this is configured in the options in the Administration panel. Reviews can be submitted by readers, and, once a review gets approved by the Administrator, the website displays it on the Article page, along with the Article text.

Yet another very important feature includes a facility to assign certain products to articles. Once a product gets assigned to an article, a link to the product information page appears underneath the text of the article. This feature works really well for SEO, and also, it helps customers who would be interested in products that are described in the associated article to find them easily.

This solution, which is available for free and can be downloaded from the osCommerce website (`http://addons.oscommerce.com/info/1026`) can address the needs of an online shop by allowing posting articles to the website, running online magazines, creating buying guides, and so on.

Third-Party Content Management Systems

Besides the built-in content management systems, osCommerce can be integrated with a number of third-party content management solutions. In this case, the website will be supposed to split into the website itself and online store. Of course, for proper visitor-to-customer conversion both parts should be linked together.

For example, the main website may contain some very detailed information about the business, products, buying process, usage practices, etc. and each page containing any product related information may be linked to the corresponding page of the osCommerce online store where the customer can actually buy a product. This approach is useful for more expensive and complex (or very new) products where customers would require a lot of additional information before they are ready to commence with the product purchase.

It's obvious that both the main website (based on a third-party CMS) and the online store (based on osCommerce) should have similar or the same design and be linked to each other.

Also, if the main website has any registration or login facilities user accounts should be shared between the two parts of the system for user convenience. So by logging into the main website, the customer would also get access into osCommerce Customer account and vice versa.

Another important point here is that osCommerce session should not be lost when the customer navigates back from osCommerce to the main website.

Having the same or a similar design, preserving osCommerce session ID, and having shared customer accounts are the key features of successful integration between osCommerce and a third-party CMS solution.

There seem to be no existing open-source contributions that would integrate one of the most featured and flexible CMS solutions with osCommerce. There are commercial products that allow utilizing benefits of the shared customer account between osCommerce and Typo3. You may want to check with your osCommerce consultant regarding the most suitable and cost effective option.

A solution based on the common customer account principle integrates osCommerce with Joomla CMS. This solution is called osCommerce Bridge. It combines customer registration and customer login features of both osCommerce and Joomla together.

PHP-Nuke can be merged with osCommerce in terms of customer login and registration as well. The corresponding solution is called OSCNuke and integrates osCommerce as one of PHP-Nuke's modules.

It should be noted that for better search engine optimization and visitor-to-customer conversion, all published text should be linked to osCommerce products where possible.

Built-In and Third-Party Blog Solutions

There is one blog contribution available for osCommerce at the moment. It can be downloaded from `http://addons.oscommerce.com/info/4808`.

It allows for posting short and medium updates, news, and comments in a blog. They are sorted by date of post and then split into groups, each group covering one month. All information can be published on the website afterwards, on a special page. A link to such a page can be added to the Information box of the site.

This solution has a built-in support for RSS. Website visitors can sign up to receive updates about new posts via their RSS reading client software.

Like any blog, it allows for comments to be made by its readers. Comments can be posted on a per article basis, and then the Administrator has a facility to approve or not approve comments made by the readers.

These features can be seen on the following screenshot.

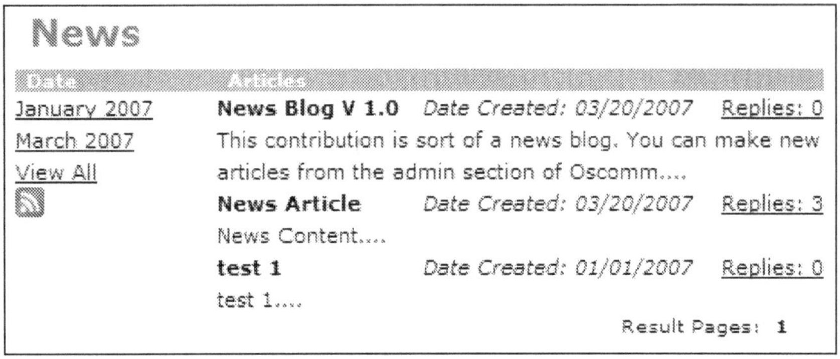

Since it's still a very new add-on to osCommerce, integration with a third-party blog solution is a better choice for businesses.

The blog solution can be either installed as a separate part of the website, or a hosted blog solution that can be used to publish blog posts.

If the Administrator of the online store decides to have a blog solution hosted on the same server where osCommerce is operating, the best idea would be to install the blog into a sub-folder of the osCommerce online store. This way search engines will consider both osCommerce and the blog to be parts of the same website, which will eventually improve osCommerce indexing and page ranks because of all the keyword-rich content published in the blog.

Besides links to the blog from the osCommerce website (and back) blogs can be integrated into osCommerce using RSS feeds. Then the latest (most popular) posts in the blog will be imported by osCommerce in a certain format (RSS) and published in the osCommerce online store. For example, links to the latest/most popular blog posts can be published in the new Information Box in osCommerce.

The contribution that can be downloaded from `http://addons.oscommerce.com/info/2692` allows for reading the RSS feed from the blog or any other news feed and publishing links to the source of the content in the information box.

To install, use, and customize blog solutions that can be presented to the customers as a part of the osCommerce website WordPress can be used. WordPress is a fully featured blog solution with multiple add-ons created especially for it.

osCommerce Blog
osCommerce fixes, improvements, news, and reviews

Archive for February, 2007

« Previous Entries

Switch to osCommerce
Tuesday, February 27th, 2007

Having had a plenty of customers recently switching from other Ecommerce solutions to osCommerce, or willing to switch from other versions of osCommerce to our TrueLoaded, we decided to publish some details of this mysterious (as referred by a customer) process to make it easier for our customers to understand what exactly is going with their online shop.

There may be many reasons why an online store owner would like to change Ecommerce platform and start using osCommerce. Most of the customers report the lack of features and not enough flexibility with their current solutions, others complain about not being able to support their sites, when with osCommerce you get support of the whole development community. And even though "plain" osCommerce is perhaps not the best solution for online retail business - it is the relatively big retailers who contact us to have their businesses backed by osCommerce solutions. As osCommerce can be enhanced with the features suitable for business management that not many other Ecommerce solutions have.

As it was easy to guess the switch usually consists of several steps. The main goal behind this process is to make it as smooth and seamless for online trading as possible.

And the first step is to ensure the Hosting Platform for the new web site is suitable to host osCommerce.

 Search

You are currently browsing the osCommerce Blog weblog archives for February, 2007.

Pages
» About

Archives
» March 2007
» February 2007
» January 2007
» December 2006

Categories
» Miscellaneous (6)
» osCommerce Fixes (4)
» osCommerce Marketing and Sales (5)
» osCommerce Modules and Services (7)
» osCommerce News (6)
» osCommerce Reviews (3)
» osCommerce SEO (2)
» osCommerce Tips and Tricks (9)

The Advanced Administration panel allows for easy management and content writing. Readers can of course read articles, search articles, leave comments, and sign up to an RSS feed.

WordPress is an open-source solution, the same as osCommerce. The two are quite easy to integrate together. There is a separate contribution that integrates WordPress with osCommerce, and can be downloaded from `http://addons.oscommerce.com/info/3886`. It adds an information box with the latest posts extracted from WordPress and contains links back to the blog. In order to integrate WordPress with osCommerce, it is possible to use the previously described contribution that downloads any RSS feed and puts it into an information box.

RSS integration allows for not only integrating osCommerce with the blog installed as a part of the same website, but also with literally any other blog (or a CMS system that allows for RSS feed export). For example, a blog hosted by Blogger.com can be easily integrated into osCommerce using the same contribution as already described.

Attracting Customers Read and Write Articles

There's no better way to attract customers reading articles than publishing original content.

In order to attract customers leaving comments in the blog, the author should communicate with the readers by asking questions and inviting them to participate in dialog. Answering comments and questions left by the customers in the blog is not only polite but will also demonstrate to the readers that the author cares about their opinion and comments and will stimulate them to do it in the future.

The site owner may also run a contest for the best article sent by customers of the osCommerce online store. To make it easier for customers writing articles several topics may be proposed for writing by the Administrator of the online store. There may be some professional copywriters and journalists among the customers of the online store who would gladly participate in the contests or will simply agree to write articles and publish them in the online store content management system for certain discounts or free product samples.

Forums and Galleries

Online forums are probably one of the most potentially content-rich extensions of an online store that can not only help users and customers of the online store discuss particular products and services, but also get virtual friends sharing similar interests and discussing various topics not related to particular product or services.

Online forums can be used by the osCommerce store to build a virtual community that addresses the interests and needs of the target audience and existing customers. Customers will be coming back to the forums from time to time to read new posts and participate in discussions. No additional advertising expenses are required to bring the customer back to the forums if the customer is interested in the discussion topics.

The online store can advertise its products and services in the forums as banners.

It doesn't necessarily need to be a new virtual community—it may be easier and make more sense from the business point of view to integrate an online store with an existing forum to give new forum members and online store customers more facilities to participate in various discussions online.

What are the topics to discuss in an online forum that belongs to/is integrated into an online store?

- Current product range and new product releases
- Customer experience
- Service improvements and changes
- Online store announcements
- Support and FAQs

To attract more customers to participate in the forums, links to the discussion threads should be put alongside pages of the online store. Every product information page may contain a link to a specially created thread in the forum where the customers can discuss it. Also an online forum solution should be integrated with the rest of the online store—this means that some recent posts on the forum should find their way to one of the information boxes of the online store, and also user accounts should be shared between the online store and the forum solution.

Along with cross links between forums and online shop, and design integration, those are the two most important tasks of successful integration between an online store and online forum solution.

The moderation task should be seriously considered by the online store owners and forum moderators assigned and given permissions to edit or delete posted content.

Integration with Third-Party Forums

If the store owner decides to integrate a third-party forum with the online shop, one should ensure the latest posts can be exported from the forum to be imported into the online store, and that the third-party forum has a technical facility to preserve the session ID of the osCommerce online store when the user navigates back and forth.

It may also make sense to check if the chosen online forum allows for having custom design skins. In that case, making it look like the original online store will create an impression that the customer is dealing with two parts of the same website.

Integration may include the following steps:

- Import the list of main forums topics into osCommerce (for example as an information box in one of the side columns).
- Import the list of latest posts into osCommerce (for example as an information box on the main page in the middle column).

- Preserve session IDs of both osCommerce and third-party forum where possible.

- If possible, create a design skin for the third-party forum to make it look to users similar to the original online store.

Integration with Built-In Forums

Integration with the built-in forum solution doesn't make too much difference compared to the integration with third-party forums, except for one important feature: merged user accounts.

Yes, once logged into a user account in osCommerce, the customer would not want to log into the forum yet again and vice versa. Merged user accounts help customers to easily navigate through the online store and the forum, buying products online, and discussing bought products, asking for support, reading industry news, etc.

Most of the modern-day online forum solutions allow for design skin integration. And since the online forum files are often located on the same server and no considerations need be made regarding other design skins, the design integration task becomes easier to accomplish.

osCommerce can be integrated with the phpBB online forum solution. The main task of the integration is to provide a smooth switch between the two, so that the customer, should they be logged in either osCommerce or phpBB, would not need to log in again when switching to either phpBB or osCommerce and back.

Of course, this also assumes that a registered customer or even a guest visitor would not lose their shopping cart content if they have products in the shopping cart in osCommerce, and then switch to the online forums part of the site, read some topics there and then switche back to osCommerce.

Yet another task is to link forums to osCommerce by listing the latest/most popular/ "sticky" posts in one of the information boxes of osCommerce.

There are several solutions that are applicable, though for a complete integration one may want to use contribution called "phpBB-osCommerce Bridge" that can be downloaded from `http://addons.oscommerce.com/info/4710`.

Photo Galleries

Photo galleries can be integrated into forums. This way members of the online forum can not only post textual content, but also upload pictures and discuss them.

Very strong moderation activities should be performed regularly to avoid turning the forum and photo galleries into a storage for pictures that are not allowed by the policies of the online store and/or the forum.

As with the forum, the main idea of using photo galleries is to make users and customers interested in visiting the website more often, participate in discussions of uploaded photos and pictures, and upload pictures themselves.

Naturally, photo galleries can be used better to increase customers' interest in the product range offered in the online store where customers of the online store can create pictures of products they buy or with the help of products they buy and upload them for review by other customers.

For example, an online store that sells digital cameras and corresponding equipment can run a photo contest for the best photo in several categories submitted by its customers. Each uploaded photo would have to have a description and a link to the digital camera product used to capture the image.

Another example is an online store that sells greenhouses. The owner of the online store can launch a photo contest in several categories including the best installed greenhouse, the best grown plant, etc. Again, each photo post in the Photo gallery would be required to not only have its description, but also a link back to the product information page of the online store.

One more example would be an osCommerce online store that sells bakery and pastry online. The photo gallery would feature pictures of the best parties submitted by customers of the online store, with back links to the products from the product catalog used to make each party somewhat special.

It doesn't necessarily have to be a contest, it's just that it works better attracting customers to submit more pictures for inclusion into the Photo gallery if there's a prize draw announced.

Photos of real products taken in the real-life environment not only attract more visitors to the website, but also serve as one of the best recommendations to the new customers who are looking into buying some products from the online store.

Even though there are Photo Gallery add-ons for osCommerce, the best results might be achieved by integrating the built-in Photo Gallery features that are parts of the existing Online Forums solutions (`www.phpBB.org`, `www.vBulletin.com`).

The main reason is to make it easier for customers and members of the forum to discuss certain submissions having logged in once as the customer of the whole system. Also, it will be easier to support the integrated system in the future.

Summary

In this chapter, we have reviewed various ways to improve online sales with the use of dynamic content.

Adding proper dynamic content solutions to an online store makes it more attractive both for the target audience and for search engines. Allowing customers to contribute content by posting reviews, testimonials, articles, forum posts, photos, etc. not only helps to freshen the contents of the website but may also help to increase conversion rates from visitors to customers. Strong and continuous moderation should be put in place.

The two most important principles are design integration and user account integration. The design of all parts of the online store, including integrated solutions should have the same or similar design in order to continue to promote the brand of the online store. Also, for more convenience, users should only have one account, which should be valid if the users want to enter any other part of the website.

Search engines revisit the online store more often and index it better if its contents change, Also, real-life experiences described by other customers are sometimes referred to as the best recommendations that a customer can get.

Dynamic content helps online stores to get more visitors and convert more visitors into customers and more customers into returning customers.

5

Building Customer Confidence

Once a prospective customer visits an online store, there are reasons to buy or not to buy products. Product price is one of the most important factors of course, but yet many other factors also affect a customer's decision.

The customer has certain needs and is trying to satisfy those needs by buying products online when he or she visits the online store website. Hence one of the most important factors affecting the purchase decision is the customer's confidence in the fact that the product will address his or her needs now and possibly in the future.

Another very important factor is whether the customer feels comfortable about buying online in general, and buying products online from that online store in particular.

In order to convince customers to buy products, an online store has to buy their confidence in the first place.

Comparing online and off-line buying processes, it's easy to see why customer's confidence is one of the key factors affecting the buying decision:

- When buying offline, the customer can see, touch, even smell and of course often try the product—which is impossible when buying products online.
- When buying offline, the customer can ask for advice from the store staff—when buying online the customers are dealing with the website, not a real person.
- When buying offline, the customer enters a real store, which has been standing in its place for a while, and is supposed to stay there for a while too—websites are much easier to create and close.

- When buying offline, the customer can return the product at any moment according to the consumer regulations that act in that country or territory—online purchases are supposed to be protected by the same regulations, but since a website is only present in the virtual space, the customer may have certain concerns whether standard regulations will be applicable.

- When buying offline, in a store, the customer can pay in cash, or using cards, checks, etc. and the money goes from "hand to hand" without much risk—when buying online the customer often trusts personal information to the online store, including contact information, credit card details, etc.

- When buying products offline in a store there is no shipping fee involved if the product is in stock and the customer can actually take that product home immediately or pick it up from the warehouse.

Having listed all those benefits of buying offline, we understand how important it is to assure customers that buying products online is a secure, easy, fast, and safe method of purchase.

Providing customers of online stores with information that helps building their confidence is an important task for any online store manager. Without that information, many customers would simply skip buying products from the online store site, and will either place an order with one of the competitors, or buy products from their local store or supermarket.

The default osCommerce installation allows for editing information about products and the online store in general. Product information (like product name, description, image, price, etc.) is edited in the Administration panel of osCommerce. Information about the online store and various policies can be edited in the language files. Language files can be either edited in a text editor, or using the Define Language tool under the Tools menu in the Administration panel of osCommerce.

In this chapter, we will review various aspects of providing customers with detailed information about the products, and about policies of the online store and business in general. We will also consider the best practices in taking and processing orders.

Ensuring Server and Database Safety

But before we proceed any further, let's stop for a while and review the security and safety aspects of buying online with osCommerce.

Certainly every customer expects the online purchase process to be secure, and important information such as credit card details, personal details and addresses, purchase history, etc. not to be available to any third party without the authorization of the customer. The same goes for online store owners, who expect information about their customers, orders, and product catalog to be securely stored in the database and not become available to the public.

In e-commerce business, the responsibility for preserving sensitive information safe is put squarely on the store owner's shoulders. Different countries have different e-commerce laws and requirements, but here's the list of the most common requirements for the safety of sensitive customer, order, and product data:

- Physical access to the servers where the database is located should be limited to the authorized personnel only.
- Highly sensitive data, such as customers' credit cards information should not be stored in the database of the online store.
- Sensitive data such as customer details, order history, etc should be stored in a secure database with access limited to the registered customers and authorize personnel only.
- The web server and database server should communicate using secure channels.
- During the customer registration and purchase processes, the customer's browser and the web server should communicate using secure channels.
- The web server and database server should be protected from intrusions from outside.
- The login and password information should be secure enough, and should be changed from time to time following a developed data protection procedure.
- Any database with important information should be backed up regularly to ensure data safety.

Correspondingly, an online store requires a secure server, secure communication between the parts of the system, and also between the customer's browser and the web server. An online store also requires regular data backups, and passwords to be regularly updated. Also, the server where the online store is located should be periodically checked for all sorts of vulnerabilities.

While the store owner can take care of most of these tasks or buy corresponding services from hosting companies, an easy and effective way to check servers for vulnerabilities is to sign up to a service that scans a web server, finds possible threats, and reports those automatically.

One of these services is ScanAlert's HACKER SAFE certification service. The service itself doesn't require integration into an online store or a website—during the sign up/account editing process it is possible to specify the URL/address of the server that should be scanned for security issues.

Once the registration is complete, the service starts scanning the web server on a daily basis and reports vulnerabilities, if found, to the webmaster or web server administrators via email.

If there are no serious issues found, a corresponding message along with the HACKER SAFE logo will appear on the website's pages where the webmaster has integrated a little piece of HTML script. Depending on the subscription level, and also on the severity of vulnerabilities found, the logo may change or may even temporarily disappear from the website's pages.

Services like ScanAlert's HACKER SAFE are not only useful to maintain the server's security in order, but also improve the customers' level of confidence in the website, and the safety of the customer's account information if the customer was to create an account or place an online order.

Information about the Business

Without personal contact, where the customer can "meet" the shop staff in person and actually get to know the shop itself, putting comprehensive information about the shop on the website is essential to improve the customer's confidence in the online store.

There are always some people who are so used to buying online that they would probably not require to know everything about the business and the team behind it. But there are always some other, more suspicious, customers, who wont buy products online until they have been assured they are buying from a real business and not from just a one-day fake website.

What kind of information about the business can be displayed on a website to virtually "introduce" it to the customers?

Usually that information would be split into general information about the business, and information about the team that stands behind the business name, and would of course include contact details as well.

Information on the Main Page and Landing Pages

When a user first visits an online store—the first impression, the very first page affects the decision to stay and possibly place an order or leave and try some other websites. Of course, if the user is looking for a specific product and the price is right, it's much easier to convert the visitor into customer. But still, the power of the content of the first page that the visitor sees (either the main page of the online store, some category or product page, or one of the landing pages) should not be underestimated.

The main trick here is to keep the balance between different bits of information that one would like to put on the main/landing page. To start building a prospective customer's confidence in the online store, the main or landing page should have (besides products and special offers, etc.) at least some very basic information about the online store itself and the company behind it, about organizations that the online store is a member of, about payment methods available on the website, and about security measures enabled to protect customer and order information.

Business Information—About Us Page

This is where information about the business in general and the online store in particular should be published on the website. It makes sense to move most of this data into the About Us page of an osCommerce online store. It also makes sense to add a short paragraph containing the most important facts about the business to the main page of the website or to one of the side columns, and then add a link to the About Us page to ensure the customers still get some of the most important information about the business they may be looking for, but at the same time it should not occupy most of the main page or other functional pages. No matter how important it is to provide such information and improve confidence, proper product placement and promotion are far more important for an online store.

Usually, every business owner would know what to add to the About Us page. But still, here's the list of the bits of information the customers might be looking for when they open the About Us page:

- Business name, official company name, and company registration numbers—if the online store belongs to a company of course

- Business history, featuring years in business (which it only makes sense to highlight if the company has been a long player in the market)

- What the business of the company is about, what is its mission

- Recent company news and latest achievements (like awards)

- How to contact the company—sometimes simply a link to the Contact Us page where more details can be discovered.

Contacts (Addresses and Phones)—Contact Us Page

We have put this into a separate topic to underline how important it is to provide customers with information about how they can contact the company in as many different ways as possible.

No matter what the reason is for contact, whether it is a prospective sale or a complaint, or a request for customer support, the easier it is for the customer to contact the online store, the more positive effect it will make on the customer's opinion about the services provided in particular and the company in general.

A real business would not mind putting some general contact information (like company name, postal address, and phone numbers) on the pages of its website. This information doesn't need to be too large of course, neither does it need to become the main part of the page.

It can be either put as a relatively small piece of text in the bottom of the website, or even put it into the header of its pages, as in the following screenshot that shows an online store's main page. Even though it's not an osCommerce-based online store, it makes a good example of how a website can look if it has its address and further contact details on the main page.

The following information can be put online about each office or warehouse that the company behind the online store owns or operates from:

- Business name (if different from the company name), and a brief description of whether it's an office, warehouse, or some other part of the company's infrastructure

- Postal address, including country, for when the company has international presence

- Map, or rather 2-3 maps at different scales

- Driving directions, including traveling by car, train, plane, or other means of transport if it's an option

- Phone and FAX numbers, including country code; free phone numbers can be highlighted, and customer support phones and other contact details are especially important

- Email addresses and/or links to special fill-in forms that the customer can use to send a message to the company

Once again, the more information about the company's physical existence and physical presence in the specified locations can be given to the customer, the easier it will be for the customers to buy from the website with no worries.

Visual Image behind the Business Name

The best way for an online store to make its business look real in the Internet would be to publish photos of its office(s), warehouse(s), products, and staff.

Photos should be clear, look nice, and should make an impression of photos of real objects and people as well. The company's brand should be featured in as many photos as possible.

Photos of the following may be published to improve customer's confidence in the online store as a real business:

- Office or show room photos, from the inside and outside

- Warehouse, from the inside and outside

- Delivery vans, if applicable

- Photos of product lines and just photos of multiple products grouped together

- Team photos or individual photos of team members with short description about each person; by the way such photos can also be added to the Contact Us page where the phone numbers are located as well, so that when a customer calls in and asks for any sort of advice or information, the customer will see who the person answering the call on another end of the line is

Memberships and Regulating Authorities

It has become a common practice among online shops to build customer confidence by promoting the fact this or that online store is either a member of a certain organization with a high public trust level, or has been certified by such an organization as a secure, responsible, professional product and service provider that meets high trading and service providing standards.

Seals and Awards

Being a member of such organizations or being certificated by them is especially important for new online stores that do not have a record of many years in online business, to prove their professionalism and ensure the security and safety of their online purchasing processes.

Once an online store is certified, it usually becomes possible to put a graphic image (the so called seal) on its pages to announce and prove the fact of certification to its visitors and customers. Such a seal is then linked back to the website of the certifying organization, to a page that usually contains information about the business behind the online shop and about the online shop itself. A common practice is that the seal is provided as JavaScript or HTML code that can be downloaded from the website of the certifying organization once the certification process has been successfully completed.

Even if the actual certificate is provided in print, it makes sense to scan it and upload to the website — the same as a brick and mortar store would place copies of its certificates and awards in the window.

For the customer seeing the online business being a part of an organization with a publicly recognized high level of standards and requirements to its members means that products and services provided by that online business will also be of certain high quality and standards, and that if any problem arises, the customer will be able to complain and that complaint will be heard and dealt with professionally and in a timely manner.

We will review several of the broad range of privacy and security seal programs that are available to online merchants in different countries and world wide:

- TRUSTe Web Privacy Seal is provided by www.truste.org. The seal helps building confidence with consumers and increases turnover by letting end customers know they can trust an online shop with their personal information. Displaying the seal on the website is not all about The TRUSTe program. There are strict privacy principles (privacy policy documents need to be approved by TRUSTe, notice and disclosure of personal data collection and use practices should be made available on the website, and others) followed by all participating companies, along with the so called TRUSTe Watchdog dispute resolution process.

  TRUSTe performs audit of websites, and gives advices on how to improve privacy and all policies to comply with best practices.

- Shopsafe logos are provided by www.shopsafe.co.uk (there are also US, Australian, and New Zealand versions of the program). The service is free, and not only checks the website for various security issues and high standards of online trade, but also lists participating online stores in its own directory.

Shopsafe not only looks into the security of online transactions and customers' data, but also into whether the online shop has a wide range of products, whether prices are clearly visible on the website, whether the website is not just a copy of some other site, whether there are contact details, including address and phone number available if the customers would like to get in contact with the online merchant, whether all delivery, privacy, returns, and other policies can be easily found on the website. Last but not least, Shopsafe checks if the business is based in the country Shopsafe issues logos for (USA for shopsafe.com, UK forshopsafe.co.uk), and if the online store delivers to, at the least, addresses in that country.

- TrustedShops.com and TrustedShops.de are mostly available for companies that trade or are going to start online trading in European countries. The service (membership) has several levels, each with certain additional features available to the online merchants. To become a member and get the seal of approval, the online merchant needs to get a certificate from TrustedShops.

  The certification process includes passing through a series of tests that are individually prepared for each online store by TrustedShops. Only after successful final acceptance of the shop, will the online merchant get the right to put the seal on the website.

- Those online merchants who also trade actively on eBay, may want to put their "eBay PowerSeller" icon on the pages of their online store. Being an eBay PowerSeller means the online merchant has managed to achieve and maintain at least a 98% positive feedback rating. Therefore the presence of the logo on the website can once again reassure customers the service they will get and the products they will buy will be of high quality. Quoting eBay, customers *"can be confident that they are transacting with an experienced eBay seller who has proven that they're committed to customer satisfaction"*.

- SafeBuy.org.uk, or rather its SafeBuy Assurance Scheme, is designed for online merchants and their customers in the UK. A SafeBuy logo displayed on a website tells the customer the website is safe and trustworthy. In the event of any unresolved dispute between a customer and online merchant SafeBuy will act as mediators at no charge to either party.

  Effectively, it creates a body to whom the customer can complain if the issue can't be resolved by the customer and online merchant's mutual agreement.

  Among other requirements, online merchants are meant to respect corresponding European terms of sale of goods and data protection acts, provide the necessary security for processing credit cards, provide their physical location and contact information publicly on the website, display and clearly explain all prices included into order totals, and provide clear explanation of delivery procedures, not use SPAM for marketing purposes, etc.

- buySAFE.com provides, besides the certification process similar to those organizations already mentioned, yet another facility for end customers to make their online orders as risk-free as possible. buySAFE actually insures transactions (when, dependent on the status of the online merchant, it's the customer or the online merchant themselves who pay the fee for the transaction guarantee).

  Therefore, the customers gets virtually risk-free online shopping experience, and those online merchants who are certified by buySAFE and have the corresponding logo on their website can significantly increase their turnover by getting online orders from those customers who would hesitate to place an online order under different circumstances.

There are many other programs and organizations that we could not mention in this book. But what is important and what is common between all of them is the main principle of building a customer's confidence in online shopping by reassuring the customer about certain high standards of online trading the online store complies with, and making the whole online shopping experience as risk-free as possible.

Professional and business awards nowadays also often come in downloadable format from the associations or organizations that issue such awards. Even if an award comes printed, or as a physical sign, sculpture, etc., it still makes sense to take a photo of it and place it on the website's pages.

Security (SSL) and Business Identity

Yet other types of seals that improve customer's confidence are security seals and business identity seals. Some companies, like Go Daddy for example, provide a combined service and ensure both the security of the online purchase process and the business identity of the online merchant, at the same time.

Usually a security seal comes with any SSL certificate. Such SSL certificate issuing organizations as VeriSign, Thawte, GeoTrust, GoDaddy, etc. have different SSL certificates and correspondingly different security seals are available to online businesses. The seal often comes as JavaScript/HTML code that can be inserted into any page. The snippet of code then downloads an image and any additional information from the SSL issuer website and displays it in the pages of the online store. Various types of security seals come with different SSL certificates.

Obviously, the more expensive the certificate is (and prices may differ from about $19.99 per year to about $400 per year, and even higher), the more complex the security seal that comes along with it, and the more aspects of online trading can be certified.

Obtaining a security seal may include several levels of authorization to ensure the SSL certificate and the seal are being sent to the company/person who really runs the online business/website and not to someone else. This may include sending several emails back and forth, and some of them only to the email addresses associated with the corresponding domain name, receiving letters and phone calls, etc.

Even more advanced service is provided by companies and organizations that certify business identity. Information about the business is checked — business name, addresses, phone and fax numbers, professional references, and many more things.

A Better Business Bureau program called BBBonline (`www.bbbonline.org`) provides services that help end customers get information about the business body that actually runs the online store, to ensure they are buying products from a company that complies with certain standards for ethical online business practice.

Also important is that a BBBonline membership means that the company agrees to resolve any disputes with its customers through BBB's dispute resolution program, so the customers are not only provided with business identity information but also are given a facility to complain and be heard and get any dispute resolved efficiently and to the mutual satisfaction of the end customer and online merchant.

Participation in BBBonline is limited to the USA and Canada only, though as said on the `www.bbbonline.org` website "the company must be based or have a physical presence" in either of those two countries. Therefore companies with their headquarters located in other countries, who have subdivisions in the USA or Canada can apply.

Conveniently enough for end customers and online merchants there are several ways to confirm business identities. Like for example, seals supplied along with SSL certificates. GoDaddy.com have several products that include business identity verification along with a regular SSL certificate. The SSL certificate just won't be issued until the company's identity and real existence are proven. Business identity information can be then displayed in a special animated SSL seal that online merchants can put on their website. Similar services are available from GeoTrust. com, and several other SSL certificate issuers.

Where Should We Place the Images?

The seals and awards can be inserted into any page of the website. In the case of an osCommerce online store, there are several pages where the seal can really make a difference.

The corresponding image can be inserted into the main page of the osCommerce online store to assure the visitors, from the very first glance, that the website provides professional services and its services and products meet the high standards of certain organizations and/or has won certain professional or business awards.

Such images can be also added to one of the side columns (if any are present in the design integrated into the osCommerce online store). They can either be placed along with the Information box, or along with the Shopping Cart box. Or the security seal could be added to the footer of the online store, usually along with its address and links to information pages (like About Us, Contact Us, Privacy policy, Terms and Conditions of use, etc.). Location of the security seal image on the page may depend on which page the customer is looking at.

It also makes sense to add seals and awards images to the About Us page of an osCommerce online store.

Certain business or professional awards can be placed on the corresponding product or category pages to demonstrate to the customers the professionalism and high quality standards provided by the online shop in that particular product range.

And of course, it's very important to place security and business identity seals on the Shopping Cart and Checkout pages, because those are the pages where some customers actually hop off the purchase process.

Of course, the seal and award images should not take customer's attention away from products and especially from the elements of the page that actually allow customers to make a purchase, but, at the same time, those images should help to ensure customer's confidence in making the purchase. So it may make sense to put such images on the main page, side columns on other pages, product pages, shopping cart, and checkout pages at the same time.

What Makes the Difference?

What really makes a difference to the customer and what makes the customer choose this or that online store to make a purchase is a combination of various factors. Some customers know what they are looking for and simply compare prices to choose the best price and the most reliable service provider. Other customers may not know what exactly they are looking for and may be browsing through several sites to find the product that may suit their needs.

In either case, making sure the customer will receive appropriate products and professional service and that the customer's online purchase experience will be positive and secure is one of the most important tasks of an online store owner.

Some researches though demonstrate that sales figures do not change that much when an online store announces it has become a member of a certain organization or has been certified to meet the high standards of certain public organization or company. But it depends mostly on how well known the organization or certification company is, and how valuable and well known their certification is to the target audience.

An online store owner should avoid trying to get the website certified in as many organizations or companies as possible, but rather concentrate on getting the website certified by one or a very few that really make the difference to the end customers.

Multilingual Aspect

In an ideal situation, information about the business that stands behind the online store should be provided in as many languages as are used in the territories in which it operates or are used by its target audience. Website visitors will welcome the facility to read general information about the business in their native language. More visitors will become customers if they can access the online store in their native language.

osCommerce has a built-in support for multiple languages and comes with English, French, and German languages enabled by default. But since business information is very specific, every store owner who's willing to operate internationally should have it translated by professional translators and published accordingly on its pages.

It's a very important task to ensure the information in different languages is always up-to-date, and once some text or page gets changed in the default language, it is also updated in all other languages. It's an common mistake that causes misunderstanding and confusion when one and the same page has different content in different languages.

However, there are cases when the store manager would intentionally put different content for one and the same page in different languages. This is because the store operates not only in different languages but also in different territories. Terms and conditions, shipping rates, and other information may be different in different territories. Correspondingly, page content changes when the customer changes language. Even address details on the Contact Us page may be different.

Only professional translators or native speakers should be used to translate such important information. Mistakes and incorrect translation may also cause misunderstanding and confusion, and eventually result in unsatisfied customers. Using online translating services to translate pages in default language "on the fly" is inappropriate because the present level of such services is not anywhere near the quality of services that can be provided by certified skilled professionals. By using online translating services to translate pages, the store owner will demonstrate clear disrespect to the visitors who read in other languages.

In osCommerce, languages can be switched on any page if the Languages information box is enabled in one of the side columns, or in the header of the pages. Some osCommerce store owners prefer to move this piece of code into the header part of the page, so that it's easy to find on the page and easier to switch to another language at any moment. Usually, the Language box contains icons of corresponding flags to make it easier for customers to switch to the desired language. If the website operates in more than three or four languages, it may be a good idea to give customers a facility to select the language in a drop-down box, because having many language icons either in a side column or in the header may distract from the layout of other design elements of the page.

A useful feature that comes built into osCommerce is the facility to change language to the one set in the customer's web browser as the default locale automatically when the customer enters the website. It's a very good marketing approach as this eliminates any confusion if the customer is not familiar with the default language of the website and has to browse through the page looking for language switch controls. But even with such features in place, it should still be possible to switch languages manually. The reason is simple; it's not always the case that the default locale in the customer's web browser can be determined correctly, and therefore some customers will still have to switch to the desired language manually.

Another approach is switching languages based on the customer's geographical location. It is possible to determine the customer's geographical location based on the IP address. Each country or territory usually has certain ranges of IP addresses assigned to it, so by knowing the IP address of the customer it's possible to find out the territory the customer is visiting the site from. Correspondingly, knowing the territory (country here), it is possible to some degree of correctness to determine the customer's native language. The cause of possible mistake here can be in wrong association between the IP address and the territory, and also in having several languages in use in the territory the customer is browsing the site from.

There is a contribution for osCommerce that is available from `http://addons.oscommerce.com/info/1096` that allows for determining country of origin by customer's IP address. This contribution was originally designed for the "Who is Online" page in the Administration panel of osCommerce, but of course it can be easily used to determine the customer's country of origin when the customer first opens any page of the website.

To minimize mistakes, it's better to combine the two methods together, i.e. determine the customer's browser's default locale and also determine where the customer is browsing the site from and only switch the language automatically when both methods give the same result.

Customer Information

Sometimes before making a purchase, during the checkout process, and after placing an order, the customers may want or may be required to read the terms and conditions of trade, or policies of the online store. Here, we will review the more or less typical set of documents that an online merchant may have to publish on the website, and also review typical content of such documents.

Terms and Conditions, and Policies

The Terms and Conditions of trade document is probably the most important one, and it describes how the customer will be treated and what sort of obligation the online store agrees to undertake to fulfill the customer's orders, how the online store protects customers and its own rights, and how this corresponds to the law. To some degree this works as a contract between the online merchant and the customer.

It's important to inform the customer that rights granted by law are not affected by the Terms and conditions of trade of the online store.

Terms and conditions are usually put on one of the information pages, and a link to that page is usually put into the Information box in one of the side columns or into the bottom of all pages where other important links can be located.

Also, and this is required by law in some countries, the Terms and Conditions document can be made a part of the checkout process and the customers should confirm they have read and understood the document before placing an order.

Changes to the Terms and Conditions document, the same as to other documents that regulate relations between the online store and the customer should be announced on the website and made part of the news archive, so that returning customers could easily locate them on the website when they return to check their account, order status, or place another order.

The following can be put into the Terms and Conditions of trade document:

- Contract definition—i.e. what is defined as a contract between the customer and the online store, and how each side is supposed to fulfill the contract.
- Data protection—details about how customers' sensitive data is protected and what are the security measures taken by online store to protect it.

- Copyright information.

- Disclaimer — this paragraph explains how the online store would deal with claims of certain types (like for example, incomplete product descriptions, mispriced products, etc.).

- Definition of means of communications — in most of the cases the online store will deal with the customers via electronic means of communications, like email or the website itself.

- Liability and indemnity definitions.

- Alteration or amendments to the document usually describes the way the current Terms and Conditions document can be altered or modified or completely replaced by the online merchant.

- Definition of Force Major and also obligations that the online store and the customer should fulfill in case of events beyond reasonable control of both sides.

- Governing law and jurisdiction — this paragraph usually defines the governing law and which courts lawsuits should be submitted to, should it get to that stage.

It is essential for online merchants to seek for legal advice when creating their Terms and Conditions document, so that the online store and its customers feel protected by the document.

Policies: Privacy Policy, Billing Policy, and Shipping Policy

All customers will be able to see the available payment and shipping methods during the checkout process.

But whether or not certain payment methods are accepted by the online store, what are the payment terms (for example if the customer is charged immediately or only after the stock has been allocated or the whole order has been dispatched, etc.), should all become a part of the Billing policy document. The billing policy may also contain logos of payment methods supported by the online store, account details for bank transfers, addresses for checks, etc. After all it's an HTML web page, which provides webmasters with endless customization facilities. But the point should always be about making it, as well as other policies, comprehensive and easy for customers to understand.

The Shipping Policy document is to some degree similar to the Billing Policy one, though it contains all the information about delivery options. Besides description of each shipping option, the Shipping Policy document can also contain shipping fee tables, useful phone numbers, and tracking links for items already dispatched. The Shipping Policy document can also advise on what to do if the order is lost after it has been dispatched, what would happen if the customer is out when the order arrives, or which regions/countries the online can store deliver the goods to.

It's fairly important to assure customers that online orders can be returned back to the online store in case of faulty products, or if a customer doesn't like the product, or the customer's mind changes, or because of any other reasons explained by the governing law. Any restocking fee policy should be explained as well, so that the customers would know how much they could be charged if returning ordered products back.

Often the return and refund policies are combined with the Shipping Policy to make it is easier for customers find all the information in the same place. And often, along with the returns and refunds policy goes the warranty policy that explains various warranty conditions for different products sold in the online store.

Help and Assistance

Quite often there's so much information available online, that a website visitor is quite confused and experiences some difficulty making a choice between several similar products, or simply finding a solution or a product to address certain needs.

That's where it's fairly important to give the visitors of an online store a helping hand, and advice if they are looking for it.

Buying Guides

Buying guides are sets of articles that can help a customer to make a choice of a product that will satisfy certain criteria and address the customer's needs. Buying guides on their own do not have to promote specific products. Instead, it's better to concentrate on determining what the customers need and to provide corresponding advice, based on the product range sold online.

Buying guides can be specific for specific categories of products. For example, an online store that sells all sorts of home appliances would have several buying guides—for cookers, hobs, extractors, dish washing machines, washing machines, coffee makers, and so on. A buying guide should explain the benefits of the solutions and approaches that are implemented in particular products, and also how those solutions can solve problems that customers experience, or address their needs with a better service than they currently have.

By providing customers with buying guides, an online store not only helps the customers to make their choice, but also shows the importance of them making the right choice.

Generally speaking, a sale is a good sale when the customer feels happy or satisfied right after buying products or services, and also, in the future as the product or service the customer has bought actually helps the customer and does exactly what the customer wanted and expected from such a product.

Buying guides are not very difficult to implement in osCommerce.

First of all, the online store manager needs to define which products the buying guides will be created for. Usually it's not difficult to do—actually in most cases a look at the list of top categories would be enough.

Secondly, there needs to be an expert who will actually create the buying guides. There could be several people writing different buying guides, dependent on what their expertise is about. A person to write a buying guide should be someone who has personal experience with such products, and also has experience selling such products to customers (either on the phone, online, or in the show room). Knowledge of what solutions customers are looking for, and what each feature, technology, or approach actually means is essential. When describing some features and solutions in buying guides it makes sense to add links to the product, that have that feature or solution in place. A link to the `advanced_search.php` page with certain parameters (category, manufacturer, product name/model) will do the trick.

It is possible to use one of the CMS add-ons for osCommerce to create buying guide pages. Links to all buying guides can be either put into a special information box called Buying Guides, or put onto a special new page and a link to that page added to the Information box, so that customers can easily locate it on the pages of the osCommerce online store. It also makes sense to add links to the buying guides both to the Advanced Search page and to the Advanced Search Results page. In the latter case, it's a good idea to highlight buying guides on the Advanced Search Results page if no one product is found according to the customer's query. Finally, a link to the corresponding buying guide can be put on the category page (an add-on to osCommerce that allows for category descriptions would have to be installed) and also on the product's page. Buying guides should be also made available in downloadable format (PDF, DOC, RTF, etc.) so that customers can download them and read them later. Especially with more expensive products it's always a good idea to give customers advice and also some time to think and choose the option that best suits them. Buying guides are also very good for SEO, as a buying guide will contain plenty of valuable consistent keywords, and content related to the products offered in the online store.

FAQ

Frequently asked questions (FAQs) are questions that many customers ask (or would like to ask). These can be summarized and can be put together with answers in the so called FAQ. Also, any questions the online store manager wants to answer to help customers to learn more about the products that are offered online, about the services provided, etc. can be included.

A FAQ is a set of pages each with one or several typical questions and detailed answers to those. Questions, if there are many, are often grouped into question categories to make it easier for customers and the website's visitors to find the answer they are looking for. For example, the FAQs of osCommerce online store can have the following categories: Our products, User account and security, Checkout process and payment methods, Order tracking and delivery, Warranty and returns.

Questions put into the FAQ are usually quite short, but of course the answers should be long enough to provide the customer with comprehensive information.

Link to the FAQs page can be added to the Information box of osCommerce. Links to the different sections of the FAQs can be put on different pages of the osCommerce online store, and correspondingly, on the account registration page, checkout shipping page, checkout payment page, checkout confirmation page, etc. It's a good practice to open such links in a new window, so that the user doesn't get distracted and can continue with the purchase process.

There are several contributions for osCommerce that allow for creation and management of FAQs. They can be integrated into the Administration panel of the osCommerce online store, and allow for creating sections, questions, and answers.

A contribution called FAQDesk can be effectively used to manage those frequent questions and answers that the online merchant would like to present to the customers and website visitors. That contribution can be downloaded from `http://addons.oscommerce.com/info/1106`. Once installed, it allows for creation of categories of questions in the Administration panel of the website, and of course for posting questions and answers into those FAQ categories.

FAQ categories can be configured to be displayed in an information box in one of the columns. There can also be a special information box with the latest FAQ posts.

Each question can have a corresponding short and long answer. For convenience, short answers can be displayed in the FAQ listing in the FAQ category, while the long answers can be displayed on the FAQ details page. A special "sticky" option is available for the Administration of the online store to mark certain FAQs to appear at the very top of FAQ lists in FAQ categories.

An important feature for FAQs is search, especially for those FAQs where there are a great many questions and answers. Often, especially if there are many questions and answers available, customers may choose to try the search feature to find the Q & A they are interested in, instead of browsing through several sections of FAQs.

It's fairly important to learn to listen to customers when they ask questions, either on the phone, in the store, or via email or live chat. Collecting questions, grouping them together, and giving descriptive answers can help answer similar questions from other customers, and also show the customers the level of professionalism the online store possesses when it comes to the products offered online, or to the services provided before, during, and after sale.

Live Support

As in a regular store, a customer may need some assistance with products, or some clarification about certain services or specifics of the ordering process. In a regular store, the customer would ask a sales adviser for help. Many online stores put the phone numbers of their Sales team on the website so that the customers can pick up a phone and make a call (often absolutely free of charge) and ask for help.

But with online stores, one more facility can be employed that can help the customers contact the Sales or Support team easily, and doesn't even require making a phone call. This is the Live Support/Live Help feature.

The live support feature is actually a Chat feature. In its simplest implementation, it allows an online chat between the customer and a Sales advisor/Support team member. It opens a new browser window where the customer can post some short messages and the sales advisor can answer also by posting messages.

In osCommerce, the Live support feature can be useful on the main or landing page, on the search results page, and on the product information pages as well. If it's added to the website, it's essential to have one or several persons or even a whole team available to answer Live support requests from the customers. Unfortunately, many store owners enable the Live support feature and then do not assign enough human resources, which results in unhappy and unsatisfied customers waiting in a queue for a chance to chat with a sales advisor or a support team member.

The Live Support features gives customers that level of confidence that it is always possible to ask a live human being for help or advice, as they can in a real store.

There are several open-source/free and commercial solutions that can be integrated into osCommerce. One of the most popular ones is called "PHPLive!" by OSI Codes Inc. It is available from `www.phplivesupport.com` as a free trial, hosted, or downloadable version. Once installed to the website, it updates the database by creating certain additional tables and can be used straightaway after the automatic installation. The before-launch configuration process includes creation of one or several departments (for example Sales, Support) and then one or several user (operator) accounts in each department. A feature that is simple but certainly good for building trust allows uploading photographs of system operators.

Integration into osCommerce is really easy and straightforward. In order to do it, one has to log into the newly installed/hosted PHPLive! Administration panel, and make the system generate a certain HTML code that can be then inserted into any page/information box of the osCommerce website. It's as simple as that!

Afterwards, every user that has reached a page where PHPLive! has been installed, sees a specially generated image that indicates whether Live Support is available at the moment, or if there are no active operators and the user can only leave a message (actually it sends an email) to the Support team.

Product Catalog

The customers come to an online store website to buy products or services. It's their main point of interest. The value and effect on a customer's decision to buy or not to buy of the quality and completeness of the product catalog cannot be underestimated. Contents provided to the customer should not only call to action (to buy products or services) but also be properly organized and detailed enough so that the customer can easily find the desired products and get all required information about them.

A well prepared product catalog is:

- Well structured
- Easy to search through
- Informative and reasonably detailed
- Easy to read and contains clean and sharp product images

Category Tree

The category tree is one of the key navigational elements in an osCommerce online store. All products are usually grouped into categories. The category tree may contain several levels of categories.

It is important to understand that the category tree, often being put at the top of the left-side-column, is one of the first design elements the customer will see when he/she opens the website.

Depending on how well it is organized, the customer may literally be lost from the very first moment, after a few clicks, or on the contrary, may easily find the desired products.

If the online store has about ten top categories, in that case the category tree should not be too long; ideally, it would not occupy more than a third of the screen's height and contain all top categories. On the contrary, if there are many more top categories in the online shop, and also sub-categories, it makes sense to list all top categories there and also add some of the sub-categories (the ones with featured or best selling products), so that customers and search engines could get easier access to Product Listings.

Too many levels of categories is not a good practice, ideally, there would be no more than three category levels, or even two levels, if it's possible. The customer should not feel lost in the category tree, as the customer has come looking for products. If the category tree contains too many levels, it makes sense to ease access to the actual products for the customers. In order to do this, some featured or best selling products can be listed on the category details page, along with the category description and a listing of sub-categories.

Category names in the tree should not be too long, but self-explanatory at the same time. Too general or too specific is not good; better use something in between the two.

Categories in the tree can either be sorted alphabetically, or by their importance. Certain categories may contain products that the store owner would like to sell, but from another point of view, other categories may contain the best selling products, so it makes sense to give such categories more priority. Of course, priorities may change with time, but it's better not to change the category tree too often so as not to confuse returning customers.

Page Load Speed Issues

Many osCommerce store owners complain about the speed of their osCommerce websites. Often the end customers bring it to their attention; sometimes the slow down is even noticeable in the Administration panel of osCommerce.

Customers do not like to wait, neither in a real store, nor when browsing through an online one. Slow response and long page load time may affect the customer's decision to stay on the website or to leave trying to find another online store selling similar products.

Some researches say customers would not usually wait more than four seconds to see a page fully loaded! Quick loading pages not only make the browsing experience more pleasant, but also demonstrate to the customers the store owners take their online business seriously, and invest in the infrastructure of their hosting platform and in website development and optimization.

An osCommerce online store that was started several years ago and has been fast all this time has suddenly become slow—how is it possible? Or why would a very new osCommerce site demonstrate bad performance?

There could be a number of issues with both the hardware and software that affect the performance of an osCommerce online store. Here is the list of what should be checked to make sure your osCommerce-powered business doesn't lose customers because of poor website performance:

- Web server average load and hardware configuration—the web server may need an upgrade (additional RAM or new CPU for example) or maybe its hard drive is full and needs cleaning.
- Database server configuration—MySQL needs to be optimized to work in the most efficient way. Mostly this relates to using cached queries. More on MySQL server optimization can be found at `http://dev.mysql.com/doc/refman/5.0/en/optimizing-the-server.html`.
- Database structure optimization—in older osCommerce versions not all database indexes were properly implemented. For example, almost any osCommerce website requires database indexes for tables that are used for 'Best Selling' and 'Customers Who Bought This Product Also Bought' features, and these indexes were often missing in old installations of osCommerce. Here, one can find more information on how to build and use indexes: `http://dev.mysql.com/doc/refman/5.0/en/optimizing-database-structure.html`.
- Number of database queries per page—osCommerce allows for monitoring not only page loading time, but also the number of database queries used per page. The corresponding contribution can be found at `http://addons.oscommerce.com/info/4643`. Obviously, the more queries are run against the database, the slower the page will load. So caching parts of the pages that do not change too often can help improve page loading speed and overall osCommerce performance. Some osCommerce standard features and contributions can be optimized, and the number of database queries can be reduced by rewriting the script. For example, to display the list of featured products, standard osCommerce would query the database to retrieve the name of each product. But the database query could be changed, so that both the list of featured products and also their names and descriptions are extracted from the database at the same time, in one go, as only one query.

- Product images — usage of thumbnails can improve the Product Listing page loading speed, dramatically. And also improve the loading speed of other pages where image thumbnails can be used instead of full-sized images.

- PHP scripts — PHP scripts can be optimized with tools like PHP Accelerator. As it says on the PHP Accelerator website (`http://www.php-accelerator.co.uk`), it "...provides a PHP cache, and is capable of delivering a substantial acceleration of PHP scripts without requiring any script changes, loss of dynamic content, or other application compromises". There are several PHP Acceleration solutions. More information about those and also links to the corresponding websites can be found at `http://en.wikipedia.org/wiki/PHP_accelerator`.

- HTML pages size — it's obvious that the larger the page is, the longer it takes for a web browser to download it from the web server. Also, larger HTML pages put more workload on the web server that in its own turn slows down overall website performance. In the latest versions of osCommerce, a special page compression feature has been implemented that compresses the page on the web server side, and then the web browser decompresses the page on the end customer's side. This feature can be turned on in the Administration panel, Configuration section, GZip Compression menu. If the web server supports GZip compression, it's better to turn that feature on to improve website performance and page loading speed for end customers.

Search and Search Results

When an online store has many products, the search function and search results display page become an essential part of the online ordering process. To order a product, the customer has to first find the desired product in the product catalog.

osCommerce provides Quick Search and Advanced Search features by default. There are several improvements that can be implemented to make it easier for customers to find the products they want.

First of all, the Quick Search box can be improved with the auto-suggestion feature (similar to the auto-suggestion feature in Google toolbar). This helps customers to not only specify their search criteria faster, but also find products by name or model even if the customer doesn't exactly know it. The module for osCommerce called "AJAX Search Suggest" can be downloaded from `http://addons.oscommerce.com/info/4144`. Once installed, it integrates with the "Quick Search" information box, and whenever the user starts typing a word in the free-type text field, the contribution lists matching products (the ones with product name starting from the typed sequence of letters) underneath the Quick Search box. An alternative solution, another contribution, can be downloaded from `http://addons.oscommerce.com/info/3413`.

Secondly, additional filters (like category or price) can be added to the Quick Search box, so that customers could search not the whole product catalog, but rather a certain category or price range instead.

An osCommerce contribution available at `http://addons.oscommerce.com/info/4352` allows for a price filter to be added to the "Quick Search" box, simplifying product search for customers, especially if the online store has plenty of products in the catalog.

Finally, the relevance of search results means a lot. The more relevant the search results are to the search terms, the more chances are that the customer will find the desired products and make a purchase. By relevancy, it's possible to understand presence of the keywords and key phrases that the customer searches for in product name, description(s), attribute names, etc. The more occurrences of a keyword are in a certain product — the more relevant that product would be to the search terms.

When a search brings up multiple products, the customer only faces the problem of choosing between those found products. But what if the search results contain no products at all? What if the customer's criteria (either set in the Quick search box or in the Advanced search page) didn't match any of the products listed in the catalog? In such a case, the resulting page should not only contain the "products not found" message, but also, preferably, the following:

- The search form with all fields pre-filled with the previously specified search terms
- Suggestions on how to improve search criteria
- Links to the most popular categories, products or searches (if corresponding statistics are available), or to the products the store owner would like to promote
- More product catalog filter options (by manufacturer, by price range, etc.)

Information in Product Listing

The Product Listing page is what the customer sees when either choosing one of the categories in the category tree, or searching for some products, or using some filters that are intended to help the customer to ease the product finding process.

It is on the Product Listing page that the customer makes the first step in a series of decisions that may or may not lead to the purchase. Therefore, the Product Listing page should contain just enough information for the customer to be able to make that decision.

Products Per Page

First of all, there should be enough products listed on the page, but not too many at the same time. By default, osCommerce brings up ten products per page. This setting can be modified in the Administration panel, Configuration section, Maximum Values menu, Search Results variable. But whether the number of products per page should be increased, decreased, or left unchanged depends entirely on nature of products being offered in the online store, and on the number of such products in the product catalog. It may also depend on design aspects because naturally, a grid view will allow for listing more products per page than a list view.

Some products require more space on the Product Listing page to be noticed by customers than the others. If products need a bigger picture so that the customer can see some important details, a short description, or maybe some detailed technical specifications to be displayed to make the customer satisfied with the level of information provided, and there is a relatively small number of items in the product catalog, it makes sense to put less products per page but provide customers with more information about such products to make the choice easier.

In either case, the rule of thumb is simple: most customers do not like longer pages, and even if the page is longer than the screen size, they do not like to scroll for more than one mouse wheel turn. Correspondingly, the number of products per page can be calculated by dividing approximately 1.5 of the estimated average customer's screen size by the height of the screen space required to display an average product in the listing.

Product Information in the Listing

By providing certain information about products on the Product Listing page, the store owner resolves two tasks: keeping the customer interested in the products, and building the customer's confidence in the fact that the products listed there will satisfy the customer's needs at present, or in the future, and that this particular online store is the right place to buy such products. As to what can be displayed for each product in the listing, it depends entirely on the nature of the products.

For example, for an online store that sells jewelry, displaying product name, price, and, most importantly a nice and sharp picture of the product will be enough.

For an online store that sells industrial equipment, it will be essential to display product category, name, picture (though this is not always needed because the name can describe the product well enough, and also the level of customer's awareness of the product will be high enough) and some of its key specifications.

A website that sells kitchen appliances would be expected to mention product category, manufacturer name (and sometimes logo), product name (or, often in this industry, model or product code), and several most important specifications or features of the product (or its short description).

As we can see, the content of the Product Listing page depends on the nature of products being offered online. If an online store has products of several different types to offer online, the content of Product Listing pages may be different for each category/product type.

In almost all cases, product price will be also displayed in the Product Listing, unless it's hidden for particular reasons. The "Add to Cart" (or sometimes "Buy Now") button may or may not appear in the Product Listing. The same goes for the "More Details" button. It should be noted that it makes no sense and only confuses the customer if both the "More Details" and "Add to Cart" button actually lead to the Product Information page (which often happens in osCommerce when a product has attributes). If you still want to have the Add to Cart or Buy Now buttons appear in the Product Listing even if products are likely to have one or several attributes, you should add attributes to the product listing. See `http://addons.oscommerce.com/info/1098`.

osCommerce has a built-in facility to control what's displayed on the product listing page. A menu item Product Listing, which is available in the Configuration section of the Administration panel of osCommerce allows for certain database fields to be displayed or hidden on the product listing pages in osCommerce. Fields like product image, manufacturer name, model number, product name, price, quantity in stock, and weight can be enabled or disabled on the product listing page, or their order can be easily changed.

In addition to the standard fields, the following may be displayed on the product listing page too: product category name, product description, product key technical specifications, and manufacturers logo.

It is essential to note that extra clicks may ruin the sale. The less clicks the customer needs to make to reach the page where it's possible to make the purchase, the better. Of course, this only applies if the customer is well informed about the product up to that moment. So, if the online store has only a little information about its products or the products do not require a very detailed description because they are either well known or everything can be explained by showing bigger sharper picture and several key characteristics of the product, the link to the Product Information page from the Product Listing page would be redundant.

Product Comparison

A facility to compare several products is highly appreciated by customers as it's often quite difficult to make a choice between similar products and seeing them all with their main characteristics in one list can help to exclude the unwanted ones and narrow the search to only one of a few desirable products.

A comparison feature is usually made part of the Product Listing page. Two or more products can be marked with check boxes and then a special button can be pressed to open a pop-up window that contains information about the selected products and allows for removing unwanted products from the list.

There is a contribution for osCommerce (available at `http://addons.oscommerce.com/info/2192`) that allows for side-by-side product comparison. It can be configured in the Administration panel of osCommerce to compare products by certain fields only. Interestingly enough, the list of fields also includes available attributes of products.

Individual Product Page

By default, in osCommerce each product has its own Product Information page. It basically contains the product image, description, link to product reviews, product attributes, if any, and of course product price and the "Buy Now" button. But sometimes, the default content of the Product Information page may not be enough to buy customer's confidence in the product itself and in the online store's ability to provide proper service, and this is then a case that calls for improvements.

Name, Price, Descriptions, and Attributes

Product name is usually the first thing a customer can see when the page opens. When selling more tangible products the name means a lot because it is often already familiar to the customer, or may already contain some information about the product itself. That is why it may be useful to include product category and/or manufacturer into the product name on that page.

Product price often follows the name and should not only be easy to notice, but also clear enough to tell the customer what is paid for exactly. For example, the price shown can:

- Be either for one product or for a box of 20 products
- Include or exclude taxes (in that case a short explanation displayed near the price figure will be just fine)
- Include or exclude delivery costs, and configuration of attributes that the customer has selected
- Be a recommended retail price displayed along with the sale price, or a sale price that it limited by certain time frame or last until the free stock lasts

All this information should be explained to the customer to avoid any confusion. At the same time, it should not confuse the customer with too much information given in the same area of the page. Layout and design pattern is something we will discuss in the next chapter of this book.

Of course, the description of any product should be "selling" the product in the first place. But to sell the product to the customer, the customer should be first given precise and detailed information about the product and how the product can address the customer's needs now and in the future. Making the customer confident in product suitability is one of the easiest and best ways to win the sale.

In osCommerce, products usually do not have short descriptions. There are several contributions out there that enhance standard functionality and add more descriptions (text or HTML) to the products.

For example the "Products Short Description" module (available at `http://addons.oscommerce.com/info/3123`) allows for entering the short description of any product and for displaying it through the Product Listing pages of osCommerce. Another contribution called "Short Description in products" (available at `http://addons.oscommerce.com/info/4452`) copies the first 80 to 200 characters of Product Description and uses it as short description through all Product Listings in osCommerce along with a "read more ..." link that leads the user to the Product Information page.

The short description should be really short (so that it would be possible to use it on, for example, a Product Listing page) and ideally, describe the most important features of the product and/or services supplied along with the product. It can contain the main technical characteristics, a warranty promise, and should give the customer at least one reason to buy a product.

The long description contains more marketing information, and more information about specific features or details of the product. It can contain information about how to best use the product, and even some reviews and testimonials provided by other customers. It should not be too long though, so that the customers do not feel lost when they open the Product Information page and bored when they read it. Fortunately, osCommerce allows the adding of HTML formatting tags into the product long description, so it's possible to highlight the main features or some of the most important paragraphs of the long description, or even add some photos and additional images directly into the long description that would help to better describe the product, and its benefits and features to the customers.

Some store owners prefer to list the main features of the product separately from a more marketing-oriented long product description. This is just a dry list of the main features sorted by their importance to customers. Even though it is not very sale oriented, the main features list helps customers choose the product they really need, and any help is always appreciated by customers. Of course, not every website would need to list the main features of their products because it very much depends on the product nature, and the amount of information about each product should not be excessive.

Yet another important requirement here, and this is what many online store owners forget, is explaining to the customer what actually this or that main feature does for them. The problem many store owners face is that being professional in the business and dealing with certain products and technologies daily, they understand what each specific term or product function means and do not require more detailed explanations. But potential customers may not have such knowledge or experience and will require some guidance on how to use those features and what those features actually mean.

Some sort of glossary available for those terms and feature names would be very much appreciated by the customers. As an example, an online store that sells electronic products (like digital cameras, etc.) could put the following terms into its glossary: Megapixels (effective), Image Resolution, Optical Zoom, Digital Zoom, LCD Screen Size, etc. Putting in a description and general recommendation for each term or feature can win more customers' confidence in the products and effectively in the online store that sells them. We will repeat it yet again here: customers buy products to address certain needs and explaining to them how to do it with the help of products being offered online helps sales a lot.

In order to make the page neater and not so long with all those descriptions, features lists, attributes, and other design elements, it's possible to use a multiple information tabs feature.

A contribution for osCommerce called "Product Tabs" allows for entering various product-related information into different information tabs in the Administration panel of osCommerce. This information is then displayed accordingly, in several tabs on the product page, each tab containing its individual piece of information describing or somehow related to the product. The module can be downloaded from `http://addons.oscommerce.com/info/2610`.

When dealing with product attributes, the effect they can make on product price is very important. The customer should be given a clear explanation of how this or that attribute affects total product price. Attribute price in osCommerce is usually the price difference that it adds to the main product's price, e.g. if a product costs $20, one of its attribute values may add nothing to the product price, and another can add $3.

Some customers may find this a bit confusing, and it might be much easier for a customer to figure out what the actual product price would be if each attribute value was associated with the total product price the customer would pay, should that attribute value be chosen. There is the "Actual Attribute Price" contribution, available at `http://addons.oscommerce.com/info/1716` that changes the way the price is displayed on attribute values, so that each attribute displays the full product price associated with it. Of course, this particular solution is only suitable if only one of the product's attributes affects its price. If product price depends on multiple attributes, it may make sense to consider such a product as a complex configurable product, and deal with it accordingly. We will get back to this topic in later chapters of this book.

Images

Product images play a highly important role in almost any e-commerce business as being unable to touch and look at the product, the customers require at least product photographs to form an impression about the product and see if the product is something that they really need.

In a default osCommerce installation, it is possible to have only one image per each product. The image is uploaded in the Administration panel. Image size can be set differently for the Product Listing page and Product Information page.

Several problems may affect product images when they get resized by the web browser:

- The image may lose its proportions and instead of a nice photograph, the customer would see a distorted one.
- The image may become blurry.

- If each product has a really sharp and nice photograph, the Product Listing page, even though it contains smaller images of all products, will still be quite heavy because actually only the visual size of each image will be changed, not its real file size.

One of the best ways to fix these problems is to have several images for one and the same product. A product image may have up to three (or sometime even four!) sizes: small (for Product Listing pages, information boxes—like best selling products, new arrivals, etc.), medium (for the product information page), and large (for the "Enlarge" pop-up window).

There are several approaches, each suitable for online stores with different product ranges and also different numbers of products.

The first approach is to allow uploading of up to three (or even four if a very small image is used on certain product listing pages or in the information boxes) images per product in the Administration panel. This assumes each thumbnail image is created by the Administrator of the online store and then uploaded into the database. It makes sense to upload only high quality images, taken by a professional photographer, if available. Resized images may become blurry, so additional sharpness filters applied to the images before upload may improve their look.

A variation of that approach is to make the system generate thumbnails and medium-sized images automatically from the bigger size images uploaded in the Administration panel. Such an approach would allow the Administration of the online store to easily update product images through the product catalog, but at the same time may not result into a pure optimal resized image quality displayed to the customers.

An osCommerce contribution available at http://addons.oscommerce.com/info/1484 automatically creates thumbnails of the original product images and stores them in a special sub-folder of the "images" folder of osCommerce. Thumbnails are especially useful on Product Listing pages, making the pages load faster and also making smaller images look better and smoother (since web browsers produce a lower quality reduced size copies of bigger images compared to thumbnails generated by that contribution).

Yet another approach is to store small, medium, and large images in special folders on the web server and use product model as the image file name, then, depending on if the online store should display small, medium, or large images, take the file with the name equal to the corresponding product model from the corresponding folder on the web server. This method is especially suitable for online stores with plenty of products in the catalog, where it's easier to manage product images in bulk than one-by-one.

Quite often, one image per product may not be enough for customers to make a decision about the purchase. Either product details, special features, or methods of use (serving suggestions for food, for example) can be added as additional images to the product. At the same time, there's no need to add more images to the product if it doesn't require them—overloading Product Information pages with extra information is never good and may make it look confusing to customers.

Two quite popular solutions based on freely available contributions can be used. The first is the "Extra Images" contribution and allows for uploading of any number of additional images per product. It is available from `http://addons.oscommerce.com/info/1289`. It adds a menu item "Extra images" into the "Catalog" section of the osCommerce Administration panel. Adding more images is really easy—the Administrator just has to select a product from the drop-down list and then upload up to four additional images at a time, any number of times.

Then another one, "More Pics", can be downloaded from `http://addons.oscommerce.com/info/1611` and allows for up to six additional images to be uploaded per product. Images are uploaded directly on the Edit Product page in the Administration panel.

Keeping in mind the fact that the customer cannot handle the products and evaluate them before the purchase, virtual 3D product demonstration can be of a great value when selling products online. A link to the virtual product demonstration can be put on the Product Information page along with product images, so that the customer can not only see static photographs but also a 3D model of the product, play with it, and explore from all sides and angles to ensure the product is exactly what the customer is looking for.

The same goes for short video clips that may explain how to use certain features of the product.

Product Reviews

Product reviews given by real customers and explaining their real experience with the products bought online are very important for prospective customers who are going to buy products from the online store.

It should be made very easy for customers to leave a review, and the online store owner should attract more and more customers to leave their reviews on products purchased online. Therefore, a corresponding form can be placed in the bottom of the list of reviews on the Product Information page. If there's any special prize to be won by leaving a review on a product, this information should also be made available on the Product Information page. To avoid SPAM reviews, it would be useful to install a special contribution that protects the online store from wrong reviews, and various SPAM messages by allowing the Administrator of the online store to first approve a review before it gets published on the website pages.

Approved reviews (or at least some of them) can be displayed directly on the Product Information page. Customers may decide not to go to a special page just to read reviews from other customers, and, should reviews be left on a separate page as in standard osCommerce, customers may miss that important information. At least short extracts from product reviews should be shown on the Product Information page, and links can lead customers further to a separate reviews page if they wish to read more details.

Placing Orders

Once a customer has selected one or several products and made a decision to place an order, there's still a chance the customer will be confused or not confident enough to complete the order, and will just close the web browser during the osCommerce Checkout process or go to another online store. One of major tasks of any online store manager is to ensure the order placement (checkout) process is smooth, straightforward, and secure.

Security and Confidence

Customer accounts in osCommerce are protected by passwords. So only if the customer knows the user name (email address in osCommerce) and password, can the customer get into the account. Since customer account pages contain sensitive information about the customers themselves, and their previous orders, they (the pages) should be protected by SSL certificate to ensure the security of the connection between the web browser of the customer and the web server.

Once the customer has registered an account or logged in to proceed to the Checkout pages, this connection should also be secured by SSL certificate so that the customer's order can be placed securely and with no risk of having someone else accessing such data as customer personal details, addresses, order summary, and credit card information.

Even if the online store doesn't take payments online, customer accounts and orders should be still protected by SSL.

And here goes the first very important point, where the customer may either proceed further with the Checkout process (or creating a new account) or simply go away. Web browsers display the SSL padlock sign if the web page is secure. Customers are used to seeing the SSL padlock in their browser; they know they can enter their personal details with no or at least less risk on such sites. But the web browser may not display the SSL padlock or, like MS Internet Explorer 7 even advise the customer to leave the site immediately if the SSL certificate is not valid. Also, there may be extra warnings that can cause the same effect on the customer.

The online store manager should be aware of the list of possible reasons why the web browser would not display the SSL padlock or would generate a warning message:

- The domain name of the website doesn't match the domain name registered with SSL certificate – this may happen if, for example, if the website uses its own domain name for SSL protected links (like `https://www.domain.com`), but the web server where the online store is installed has a different SSL certificate installed (even `https://domain.com` would be considered a different domain), or it has a so called shared SSL certificate installed – like `https://ssl.webhosting.com`.

- The web server simply has no SSL certificate installed.

- The SSL certificate is out of date, or its issuer is not known to the web browser – it makes sense to use SSL certificates from the major well known SSL certificate issuers, like Verisign, Thawte, GeoTrust, GoDaddy, etc.

- There are non-secure elements present on the web page along with secure elements, so that the web browser cannot guarantee the whole page is secure – this may happen if the page contains an image or a JavaScript or a Flash object downloaded from any other website and instead of `https://` links, that object (or those objects) use `http://` links.

All these reasons can cause the web browser to either display a warning message, or not display the SSL padlock, or even recommend the customer leaving the website as it's not secure. Effectively, the customer may lose confidence in making an online purchase at that particular online store and surf to another website that sells similar products.

Registration and Checkout Process

In osCommerce, customers have to register or log in before they can actually pay for the selected goods and place an order. The registration process is usually not very complex and only requires entering the customer's personal details and addresses, but the online store owner should simplify that process as much as possible so that the customer has as few fields to fill in as possible. All fields that are not required should be removed or disabled in the Administration panel of the osCommerce website. For example, not all online stores require the customer's date of birth. This field appears in the default osCommerce registration form and not all online store managers remove it from there if they do not really need it. Also, some osCommerce stores only deal with domestic orders. In that case, the drop down of countries can be removed from the address forms and a text label with the default country name can be displayed instead. If the online store deals with international orders, it makes sense to split the country list in the countries drop down in a way so that the first ten or twenty are the ones the orders are most often delivered to, and then all other countries would be listed alphabetically. This latter improvement can be implemented in multiple ways. For example a special "sort order" field could be introduced for countries, and those countries with sort order greater than zero would appear in the very beginning of the country list if the corresponding database queries are amended.

Each extra click, each extra field to fill in may affect the customer's decision to buy and also the customer's confidence in data safety and in the online store itself. Fortunately, nowadays many customers use the Autofill features of their web browsers or browser add-ons that make the registration process much faster.

Once the customer is registered or logged in, the customer can select the shipping method among the list of available ones. If certain shipping methods allow for tracking the status and location of the delivery, it is sensible to tell the customer about that on the Checkout Shipping page. Of course, this assumes the shipping carrier will actually send the store manager a special tracking number that will then be transferred to the customer.

The Checkout Payment page is the one where the customer expects maximum security, and minimum distraction from the process, because here the customer often enters credit card details or other important data. This page should be secured by SSL certificate, and to make the customer confident that the Checkout process is secure, an SSL certificate seal(s) can be added to that page.

Almost any payment module for osCommerce that allows charging customers online has either its own logo and/or logos of the payment methods that could be used to pay money to the online store. If a payment module accepts credit cards, it makes perfect sense to display logotypes of those credit and debit cards that can be used to make the payment. Such card logos add credibility to the Checkout payment page. Only those card logos should be displayed that can be actually used to send the money, because the customers will be confused and become angry and inpatient if they are not able to pay using a card that is announced as acceptable by the online store.

In osCommerce, the customer is given a facility to confirm the order even after the payment details are entered on the Checkout Confirmation page. All order data appears there, along with the shipping and payment order details. It's needless to say that page should be also protected by SSL. If the online store has any certificates, seals, and logos of organizations the online store is a part of that certify professionalism and the identity of the business behind the online store, it would make sense to put those on that page.

Ideally, the customer should be given a facility to read the terms and conditions of service yet again, and confirm understanding of that document by, for example, ticking a special check box on the Checkout Confirmation page.

Simplifying osCommerce Checkout Procedure

It has been noted that many end customers find the standard osCommerce Checkout process too long and too complicated. If the customer is already registered with the online store, Checkout would include the Login page, Checkout shipping, Checkout payment, Checkout Confirmation, and Checkout Success page. Add Account registration and Successful Account Registration pages to this list if the customer is not registered yet! Also, some customers simply do not want to have an account with the website, but would rather prefer to place a one-time order, and would not mind going through the Checkout process next time just to avoid having an account created for them in the database.

There is a contribution called "Purchase Without Account" available for download from the osCommerce website at `http://addons.oscommerce.com/info/355`. This contribution allows for making a purchase without account registration; the customer fills in an address and other contact information directly in during the Checkout process. This contribution is supposed to convince those customers who would prefer not to leave their account information with an online store to make a purchase.

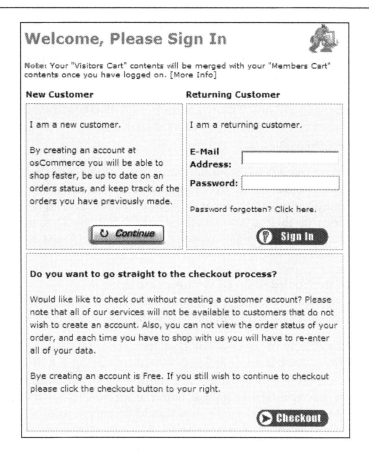

Interestingly enough, the customer is not asked to enter a password during the Checkout process, and a password is then sent to the customer in a welcoming email.

As seen in the previous screenshot customers are actually given a choice between creating new account, logging into an existing account, or proceeding with the Checkout process without creating an account. Even though it works for some customers, there may be an even better approach used by osCommerce store owners to simplify the whole account registration and checkout process. This will be discussed in more detail in Chapter 10 of this book.

There is one more way to simplify the osCommerce Checkout process, and this is using third-party Checkout processes instead of the standard osCommerce ones. We will consider Google Checkout and PayPal Express Checkout here. These two methods allow end customers to complete their orders by securely logging into their Google or PayPal accounts, using their Google or PayPal logins and passwords, respectively. Customer and order information is then exchanged between the online store and third-party server and the customer doesn't have to enter anything else to complete the order easily and quickly.

Besides store owners receiving certain bonuses from Google and PayPal for using their Checkout, this is extremely convenient for end customers who do not have to remember multiple accounts with different online stores — instead they only need to know how to log into their account with Google or PayPal. This, using the power of big brands behind third-party Checkout process, also builds the customer's confidence further.

The Google Checkout contribution can be downloaded from `http://addons.oscommerce.com/info/4556` and PayPal Express Checkout contribution can be downloaded from `http://addons.oscommerce.com/info/3647`.

At any point of the Checkout process, the customer should have access to support materials, if required. Enabling a Live Support feature during the Checkout process can not only give customers an extra level of confidence but also improve sales as confused customers would be able to chat with the support team straight away and their orders wont be lost. Online merchants should be very careful when installing live support solutions as some of these may have certain issues with being used on SSL protected (`https://`) pages. Usually, a fix would be available to allow running the same live support solution on secure and non-secure pages of the same online store. Online merchants may have to refer to the installation manuals or support forums of the chosen live support solution.

Order Processing

Accurate and fast order handling is a very important process for customers because the money for the order is often already paid in full and now the customer is waiting for the order to be fulfilled. The customers expect fast delivery, ability to track order status in general, and delivery status and location, in particular.

Processing orders fast, being responsive to customer's questions and comments, giving estimated delivery dates and keeping promises, high security measures when taking online orders, delivering ordered products in time and in a proper state, these are the key to making a customer a happy customer, a customer confident in the online store the products were purchased from, and eventually, a returning customer.

Orders can be processed in osCommerce or in ERP or a Business Management system the online merchant uses; it depends on the business model used by the online store. If all sale orders are first downloaded into ERP and then processed, it makes sense to speed up and improve this process by implementing automated import/export facilities for sale orders and customer accounts in osCommerce. There are freely available contributions that allow for export of osCommerce orders into Intuit QuickBooks software, and commercial software solutions (data links, connectors) that allow for complete integration between osCommerce and ERP/accounting/business management software. Transferring order data fast and without errors into ERP is essential, especially when an online store receives many orders per day.

Charging Practices in osCommerce

The easiest way is to always charge the customer the full amount of the order as soon as such an order is placed online. Actually, the charge is made during the order placement process, so that orders where the customer didn't pay or was not able to pay do not make their way into the osCommerce database.

Charging the customer immediately and the full amount works perfect when the online store sells products from stock. But what if the ordered products are not in stock, or not enough are in stock, and would have to be ordered from the supplier/ manufacturer to fulfill the order? In that case, good business practice would require the online store owner to charge the customer some deposit and charge the rest on when all products arrive in stock and the order is ready to be delivered to the customer. Customers may become upset if they are charged for products that are not in stock yet, for products that have not been yet allocated to their order. More than that, in some countries it would be illegal and the online store owner would have to wait until all back orders are fulfilled before charging the customer the full order amount.

Notifications, Order and Dispatch Statuses

Once an order is placed, the customer would expect to receive a notification from the website acknowledging the fact of order placement and advising of the next steps.

osCommerce sends order notification emails automatically to customers. The online store owner just needs to ensure that the format of the notification emails is fine, and that the email contains all the information about further steps that will be performed with the order to have it fulfilled.

It makes sense to have different emails sent to the customers when the order reaches different statuses. Sometimes, an order passes through more statuses than the notifications the customer gets as the order goes through certain internal order fulfillment processes. It's not only order status change that is of interest to the customer, but rather if all ordered products will be delivered and when exactly the goods will arrive.

That is why depending on order status, the notification email may contain the following information (or a combination of these depending on the business model):

- Whether the order has been received and added to the database—this is the very first notification the customer will receive via email from the online store.

- Whether the payment has been processed successfully—this notification can be combined with the previous one, or come on its own depending on how payment processing is implemented in the online store; also this notification actually confirms that the online store will fulfill the order.

- Whether the products were allocated to the order, or if some of them were put on back order—this notification usually comes later and confirms if there were enough products in stock to allocate them to the order, or if some products were put on back order; in the latter case, an estimation of the date of when the products are expected back in stock would be appreciated by customers.

- Whether the delivery team packed goods for delivery—this confirms whether all products have been allocated and received for the order, and now the order is waiting to be dispatched; this notification may contain an estimate of when the products will be delivered to the customer.

- Whether the order has been dispatched—this actually confirms the products are on their way, and usually gives the customer tracking number(s) to check delivery status and location with the shipping carrier.

Detailed information about the order, its status, and tracking numbers give customers a facility to know exactly what's happening with their order. Unawareness should not be allowed if the online store wishes to have happy customers and convert more new customers into returning customers.

Finally, all email notifications sent from the online store should contain full contact details of the online store and the business name behind it, to keep customers confident in that they are dealing with a real business.

Printable Documents

There are three types of printable documents in osCommerce:

- Invoice
- Packing slip
- Printed order

Invoice and packing slip are available from the Admin part only. Customers can print order details from the "My account" section, and also right after placing an order from the Checkout Success page if a corresponding contribution is installed. The contribution is called Print Order Receipt and can be downloaded from http://addons.oscommerce.com/info/2379.

A problem with the standard printable documents is that they may not contain enough information and also their layout may seem unprofessional to the customers.

Fortunately, there are quite a number of contributions that can improve this situation:

- PDF Customer Invoice — this contribution converts the standard HTML invoice or Packing slip to a PDF document: http://addons.oscommerce.com/info/5321.

- Professional Invoice and Packing slip contribution — this contribution adds an Invoice number (linked to Order Number), Invoice Date (linked to Order Date), and a more professional layout for Invoice and Packing Slip: http://addons.oscommerce.com/info/2604.

- Fancier Invoice & Packing slip — this contribution will replace your current invoice and packing slip with a much better, cleaner, and fancier invoice and packing slip (with boxes and shadows around certain sections and order numbers): http://addons.oscommerce.com/info/2861.

- Show Shipping Method on Invoice — this contribution allows displaying the shipping method for the order on the invoice (below the address box): http://addons.oscommerce.com/info/4084.

Summary

This chapter was dedicated to understanding why it's important to build customer confidence and how to do it. We have reviewed plenty of ways to improve the online store and, to some degree, a business model to make customers more confident about placing orders online with a particular online store.

Because the nature of online sales differs from the nature of regular offline sales, extra credibility, reliability, secureness of the online store, once implemented and promoted correctly, can improve the turnover of an online store a lot. "Visitor to customer" conversion rate can be improved, as well as "customer to returning customer" conversion rate. Also, this will eventually result in happier customers, i.e. into less workload put on the support department of an online store.

In the coming chapters, we shall concentrate on how to improve particular parts of the online store to improve online sales. Our next chapter will be solely dedicated to how to use website design to convert more visitors into customers.

6
Design to Sell

It's natural that the design of an e-commerce website, its visual look, feel, and appearance, play a major role in the sale process. Product specification and price play an even more important role, but it's the design that can make the whole online sales process smooth and easy, or so very complicated that the customer may even leave the site.

Effective design of an online store is a sales and marketing instrument and should be used accordingly, to improve the customer's experience with the online shop in general and increase online sales in particular. Visual impressions can affect the customer's decisions, and for an e-commerce website, they should help achieve the main goal—to sell goods online.

This chapter is dedicated to various aspects of osCommerce design. What design is, how to use design to improve online sales, how to optimize design for different types of customers—all this has been put together here.

It should be noted that not all advice and ideas mentioned in this chapter are available as downloadable contributions. Quite a number of those pieces of advice and ideas may require help of a qualified osCommerce consultant or web designer. Once the changes are carefully selected and properly implemented, they may pay off very soon!

But first, let's just briefly touch base about what design is in terms of osCommerce.

osCommerce site's design should not be mistaken for its functionality. Design is what the customers can see and how its pages look when customers browse the website, from the main or landing page of the online store to the checkout success page. All still graphics and animation elements of the website pages, layout of individual elements on each page of the website, fonts and colors of texts on those pages, all this is a part of osCommerce design. We will not consider design of the back end of an osCommerce website in this chapter, but osCommerce front-end design.

Main Principles of E-Commerce Design

When choosing a design for an osCommerce online store (or for any online store based on an e-commerce technology) several main principles should be taken into account. Even if the online stores already has a certain design integrated, it can be reviewed to make sure the current design is the best for helping customers with online ordering.

Main Principle: Design for Sales

Before we proceed any further, let's talk about the main principle of e-commerce design in general and osCommerce design in particular.

The design of an osCommerce online store should help the sales. It should not be applied just to demonstrate the capabilities of the web designer who created it, or how much of an artistic taste the online merchant has. It's quite often actually the case that online store owners make decisions about whether to apply this or that design to their online stores based solely or mostly on their own feelings about the design, using their own style, color, and other preferences. Or they make decisions following advice given by friends, partners, or colleagues.

While this can sometimes work, the best results can rarely be achieved that way, even if the online store looks brilliant with the chosen design integrated. There are plenty of online stores that look brilliant but do not sell that brilliantly at all.

The best way to create a design that helps sales is to look at it from the customer's point of view only, and never from any other side! Even if the online merchant doesn't personally like the look and feel of the site, the main point should always be about whether the customers will like it or not, and whether it will help online sales or not.

Decisions made about online stores should not be based on intuition or the personal preferences of decision makers. Those decisions should be based on studies and measures of target customer groups. This not only relates to design issues, but to all other aspects of e-commerce development too.

We will restate it again: No one, especially anyone who influences the decision making process on how the online store should look, should ever put individual design preferences above customers' preferences, and above whether that particular design would help online sales or not.

Design Accompanies Products

When a customer first comes to an online store, it should be quite obvious what sort of products the online store sells. The design of an online store should be related to the products it sells, or at least not confront the products.

When buying products, the customers have certain expectations of how their needs should be addressed with the products that they buy. Online store designs should to some degree "prepare" the customer, remind the customer either about the products that are being sold online, or something related to how those products can be used to satisfy customer's needs.

Alternatively, the design of an online store can be made very neutral to avoid drawing the customer's attention away from products and avoid irritating customer's sight.

Page Load Speed Optimized Design

Nowadays more and more customers would have fast Internet connection when they browse through pages of an online store. This is especially true if customers buy online from their workplaces. But some customers (and depending on the marketing strategy and target audience it can be quite a number) still have slower Internet connections at home or where they browse websites from.

The design of an online store should never make the browsing experience worse; it should always improve it, make it more pleasant to customers.

Therefore, the design of an online store should not seriously affect the page load speed of the website. If it does, the site either needs to be redesigned completely, or the existing design needs to be optimized to improve page load speed. Customers are used to an almost instantaneous page loading experience, and should the website take longer to load up its pages, the customers will more likely be disappointed, "tired" of waiting (even if it takes only several extra seconds to load a page), and the chance of them leaving the online store without making a purchase increases.

Multiple Platforms and Browser Compatibility

Depending on who the targeted audience are, the list of computer platforms and web browsers that should be supported by an online store may vary. By "supported", here we mean "looking good and in accordance to the original design". One and the same website may look different, and sometimes worse, on certain computer platforms than on others, and in certain web browsers than in others.

Most multi-platform and cross-browser design compatibility issues are related to improper page structure, or to the specifications of the corresponding computer platforms and web browsers.

A reasonable solution here doesn't require an online store to be designed in a way that makes it compatible with absolutely all computer platforms and web browsers. Instead, it requires the online store to be compatible with all computer platforms and web browsers that its targeted customers use.

Even if only 5% of the targeted customers are reported to be using a certain web browser, not having the online store compatible with it can cause almost a 5% loss in revenue—something not every online merchant can afford or would like to see.

Unity of Design throughout the Online Store

To ease browsing and purchase experience for users and customers, the website's design should not draw away their attention from products, special offers, and of course the ordering facilities. Also, to maintain and promote the brand of an online store its logo, identifiable colors, and styles of main design elements (such as information boxes, buttons, backgrounds, etc.) should be present on as many pages of the website as possible.

Therefore, it's not recommended to change design style, colors, even font sizes and types between the pages of an online store without a good reason.

For an online store with a large product range, a good approach would be to identify certain parts of the product range (like separate categories or brands) as individual mini-stores, where each mini-store would have its own color scheme or design style. Even in such a case, changing color scheme would be the best way to achieve marketing goals, leaving the design style, layout, and of course the logo of the online store intact.

Design elements should not only be present on the web pages; the logo and certain design elements should also be also put on printed documents such as invoices, packing slips, and order confirmations to further promote the brand of the online store and also help customers identify printed documents with the online orders they placed.

osCommerce has all the facilities for maintaining design unity through the whole online store, even though some online merchants neglect those opportunities and eventually lose out on converting more visitors into customers and customers into returning customers.

Design that Helps Sales

Web designs can't "sell" products on their own, it's the product itself and its price that make the difference and affect the customer's decision to buy it. But the design of an online store can very much help to sell products (just as it can confuse the customers and make some of them go away from the online store).

"osCommerce" Design—Pros and Cons

osCommerce comes with a certain default design. This includes the logo, CSS style sheets, buttons, information box designs, and a number of "standard" osCommerce images and icons that are displayed on different pages of the website (such as images on the User Account page, or the header of the website, or the Quick Search icon).

It comes with the header, left, middle, and right columns, and the footer. All or almost all bits of information are displayed in the so called "information boxes" that share the same or a very similar style of the title, border, and content.

Actually, osCommerce comes with a complete design and is ready to be installed and start selling products online right away. That's certainly a benefit of this e-commerce solution.

At the same time, the default osCommerce design, being very generic and basic, may not suit each and every online store owner, and may not help selling certain product ranges. Also, it has not been changed for several years now, and doesn't look as contemporary as it was in the past. Also, there are some design elements (like standard osCommerce icons for example) that do not help customers very much in understanding what this or that page is about, thus confusing the customers instead. Actually, and many web design and development companies would testify, online merchants often ask to remove those standard osCommerce icons and design elements from the very first.

The osCommerce standard design doesn't permit easy manipulation of information boxes or other elements; webmasters or web developers should be involved in order to make changes in the design or layout of the website.

Actually, if a website consists only of an online store, and products are either very unique or the prices are very competitive, one can afford leaving the standard osCommerce design intact — as the sales will be coming through the website anyway.

Otherwise, it may be a good idea to consider changing the design of an osCommerce online store to something that would either match the design of the main website, or accompany the product range, or make the browsing and purchase experience smoother for customers — or just implement the three tasks all together.

General Recommendations for osCommerce Design

Several recommendations could be given for the design of an osCommerce website.

But of course, detailed suggestions can only be made when the product range is established and the target audience is known.

A logotype should be present on all pages of the online store, and also on all printed and/or downloadable documents as was suggested earlier. Usually, the logo is placed at the header of the website, in the top left corner.

A banner promoting featured products or special offers, or links to pages with information about the store can be added to the header of the website. Sometimes, links to the Shopping Cart and Checkout pages are also added to the header of an online store, even though the Shopping Cart is usually present as an information box in one of the columns.

Categories (or rather top categories or the most important categories if there are many) can be also added into the header of online store, usually as a horizontal menu. Sometimes, if there are too many sub-categories they can be added as pop-up menus (similar to how menus look and feel in MS Windows).

Finally, the header may contain the so called "breadcrumbs"—clickable parent-to-child category names that indicate where in the tree of categories the user is currently located, and allow for easier navigation between levels of the category tree (and other pages of the online store as well). Breadcrumbs also play an important role in SEO.

The left column of an osCommerce online store usually contains navigational elements.

It is suggested to put the Quick Search box in there and the tree of categories (also in a box) right after it.

Since there might be multiple levels in the category tree, it would make sense to display only top categories and then allow customers clicking those top categories to see their content (sub-categories and products), and sometimes, sub-categories can be displayed right under their parent categories in the tree in order to make navigation easier for users. It all depends on how deep the category tree is, and how many sub-categories exist, on the average, per level.

Navigation can be performed in many more different ways than by categories only. For example navigation by the manufacturer (or brand, or special occasion, depending on the online store and its product range) can make a significant difference and can make navigation much easier for customers.

So the left column (in a three-column layout, as in osCommerce left and right columns can be disabled) usually contains quite some information in it, and is quite a long one. It would probably make sense to add the Information Box (with links to various information pages) there, under all other boxes and design elements.

The right column can start with the Shopping Cart box that would contain brief information about the content of the Shopping Cart, plus links to the Checkout pages. Along with the Shopping Cart box, it would make sense to add various security seals and certificates to the right column, and icons of the payment methods that could be used to pay for the orders placed in the online store. The right column can be used to display all sorts of additional information, like a Special Offers box, Featured Items, Best-sellers, also Manufacturer information (name, associated image, and links), and again can also contain links to additional information pages.

The footer of an online store can be used to display contact and copyright information, and also contain links to the information pages.

Banners (leading either of the pages of the same online store, or to external pages) can be added to the header, to the side columns, footer, or of course to the middle area of the site. The middle area (which is made wider than either of the side columns in almost all cases) contains all the most important information—products, textual and graphics content, certain navigation controls, and various forms (registration, checkout, newsletter sign up, etc.).

It's not recommended to change the general page layout from page to page when the user navigates through the online store. It may be confusing if one of the side columns disappears where the user navigates to certain pages of the online store, or if side columns change their width, or if the header changes its height or disappears.

In fact, it makes sense to change the layout of the online store while user navigates through its pages only in two cases.

First, if the user proceeds to the Shopping cart page, Customer Registration page, or Checkout Pages—in that case it may make sense to remove certain design elements that could distract the user's attention, or cause confusion.

Secondly, if there is so much important information available on certain products or categories of the online store that removing some design elements (such as side columns for example) can make it much easier for users to read that information completely, without unnecessary scrolling.

Font styles should not change from page to page either, to make a good impression on users. Ideally, font style would not be changed within a single page, having all design elements (textual and graphical) sharing the same font style.

Font size should be used rationally to highlight only the required bits of information, and also make it easy for customers to read all the textual information from the screens.

It is quite often the case that webmasters "forget" about the needs of their target audience and instead of making it easy and pleasant to read from the screens, they use font styles and sizes that look fancy but certainly do not improve the reading experience.

Font styles and colors of design elements should not distract user's attention from Product Information or from the purchase process. Instead, colors should help the user to see the most important information on the pages first, and also make it easy to locate control elements on pages of the online store (for the latter, it's especially recommended to highlight those control elements that lead customers to the purchase completion leaving other control elements less highlighted).

Product Information Presentation

Product Information should be presented in a way that makes it very easy for customers to see the main features of the product and how that product could actually help the customers to address their needs.

In osCommerce, Product Information appears in:

- Information boxes in side columns and in the middle area (specials, featured products, etc.)
- Product Listing pages (category Product Listing and search results)
- Product Information pages
- The Shopping Cart page
- The Checkout confirmation page

Where there's not much space dedicated to an individual product, only a little of the available Product Information can be displayed. Therefore, it's especially important to present that information to the customers in a way that will make the customers interested in the product, and possibly further interested in purchasing it.

Information boxes in the side columns can usually only display the product name and one image, and sometimes its price. The product name should ideally not take more than one line of text, otherwise it won't look nice in the limited space of a side column. So product names should be made reasonably long to let the customer know more about the product, but at the same time not too long to avoid breaking the design elements such as information boxes in the side columns. The product image that is displayed along with the product name should be made sharp and clean. It will most probably be a thumbnail of a bigger product image, and it's especially important to make it very crisp; if it doesn't look nice the customers may not want to click the product link to get more information about the product or proceed with the purchase. The price of the product is usually displayed along with its name. It is also possible to add certain special icons, like "new", or "hot", or "special" to indicate popularity of the product, or the fact that the product is on a special offer, etc.

Boxes displayed in the middle area of the website that contain one or several products will usually contain the same amount of information, plus they may contain also a short description and information about stock levels (if it's important for a particular website).

Product listings can be designed in at least two standard ways, and of course any number of very bespoke ways too.

Either list or grid layout can be used, depending on how many products are supposed to fit into one page of Product Listing. It's recommended not to make Product Listing pages too long, as it may be difficult for customers to scroll down to the end of the page if it takes more than one or two mouse scroll wheel turns. Grid-style layout may look similar to the following screenshot:

and list-style layout similar to the next screenshot:

Depending on the layout and the products sold online, the Product Listing may contain product name, model number, short or long description, thumbnail (again, the clearer and the crispier, the better), stock levels, prices, and of course buttons like "More info" or "Add to cart" or "Buy now" that would either send customers to the Product Information page or directly to the Shopping Cart page. Sometimes online stores allow the customers to choose the layout of the Product Listing page according to their preferences, by providing a switch between the two layouts for the Product Listing pages. Using dynamic elements of JavaScript or using AJAX technology it's possible to let the customers see the full product description when the customer hovers the mouse cursor over one of the products, and display the short description when the mouse cursor leaves the product area.

Product listing is where the customers often make up their mind on buying or not buying certain products. It's worthy to note that should the Product Listing contain only one product (say there's only one product found when doing a Quick or Advanced search, or if the category only contains one product), instead of the Product Listing page it's better to show the Product Information page to the customer to avoid one extra click.

The product Information page is obviously the most important page in the product browsing and purchasing processes. Its job is to give the customer complete information about the product, how can it be used (i.e. how exactly will it make a customer happier by addressing their needs), what its main features are, how it looks and feels, what its price and how can it be bought, and what other customers have to say about that product. Also, the very same page can give customers an idea about similar products or products somehow related to the one being browsed.

Usually, the product name is put onto the top part of the Product Information page, along with the product model number, stock level, price, and "Buy now" button. If the product cannot be bought, being out of stock, information about when the product is likely to be back in stock would be highly appreciated by some customers. The product short description can be also put into the header of the page.

The product image (medium or large rather than small) can be put along with all the information into the header, or right under that data block. Again, it should be very crisp to give the customer an opportunity to see as many of the product features from the picture as possible, without the need to enlarge it. Additional product images, featuring certain details of the product or explaining how the product is built or how it can be used are also displayed on the Product Information page, usually just under the main image. The detailed description (long description) is often displayed further below. It should not be made too long and should usually contain detailed information about products and their features, and sometimes will be joined by product technical specification for products of corresponding nature, where certain technical parameters make the difference. At the bottom of the page, there may be one more block containing product code, price options, and control buttons like "Add to Cart" or "Buy now". This will help those customers who scrolled down to the very bottom of the page in order to read the description in every detail to buy the product without the need to scroll back all the way to the top of the page. Below that block there could be a list of compatible or related products, accessories, etc, for cross-selling. The following screenshots demonstrate different variants of the Product Information page design for osCommerce.

This Product Information page has been modified a bit with respect to the osCommerce standard layout:

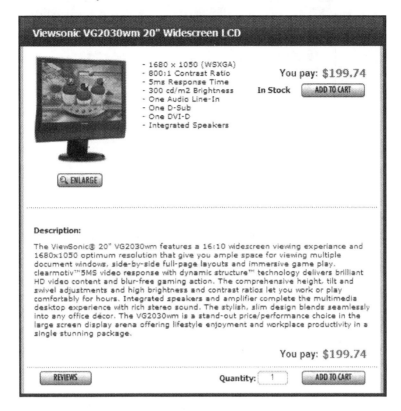

One can see a short description added to the top of the page, stock indicator, price and the "Add to Cart" button also added into the top part of the page. Also, the "Add to Cart" button appears in the bottom of the page so that after reading the description the customer doesn't have to scroll up to the very top of the page if the customer is ready to place an order online.

The layout of the following Product Information page has been left almost intact:

The next screenshot of the Product Information page contains an enlarged image of the product, stock information, information about available shipping methods, price information (including the recommended retail price), marketing product description, and product specification:

Standard osCommerce doesn't display too much information about products on the Shopping Cart page. It only displays product name, price, and additional attributes (if selected). Instead, it may be an excellent idea to display not only a thumbnail of the product image but also the short description in the Shopping Cart product list too, to remind the customers what they actually pay for.

Prices and Purchase Facilities

Almost every occurrence of a product on the website, either in the Product Listing or Product Information page, and also in the information boxes (like special, featured, new, etc.) displayed in the middle area of the site, or in one of the side columns, should be accompanied by the product's price. There can be several different prices associated with one single product: recommended retail price (RRP), current price, special price, tax inclusive or exclusive price, quantity discount price, etc. Customers should be always given a clear way to see the price they are paying for each product.

For example, an RRP price, if present (this is not a part of the standard osCommerce installation but can be easily added as a contribution—see `http://addons.oscommerce.com/info/3574`) should be struck out and its color should be paler than the color of the current product price. In the same manner, current price should be struck out if there is a special price—special prices can be defined in the osCommerce Administration panel. It may be useful to demonstrate to the customer how much the discount is (in percent) comparing RRP and current price, or current and special prices—again the amount of the calculated percent should usually be made less noticeable than the actual price the customer is to pay for product.

The final price customers are paying for product should be highlighted compared to all other price information related to the product.

Sometimes, online stores prefer to display tax inclusive and/or exclusive prices. In that case, an indication of if the prices are inclusive of tax or exclusive of tax should be displayed on every page where the product price is displayed. It's possible to display a corresponding message (or tax inclusive or exclusive figures) along with each product's price, but it may be better from the design stand point to only display one message per page. That message would explain if tax is included in or excluded from the price, and what the rate of tax is. Such a message can be shown in the footer of the website.

Design controls that lead to the purchase should be highlighted, to make it very easy for every customer to find them on the pages, whatever page the customer is browsing at the moment. An example is the **Add to Bag** button on that Product Information page that is made red and is highlighted comparing to the grayed **Continue** control button.

It should be noted that putting two blocks of buttons that lead the customer to the purchase on the Product Information page only makes sense when product description or additional images and similar design elements make the page really long (say more than 1.5-2 screens). Also, as a rule of thumb, purchase controls should never be too small, too thin, too hidden among other design elements. Therefore, it's better not to use text links for "Add to Cart" or "Buy Now" but to use clear noticeable images of buttons that the customer can press with the mouse cursor.

Design Matches Products

As was said earlier, design of an online store would ideally accompany its product range in various ways. Either the style or colors would remind customers about the products offered online, or would remind customers about something associated with the products, or what that can be achieved by using such products.

For example, an online store that sells security and protection systems for homes may benefit from choosing "police" style and color design (i.e. mostly gray, blue, black and white color scheme, certain font types, additional design elements that would make a corresponding impression of the security and order the customers can expect after buying and installing the offered products). An online store that sells picnic baskets (including food, crockery and cutlery) would benefit from choosing a design that reminds customers about picnics and spending time out (i.e. nature-like colors, maybe photographs of trees, fields, or a river bank in the header of the online store, of course with a widely opened picnic basket, and maybe some happy family photographs too).

Choosing Style

To choose a design style, one should consider how it will match with the products, or rather how the prospective customers of an online store will associate it with the products being offered online.

There can be several approaches to choosing the design style of an online store:

- Neutral—a good sample is the osCommerce standard design, which is not associated with any specific product range, but just accompanies products. A design may not be associated with products at all—in that case it probably makes sense to make it of neutral colors and style to not draw customers attention away from the product catalog

- Associated with products directly—a website that sells, for example, DVDs online can first of all use licensed photographs of actors and screens from the movies in its header and banners, but it can also use all that "movie" style in order to make an appropriate impression on its customers. For example, its boxes can have perforated film edges instead of regular osCommerce information box borders, its control buttons may have icons of a movie projector, film roll, white screen, etc.

- Associated with products indirectly — as described in the example with the picnic baskets. Also, as an example, a website that sells American souvenirs will be most probably be designed in US patriotic style, with the obvious choice of red, white, and blue colors, with American flags used in multiple design elements, so that the customers would associate products they can buy online with the country, its history, and all what's related to the very "brand" of USA.

Layout of Product Listing and Information Pages

The design of product listing and Product Information pages may depend on the products being offered online.

Of course, the obvious requirement is to make all pages look and feel so that it's very easy to locate information about the products, and manipulate controls that would lead customers to the purchase pages.

But, depending on the product type, the Product Information page may contain only a few lines of text, or quite a long description. Just compare an online store that sells MP3 players with another online store that sells D.I.Y. tools — it's obvious in the former case there will be much more marketing and technical information put on the Product Information pages than in the latter one.

A website that sells devices for machinery will most probably have a number of key product attributes listed on the Product Information pages, besides general description. The same goes for a website that sells home appliances. In contrast, an online store that sells luxury food products would rarely have anything on its Product Information pages except general or marketing description and a nice looking main picture of the product (maybe "serving suggestion" pictures too).

Product listing page design may vary depending on the type of products being sold. An online store that offers watches and related products to the customers will show crisp and relatively big product image, highlight its brand, and list key features in the Product Listing to gain maximum customer interest in the listed products. That website would benefit from displaying products in a grid on the listing page. For a selected category, it will list all products, may be even without splitting them into sub-categories. Of course, the price of the product should be displayed too, but instead of the "Buy Now" button it would make more sense to display the "More Information" button along with each product, as only very few customers would be ready to buy a watch without reading detailed information about the product, its features, warranty conditions, etc.

At the same time, an online store that sells coffee and related products may not even display a picture of each product it has on the Product Listing page—one picture per category of products will be quite enough, and then each sort of coffee may be just given a name and price on the Product Listing page along with the weight, obviously providing more detailed product data on the Product Information page. A list of products split by sub-categories with each sub-category having its picture would be a good choice for such websites. Also, because many customers would be already familiar with the products sold online, it would make sense to add the "Add to Cart" button to the Product Listing page, and quantity boxes, so that customers could select several sorts of coffee from the same Product Listing page and add them all to the Shopping Cart at once, without the need to spend time on going to each product's information page and adding products to the cart one by one.

Design Matches Target Audience

Naturally, before starting an online business, one should carefully study the market, define the targeted audience, and study it, so that products will be interesting to the prospective customers, prices will look reasonable to the targeted audience, and advertising campaigns will reach the desired target group of prospective customers.

Therefore, design of an online store should also "match" the supposed target audience. It should look attractive to prospective customers in any way. It should correspond with the lifestyle of prospective customers, and match their expectations.

Of course, it conflicts a little bit with the concept of design matching the product range, but if we look closely into this matter, we will see that the products themselves will always "match" the target audience—because otherwise the online store would be targeting the wrong audience. So there's no problem in the online store's design matching the product range and target audience at the same time.

If an online store is dedicated to, for example, products for families, its design will most probably have all soft and round design elements, soft and clean font style, include some photos of happy families, etc. Even if that online store sells video games, its design will stay the same to make it attractive to those parents who would buy those video games for their kids.

An online store that sells toddler-oriented products (merchandise, apparel, shoes, toys, games, even confectionery) will most probably be designed in a fun style, with lots of bright design elements, funny virtual page-mates, and of course photos of happy children, so that both kids and their parents would be pleased to browse through the pages of the website—as most likely both the kids and parents will be involved into the process of choosing products.

Yet another example would be an online store dedicated to selling its products to those who take sports seriously. The design of such a website will be more active, bright sometimes it can be even a bit aggressive. It can be made reminding of the spirit of exercise, strength, competition. And if it offers a broad range of products, some of them may not be 100% related to sports—like casual cloths, but nevertheless the style of the whole website will be delivering the corresponding "message" to its target customers.

One more important detail about choosing design of an online store is the default font size. Quite often, online store owners or web designers forget about the importance of all the contents being easy for customers to read for the sake of nice looking pages.

Yet without the ability to read the information displayed on the page, the customer will very likely not complete the purchase process and leave the online store. There are a lot of online businesses with their target audience including middle age and senior people. Therefore, bigger font size should be used by default to guarantee that the prospective customers will not experience any difficulties reading any text on the website.

Of course, the design of the website should be made in a way that allows customers to change font sizes using the facilities of their web browsers, so that the website still looks well with any default font size. Also, in some countries and regions there are certain legal regulations that determine how the websites should be designed to allow for their usage by customers with sight problems.

Design Compatibility

Design of an online store determines its look and feel. Of course, design is a result of a special process that includes lots of creativity, planning, and implementation work. Design is specially created to make the online store look attractive to its customers, to help selling products online.

But what if under certain circumstances, design of an online store changes such that the look and feel of the website are no longer the same as were supposed to be, or, even worse, if it changes so badly that customers can't buy products online from the website anymore, even if they do not care how the website looks and feels?

Web Browser Compatibility

There are multiple web browsers nowadays that many customers use to browse through the Internet. Web browsers also run under different operating systems like MS Windows, Apple Macintosh, Linux, etc. The most popular web browsers nowadays for Microsoft Windows are Internet Explorer, Mozilla Firefox, Opera, and Netscape. For the Apple Macintosh platform those would be Safari, Internet Explorer for Macintosh, and so on. For Linux-like systems the most popular browsers would be Mozilla Firefox and Netscape.

Statistics available for study differ depending on the type of service used to collect them, on geographical location of the target audience of the website or web service, and on many other factors. In fact, they can be different for any other online store as the target audience may have its own preferences for using certain web browsers or operating systems.

Statistics may sometimes be misleading if they are not applicable to the same target audience as the online store.

The following screenshot shows web browser usage statistics of `www.w3schools.com`—a website used mostly by webmasters and e-commerce developers, therefore they cannot be fully applicable and should not be used to make qualified decisions about support of this or that browser version by an online store:

Browser Statistics Month by Month

2007	IE7	IE6	IE5	Fx	Moz	S	O
April	19.2%	37.3%	1.7%	32.9%	1.3%	1.7%	1.7%
March	18.0%	38.7%	2.0%	31.8%	1.3%	1.7%	1.6%
February	16.4%	39.8%	2.5%	31.2%	1.4%	1.7%	1.5%
January	13.3%	42.3%	3.0%	31.0%	1.5%	1.7%	1.5%

2006	IE7	IE6	IE5	Fx	Moz	N7/8	O
December	10.7%	45.3%	3.4%	30.3%	2.6%	0.2%	1.5%
November	7.1%	49.9%	3.6%	29.9%	2.5%	0.2%	1.5%
October	3.1%	54.5%	3.8%	28.8%	2.4%	0.3%	1.4%
September	2.5%	55.6%	4.0%	27.3%	2.3%	0.4%	1.6%
August	2.0%	56.2%	4.1%	27.1%	2.3%	0.3%	1.6%
July	1.9%	56.3%	4.2%	25.5%	2.3%	0.4%	1.4%
June	1.6%	58.2%	4.3%	24.9%	2.2%	0.3%	1.4%
May	1.1%	57.4%	4.5%	25.7%	2.3%	0.3%	1.5%
April	0.7%	58.0%	5.0%	25.2%	2.5%	0.4%	1.5%
March	0.6%	58.8%	5.3%	24.5%	2.4%	0.5%	1.5%
February	0.5%	59.5%	5.7%	25.1%	2.9%	0.4%	1.5%
January	0.2%	60.3%	5.5%	25.0%	3.1%	0.5%	1.6%

Since web browsers have been developed by different companies, they sometimes "understand" the same web pages differently. Even different versions of the same web browsers can display one and the same web page in a different way. The difference in most of the cases is only about something very minor, like certain design elements moved by one to two pixels on the page, or a block of text information aligned differently. But sometimes those differences can be quite noticeable, as the page will look scrambled; for example one of osCommerce side columns may disappear, or some design elements will change their position, or disappear, or backgrounds will disappear in the information boxes making it impossible to read the text, etc.

It's not safe to suppose that "most" of the customers will use a certain type of a web browser and only have that web browser in mind when creating and testing the design for web browser compatibility.

The mathematics is very simple here. Say most of the customers of an online store use a web browser of a certain type. The figures can be retrieved from web server logs/statistics and would be quite accurate if the online store receives many visitors daily. It should be also noticed that those figures tend to change with time, as the number of customers in the Internet who use this or that web browser changes too, or new customer groups start visiting the online store. If the online store has no statistics of visits yet, one should study general statistics of what browsers are used by the prospective target audience.

With or without those statistics, it's always safe to design an online store to look in the same way independent of the web browser (either type or version of the same type) used by its customers.

We can see that with an imaginary example. Let it be that 92% of the website visitors use Internet Explorer, and 6.5% use Safari, and 1.5% use some other web browsers. A website is designed to look nice in Internet Explorer and it does work very well for those 92% of visitors converting them into customers with this or that efficiency. But if the website has not been designed to look absolutely the same in Safari, and if it has certain design issues in Safari, those who use Safari browser may think the site is broken or just not feel confident enough to buy products from that online store.

Effectively, according to the imaginary figures we have taken as an example, this will result in losing (well, actually not making, but not making a sale because of web design issues is almost the same as losing it!) up to 6.5% of all sales, or even worse, up to 8%!

If the imaginary online store has, for the sake of simplicity, a one million annual turnover, it would have given the store owners from $65,000 to $80,000 extra turnover had it been designed to be compatible with multiple web browsers.

How to Ensure Web Browser Compatibility

As said earlier, the easiest and most straightforward way seems to be to always design online stores to be compatible with all major web browsers that can be used by customers who belong to the targeted audience. That would be the best assurance and would help to avoid any issues in the future and ensure that the online store continues to receive revenue from selling its products to customers who use different web browsers.

The first step to take is to test the online store (actually, its main page, Product Listing, Product Information, Shopping Cart, checkout pages, user account pages, and general information pages) against W3C HTML standards using the W3C HTML validator. Chapter 3 of this book contains suggestions and advises on how to do it. Validation is important because all or almost all web browsers supposedly support W3C HTML format, and should the page be considered valid in terms of W3C HTML format, it will more likely be displayed in the same or very similar way by all major web browsers.

However, the best way to ensure that the online store actually looks and feels correct under different web browsers would be to test it under different web browsers. A web designer who intends to test the compatibility of an online store will more likely require two or even more different computers in order to test how the website looks and performs under different browsers under different platforms (PC, Apple Macintosh, Linux, etc).

Ideally, an online store should not go live without such tests being successfully completed. More than that, since the design of an online store changes from time to time, each such change should be checked for compatibility with multiple web browsers as well, to ensure the whole website is always compatible with multiple web browsers.

Screen Resolution Compatibility

Another issue with compatibility that online store owners should take into consideration is screen resolution. Customers may have screens of many different resolutions and even though nowadays most of the prospective customers would have better monitors and higher screen resolutions than several years ago, there still can be certain limits applied to design of an online store because of limited screen resolution of its target audience.

These screen resolution statistics is based on the statistics published by www.w3schools.com and may not be fully suitable for online store owners as it also very much depends on the preferences of the target audience.

As the report says, most customers use 1024 by 768 screen resolution. But there are some customers who still use the 800 by 600 screen resolution (almost 15%):

Display Resolution					
2007	**Higher**	**1024x768**	**800x600**	**640x480**	**Unknown**
January	26%	54%	14%	0%	6%
2006					
July	19%	58%	17%	0%	6%
January	17%	57%	20%	0%	6%
2005					
July	14%	55%	25%	0%	6%
January	12%	53%	30%	0%	5%
2004					
July	10%	50%	35%	1%	4%
January	10%	47%	37%	1%	5%
2003					
July	8%	43%	44%	2%	5%
January	6%	40%	47%	2%	5%
2002					
October	6%	38%	49%	2%	5%

It becomes an important task to gather information about screen resolutions and monitors used by customers belonging to the targeted audience. If this information is not accessible, it's better to count on the worst case, i.e. on the worst screen resolution and smallest display size to make sure even those customers with smaller/older screens will be able to see the pages and navigate through the online store without any difficulties.

Actually, customers with smaller screens and lower screen resolutions can experience two sorts of problems: the web page can be wider than the screen, or can be much longer than the screen.

The first case is considered to be the worst, since no customers really like scrolling horizontally to see missing information on the web page. More than that, if the page is much wider than the screen, customers may miss some important piece of information just because they would not think there's something else there, to the right of the vertical scroll bar.

Pages that are too long will require customers with lower screen resolutions to scroll the page vertically up to several times to see the information that was supposed to be visible to customers either without scrolling at all, or with just one scroll wheel turn. A good example would be the user registration page in osCommerce. Should it be modified to get some additional information from the customers, and should the customers have lower screen resolutions—they would have to scroll the page vertically to fill in all the required fields, which will effectively make an impression of a long and boring registration process and may change the customer's mind about proceeding further with the purchase.

The customers may feel confused, and web pages may not work as efficiently as they would if the customers had screens with higher resolution, or rather if the website was optimized for lower resolutions and smaller screens.

This leads to several suggestions on how to make an osCommerce online store look nicer and work efficiently if prospective customers are likely to have lower screen resolutions:

- First of all, the website should be tested under the worst (lowest) screen resolution as is supposed to be set on the target customers' screens.

- The pages of an online store should be built in such a way that the most important information is always aligned to the left side of the screen, or is available in the middle area, so that the right-hand-side is used for some additional, non-crucial information like promotion banners, Shopping Cart, etc. This way, should the customer have a screen with lower resolution, and should a part of the website be located "out" of the customer's screen, the customer will still see all the important information on the screen (like website logo and main navigation, category tree, search facilities, middle area with all product, checkout, and user account information).

- There is an interesting approach that changes page layout depending on the customer's screen resolution, by, for example, hiding the right-hand-side column completely when the customer's screen resolution is too low, and displaying all the "hidden" design elements (information boxes, texts, banners, etc.) in the left column instead.

- Pages should not be made too long in any case, as the less effort is required by the customer to reach the end of the page when reading some information or filling in a form—the less tiresome the process will seem to the customer and the greater the chances the customer will continue to browse through the website, complete the purchase, and come back in the future, or recommend the website to friends or colleagues.

But it would be wrong to assume that problems only come when customers have lower screen resolutions. Actually, should a part of the target audience have screens with higher resolution than the rest of the customers, it may also result in a problem, since the website would be optimized for lower screen resolutions and look "empty" on screens with higher resolutions.

The solution depends on the way the website is built; either it has a fixed width design, or a so called "ribbon" design, when instead of a fixed width the content of the page scales to occupy a certain percent of the available page width.

In the case of a fixed width design, the easiest solution would be to display additional banners on the left or right-hand sides of the page, should it be optimized for lower screen resolution and should a particular customer have higher screen resolution instead. Screen resolution can be determined on the server side (in osCommerce PHP scripts) when the customer opens any page of the website, and is forwarded by the web browser to the web server along with the request to bring up a certain page.

In the case of a "ribbon" design, there are at least two solutions. The first, is the same as in the case of the fixed width design, i.e. to display additional banners and promotions at the side of the screen.

The second solution is much trickier and may require significant additional programming effort to implement. Depending on the screen resolution, it would change the amount of information displayed on each particular web page. For example, in the case of the Product Listing page it would display some additional fields if the screen resolution is higher than the page that it was optimized for (like additional attributes, or a longer marketing description). If the Product Listing page uses grid layout, it could display four products in a row instead of the three products that are usually displayed there on screens with lower resolution.

Multicultural and Multilingual Designs

Many companies that trade online nowadays face global challenges, when instead of winning market share in one particular country or a certain region of a country they try to break into the international market. Trading internationally helps an online merchant to increase turnover and profits, but also brings up certain difficulties that local businesses may not have to deal with.

Solving those difficulties in the most efficient way is the key to success in international trading for any online merchant.

International Sales

To make international trading possible, an online merchant needs to address at least the following requirements:

- Have the website available to those prospective customers who come from countries and regions where the online store trades.

- Implement corresponding delivery methods for all countries and regions where the online store trades.

- Implement local payment methods for certain countries and regions.

- Have Product Information and prices available in the corresponding local languages and currencies.

- Ideally, have the complete website available in local languages of countries and territories where the online store trades.

- Finally, to help the sales, all local design preferences should be respected in the way the online store would look and feel for local customers.

There are many ways to run international sales.

It is possible to have all orders processed in one office, and all products delivered to any country or region from one central location. This is sensible if the products are very unique, and if the customers are ready to wait while the goods are being delivered.

Online merchants must study local markets in all countries and regions to which the online store will be delivering orders to, and make sure the prices stay competitive in the currency for each territory. So ideally, products would have different prices in various currencies, not necessarily according to currency exchange rates. At the same time, this approach leads to several issues:

- Customers can change currency or location and find products priced differently for different regions.

- If products and orders are all managed from the same office, the product cost price will be the same but product sale price will vary depending on the country or region where the customers live, therefore turnover and, more importantly, profits, will also change, sometimes leaving almost no profits at all.

Taking this into account, and also the fact that international customers, the same as local customers, demand prompt delivery and local support, the best way to run international sales would be either opening a child company and a special online store (a new front end, having all front ends linked to the same back end and the same osCommerce database) per each country or region with a significant number of prospective customers, or, instead of opening a child company, outsourcing management to a local partner who might be able to take even better care of business because of their knowledge of local markets.

Another variant is to perform customer support and order processing from one and the same office, but having deliveries done from drop-shipping partners in each country or region where the online store trades.

Delivery is a very important part of the online sale process. For companies that sell their goods internationally, selecting the best and the most cost effective local delivery method is a highly important task. It is of course possible to use international carriers, but then the price the customers would be paying for delivery could scare some of them off the website.

It is the same with local payment methods — in a number of countries there are local payment processing gateways that local customers are already familiar with. It's very important for "local image" and of course, for customers' convenience, to support those very local payment methods in an online store, for each country or region. And of course, international payment methods should be available to the customers too.

Although many prospective customers would be able to read and understand Product Information in English (or another default language), they may prefer having it available in their local language. Proper translation of Product Information is the key to successful international sales and to proper Search Engine Optimization of the website, because having important keywords translated properly into several languages significantly increases the chances of an online store to be found in search results when customers search in their local languages. The same relates to the whole website, if it is translated properly and thoroughly, so that there are no texts left in default language — this demonstrates respect and attention to the needs of local customers.

But it's not only the texts that need to be translated. It's the brand, the whole look and feel of the design sometimes that need changing to match expectations and preferences of prospective customers from different locations.

Benefiting from Cultural Diversity

Launching an online store that trades internationally is a part of the globalization process. But having said that, we should not forget about the cultural diversity that makes online trading in each country or region a bit different than in another.

Of course, there are different local regulations that an online store should comply with. These will affect terms and conditions, various policies (like returns, refunds, delivery, etc.).

But launching an online store for customers from other countries or regions is not only about dealing with the legal side of the business, or having product prices competitive in every country or region, or choosing local payment gateways and shipping carriers. It's also about ensuring that the online store looks and feels in a way that local customers will feel comfortable with, and also ensuring that the marketing and advertising of the online store is being performed in a way that will most effectively reach local customers.

Customers who belong to different cultures would expect an online store to look and feel easy and comfortable for them to browse the product catalog and place orders. They would expect the online store to "speak their language" too. The following aspects should be taken into consideration and made look and feel "local":

- Logotype and slogan (if any) — these design elements change very rarely, but still a merchant may want to change the slogan so that it would sound better for local customers and would ensure better "reach" of the target audience in every country or region where the online store trades.

- Some online stores have completely different designs for each country or region they trade in. This is explained by the fact that prospective customers belong to different cultures and may prefer different color schemes and design styles that look more "local" to them.

- Advertiseing and banners — the way special promotions and ad banners are placed on the pages, the content, and the look of those promotions and banners should be made very "local" for each country or region.

- The text content of the pages of an online store may differ depending on country or region, not only because of the translation but also because different approaches (text content) may be required to better "reach" customers who belong to different cultures.

- Finally, product marketing description may be different too, as although prospective customers would be looking into addressing similar needs, they may pay attention to different details in the product description depending on the culture they belong to.

By having those aspects of international trading properly addressed, an online store will benefit a lot from cultural diversity and will see an increase in the turnover.

Technical Aspects of Multicultural Design in osCommerce

Technically there exist three possible ways to deal with multicultural design in osCommerce:

- Have one and the same design implemented for all countries and regions.
- Have separate online stores, each with a different design, implemented for some countries and regions.
- Have separate front ends implemented for some countries and regions, and have all those front ends linked to the same osCommerce back end.

The first two solutions are self-explanatory.

It is possible to create several osCommerce front ends (catalogs), all linked to the same database, and then have one osCommerce back end (Administration panel) linked to the same database too. This will provide a facility to change the design of each front end, individually, according to the best practices for a certain country or region. The main issue the online merchant will face would be the necessity to actually maintain multiple online stores, as a change or new feature implemented in one front end will have to be replicated in all other front ends.

So effectively, even though this particular solution is better than the one with completely separate online stores (because this solution uses only one database with products and orders), in terms of the difficulties associated with maintenance and further improvements it's not much different.

Yet another way to implement multiple front ends in osCommerce would be using design templates. We will consider design templates in more detail later in this very chapter. The main benefit of such an approach is that even though design of each front end can be made different, all front ends will be effectively connected to the same database, the same back end, and also use the same front end scripts, which makes maintenance and further improvements less difficult than working with a single online store, not dependent on the number of front ends.

This solution assumes that all front ends will be hosted on the same web server.

Therefore, all separate domain names or sub-domains or URLs associated with individual front ends should be properly configured. In the case of using design templates for a multiple front ends solution, all domain names (or sub-domains) would point to one and the same copy of the online store.

Usually, in the header of the website there would be placed links that lead customers to the corresponding local version of the online store. Those links can be implemented as corresponding country flags, or as a drop-down menu with the list of countries/regions for which the online store has local versions.

It is possible to determine where the customer's coming from using the GeoIP features, and switch to the corresponding front end (domain name, sub-domain, or just a special URL associated with the country or region the customer is browsing the site from) automatically. Of course, the customer should be given an opportunity to change the front end if desired.

Design Recommendations

Certain suggestions can be given as to how to design an online store based on osCommerce.

Main Page

The main (or home) page of an osCommerce online store can be implemented in two ways.

First of all, the standard osCommerce main page can be used. It is operated from the `index.php` file, and by default displays all standard layout elements (the header, two side columns, footer, and the middle area) and their content (various information boxes, texts, links, and images). Depending on the design concept, certain standard osCommerce design elements can be absent, or the layout can be changed. It is important to remember that the main page is a part of the same osCommerce script responsible for further navigation within the product catalog, so changes in the main page (`index.php` file) may result in changes in the rest of the online store.

The second approach would be using a special HTML design template solely for the main page of the online store. That template would be easy to edit using any HTML authoring software. Its content, layout and practically anything can be changed easily without affecting the rest of the online store.

Independent of the layout of the main page, it's recommended to have the following elements displayed there: the logo, main menu links, category tree, quick search box, box with links to information pages, Shopping Cart box, and possibly additional boxes promoting products and hot offers.

The middle area of the main page is very important, as this is what the customers see when they first open the website. Its content, like the design and content of other design elements, depends a lot on the product catalog. It can contain top or featured products, the complete list of all products (if the product range is relatively small), explanation texts and images that will tell the customers what the online store is about, promotion banners, or all this together.

The main task of the main page of an online store is to:

- Inform customers about what they can buy on the website
- Promote certain products or special offers

The design of the main page should be implemented in a way that will make the customer aware of the logo (brand) of the online store, and also make the customer either read the introductory text of the website, or divert the customer's attention to certain products or categories.

As for customers, the main page of an online store is very important for search engines too, because in most cases, it is the first page a search engine bot can "see" when it gets to the site.

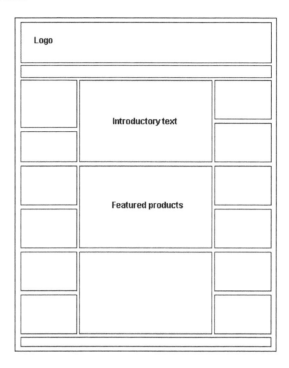

Category and Search Results Pages

Once a category is selected, the customer can see a new page that contains the list of sub-categories and products.

The following recommendations can be given for the content of the middle area of that page (the rest of the page, header, side columns, and footer would not change too much when navigating from one page to another):

- Current category name highlighted in the header of the page, with the path to parent categories, all clickable

- Title, description, and picture associated with the category — the picture can be of one of the products that belong to that particular category or to one of its child categories

- Several of the most popular products of that category, along with sub-categories

- All the products that belong to the category, with navigation controls that allow easy navigation between the products that belong to the category — though it makes sense to hide the navigation controls if all products within the category can be put on a single page
- Additional Product Listing filters, if applicable

The design of the search results page is just a bit different from that of the category page. It would not have the sub-categories section. Instead, it would display the search criteria the customer used to find desirable products. This would help the customer to quickly check if there was a mistake in the search criteria if no products were found.

Also, the search criteria box should be pre-filled with the very same query as submitted by the customer in the previous step, to give the customer an opportunity to edit the search conditions if required.

Products displayed in the search results page, the same as on the category page, can be sorted in any way by customers. It is recommended to have a special filter in place that would allow for refining search results and also sorting products within the search results alphabetically, by newest/oldest date range, popularity, or lower/higher price.

Even if there are no results found, the search results page should try to suggest similar searches or at least today's most popular products.

Product Listing

Product listing is a part of several pages, including category pages and search results pages. Product listing in some cases may appear in the main page of an osCommerce online store.

Products in the listing can be sorted in various ways. It makes sense to use featured/ not featured sorting by default to promote products marked as "featured" by the Administrator of online store.

Depending on the osCommerce settings of how many products should be displayed per page, and depending on product type, the listing can look like the standard osCommerce product list or appear as a more advanced product grid.

In either case, each product requires a name (or model), image, price, and, if fits into the page layout, description (or set of the most important technical characteristics).

Along with each product, its stock level could be displayed and also the "Buy Now" button—if the product can be bought directly from the Product Listing, i.e. if it doesn't have attributes that should be selected by the customer prior to the purchase.

Indication of stock level makes it possible for customers to see right from the Product Listing which product is and which product isn't in stock, sparing customers one more click into the Product information page.

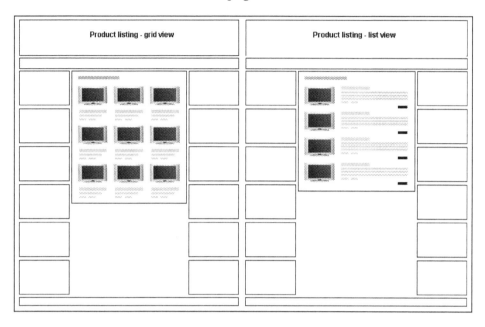

Product Information Pages

On the Product Information page, Product Information is an essentially main design element that the customer should be able to see. Product name and product model number (if present) should be displayed across in the top part of the page. It is recommended to use one of the HTML header tags for the product name.

It should be noted that on the Product Information page the customer's attention should be on the product and, maybe, accompanying products. It makes sense to remove banners that advertise anything else but similar products or services from the Product Information pages. The concept here is that the closer the customer is to the purchase process, the less extra information should be shown to the customer. This not only requires banners not related to the specific product or category of products to be removed from the Product Information pages, but also assumes there will be less and less extra information provided to the customer on the Shopping Cart and checkout pages to avoid distracting him/her from the purchasing process.

The price of the product, or rather product prices—as there can be several prices given per product, including RRP price, special price, etc.—are usually displayed under the product name, or to the right of the product name dependending on the design.

It is important to note that the current price should be highlighted (made bigger or of a different color than other prices, like RRP, previous price, etc.), so that the customer would see without a doubt exactly how much the product costs.

The product main image can be displayed aligned to the left or right side under the product name and price. It should give space for the product's short description to be put alongside, so the main product image should not be made too wide. Along with the main product image there could be displayed several additional images. Additional images are usually displayed as relatively small thumbnails, but it's possible to display additional images of the same size as the main product image, depending on the layout of the page and specifics of the product range.

The product description can be shown alongside the main product image, or directly under it. Depending on whether the product has a short or long description, and also if the product has any properties or technical specification that should be made available to customers, they can be displayed in the following order: short description, properties or technical specification, long marketing description. Alternatively, if the Product Information page has tabs, the long marketing description can be put on the first information tab, and the properties or technical specification can be put on the second tab. More tabs can be added: one with complementary products, another with accessories, yet another with information about the manufacturer or product type, etc.—this solely depends on the product type and the amount of Product Information available.

The "Buy Now" or "Add to Cart" control buttons are usually placed along with the product price. If the product's marketing description is supposed to be long, it makes sense to display product price(s) and "Buy Now" control buttons at the bottom of the page too, so that customers do not have to scroll up to buy the product after reading its description.

Manufacturer/brand information in osCommerce is usually displayed as an information box in one of the side columns. That information box should be aligned so that it can be easily seen when looking at the Product Information page. Alternatively, it's possible to display manufacturer information directly in the middle area of the Product Information page. This would include manufacturer name, logo, and can include two links: one to the manufacturer's own website and another to the list of other products that are made by the same manufacturer.

Brief information about the manufacturer and, ideally, the category the product belongs to can be put on the Product Information page for customer's convenience, and also for SEO.

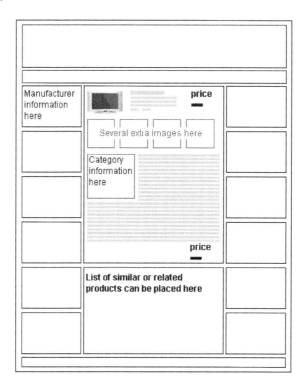

Variants of the Shopping Cart Page Design

Pressing the "Buy Now" or "Add to Cart" button on either the Product Listing page or the Product Information page adds the selected product(s) to the Shopping Cart. Depending on the osCommerce settings, the user can be redirected to the Shopping Cart page after that, or can stay on the very same page.

This behavior should depend on how many products the online merchant expects the customers to buy from the website at a time. If the customers are expected to buy multiple products at once from the Product Listing (like, for example, an online store that sells beads for jewelry making, or coffee) it's better to leave the customer on the same Product Listing instead of opening the Shopping Cart page each time the customer adds something to the Shopping Cart. On the contrary, if the online store sells, say, home appliances, it's better to open the Shopping Cart page to show the customer its content, calculated shipping fees, and estimated delivery dates, etc.

The default design of the osCommerce Shopping Cart page is not optimal. Here are several suggestions on how to improve it:

- Display small product images within the list of products in the Shopping Cart.
- Instead of the "remove" tick boxes and the "Update" button it's better to display small "Remove" icons (like little red crosses or waste bins) near each product in the Shopping Cart giving the customers a facility to remove individual products easily.
- Ideally, the Shopping Cart page would also display shipping fees, so it would allow customers to specify their location (by selecting country and region within the country or ZIP code) to have the online store recalculate the shipping fees accordingly.
- If the Discount Coupons feature is installed, the customers should be given a facility to enter a coupon code and press the "Redeem" button on the Shopping Cart page to see what the order total will look like with the discount coupon redeemed.
- Finally, knowing how much all products in the Shopping Cart cost, the delivery fee, and having applied the discount coupon (if any) the Shopping Cart page can display the order total value to the customers, without the need for customers to register or login to find out what the total order amount will be.

As was suggested earlier, control buttons should have different style or colors depending on if they lead the customer to the purchase or not. Therefore, the "Checkout" button on the Shopping Cart page should be somehow highlighted compared to other buttons to make it easier to find on the page.

Checkout Pages

It's quite often the case that customers and online store owners find the osCommerce checkout process too long and too complicated. This causes confusion and some customers may leave the online store even though they wanted to place an order at first.

Therefore, it's recommended to simplify the checkout process of osCommerce by reducing the number of pages involved in customer registration and the actual checkout process itself.

By default, the checkout process in osCommerce consists of the login page (with a choice to register for new customers and log in for existing customers), customer registration page (for new customers), customer registration success page (for new customers), checkout shipping page (optional, skipped if the online store sells downloadable or virtual products), checkout payment page, checkout confirmation page, and checkout success page. Seven pages all together in the worst-case scenario.

It's suggested to reduce the number of checkout pages to only three: Checkout page, Checkout Confirmation page, and Checkout Success page. Effectively, it means combining customer login and registration, selection of payment and shipping methods, and display of the order total on the same page.

Let's consider the Checkout page.

First of all, it's recommended to display the Product Listing (along with the images and attribute details, if any) at the very top of the checkout page, so that customers will know what they are about to pay for.

After that, it's recommended to display login facilities for existing customers, just an email address and password. But in order to make the page look more compact, login facilities for existing customers can be hidden by default, and can be opened if the customer clicks a corresponding "Existing customers login" link on the page. Once the customer has entered email address and password, the page would refresh with all other fields pre-filled with customer details.

New customers would be asked to enter two addresses: billing address (for invoices) and shipping address (optional for when the online store sells products that can be physically delivered to the customer). There should be a special control button or a tick box that would automatically copy the content of the billing address fields into the shipping address to speed up the process and not make customers enter the same information twice. Alternatively, that option can be ticked by default, hiding the shipping address controls and reducing the page size. Un-ticking the box will un-hide the shipping address controls.

The selection of delivery methods would be updated depending on the country, region, and ZIP code entered by the customer in the shipping address fields. It is possible to use AJAX technologies to reload available shipping methods and shipping charges for the selected location without reloading the whole Checkout page.

The redeem section for discount coupons could be also displayed on the Checkout page, right before the shipping methods section.

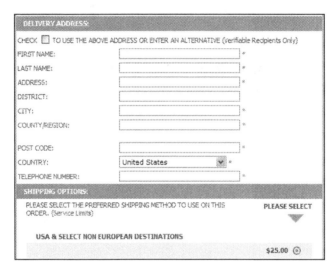

The order total would finish the Checkout page, and would be updated automatically depending on the selected shipping method (and of course taking into account order sub-total, taxes, and discount coupons). Again, it is possible to use AJAX technologies to update order total values.

Once the **Continue** control button is pressed by the customer, the website would open the next page — the Checkout Confirmation page. Basically, this would contain all the same information as the previous page, but it would not be editable, and customers will be expected to check all order information and confirm it is all correct (i.e. the list of products is correct, billing and shipping address information is correct, selected shipping method is correct, and also the entered discount coupon, if any, is correct). Order total values (including detailed explanation of costs) will be also displayed there. As a confirmation of the order, the customer will be asked to enter payment information, so the list of available payment methods will be displayed at the very end of the page, and by selecting one of the payment methods and entering corresponding payment information the customer will confirm the order.

It is important to note that if the website is protected by SSL, a corresponding security seal should be displayed on the Checkout Confirmation page (in fact on all Checkout pages) to improve the customer's confidence in placing that online order.

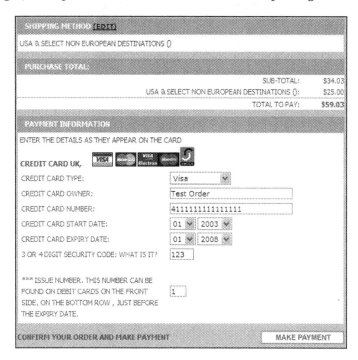

The third and final page of the optimized checkout process, the Checkout Success page, should again contain the list of products that have just been ordered, billing and shipping address, and order total information. And of course, a message that thanks the customer for placing an order and explains what will be happening with the order next.

There is no known contribution that would allow for such changes in the default osCommerce checkout process. If you'd like to have your online store modified in the way described here, you may want to seek the assistance of a professional osCommerce consultant. Fortunately, there are many individuals and companies that professionally design and develop osCommerce online stores.

User Account and Order History Pages

After creating an account with an osCommerce online store, and of course after placing an order, the customer gets access to the User Account page. It contains three groups of links: to manage account information (like personal data, addresses, password, or close the account), to view order history (the newest several orders are usually displayed on the main user account page, and the rest are available on the Order History page), and manage email notifications (i.e. subscribe or unsubscribe from the newsletters).

Unless there are some extensive requirements for the user account management, (like some sort of subscription service, or credit account functionality), the standard osCommerce user account pages are well designed and would not require significant changes.

Important Design Elements

Besides general recommendations about the look and feel of an online store based on osCommerce, recommendations could be given to particular design elements of osCommerce design. Positioning, color schemes, dimensions—all these give an online store a good or bad look, and eventually affect how many of the visitors to an online store become its customers.

Logo

The logo of an online store is one of its key design elements. It is present on all pages of the website, and also on its printed documents (like invoices, packing slips, and order details) and downloadable materials (like PDF product catalogs).

The logo is usually placed at the top left corner of the page, or sometimes in the middle of the page header. The logo of an online store should be easy to notice on the page, but at the same time it usually should not be wider than 25% of the page header.

It is important that the logo is presented by an image of the highest quality. It means that if the logo is represented by (for example) a JPEG image, its compression level should be set to such a that has absolutely no affect on the image quality.

The logo may contain a short description, or a slogan of the online store, to ensure that customers will further associate that description or slogan with the logo and with the entire online store.

The color scheme of the online store's logo should of course match the color scheme of the rest of the design elements, or rather vice versa, as the logo is the most important part of the online store's identity, and its colors and style should be used when creating other elements of design.

Font Styles and Sizes and Colors

The main requirements for the fonts used throughout the online store is to make it very easy for customers to read and understand textual information from the web pages.

Therefore, the font style and size should allow for easy reading.

It's not recommended to use fancy font styles unless its a strict requirement; however nice and artistic they look, they may make the reading experience more difficult for some customers.

Also, small letters can make it difficult to read textual information from the pages for quite a number of customers, or big letters will make it impossible to put enough textual information on the pages without breaking the layout.

Using all large caps in the textual information may not work as the customers would not be able to concentrate on a particular highlighted part of the text, because all the text will be highlighted in that case. The same applies to highlighting text with bold or italic font styles; only certain parts of the text can be highlighted in that way to grab customers' attention.

The colors used to display text should provide an easy reading experience to the customers. So, the text colors should be always checked against the colors of the background where the text is to be displayed. Customers should not experience any difficulties reading textual information from the web pages because the text colors are very similar to the background colors or the contrast between text and background colors is too low. For example, light gray text on a whiter background, or light green text on a gray background will be difficult to read.

At the same time, a part of the textual information that is not very important and is placed on the web pages for general information purposes or legal purposes only can deliberately use a color that will make it almost unnoticeable on the pages, especially compared the important information, such as product description, terms and conditions, etc. This is done not to hide that information, but rather to avoid drawing the customer's attention away from the products.

As said above, different font sizes and colors can be used for prices, to indicate which is the current price and which is the previous or RRP price. Customers should not have any doubts about that the current price should be always highlighted relative to any other previous or RRP price displayed alongside.

Quick Search Box

The Quick search box is especially important where there are many products in the product catalog, and when the product names and product description contain keywords that many of the prospective customers would use to find such products in the product catalog. If there are only a few products in the database (say less than 20), it doesn't really make sense to occupy the space on the screen with the Quick search box at all.

The quick search box can be added into the header of the online store pages or even into the horizontal bar below the header, usually on the right-hand side as the left corner is usually occupied by the logo. This will ensure that the customers always have access to the Quick search facility, whichever page they are browsing at the moment.

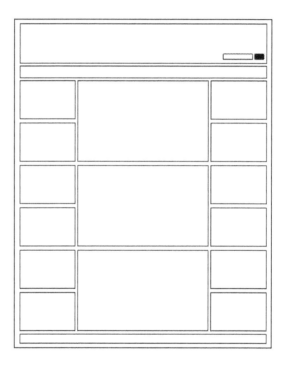

It can be placed into the left side column, usually as the very first information box, over the box with the category tree. Again, this makes sense when there are too many entries in the product catalog and prospective customers are expected to know keywords associated with certain products, but may not know where to find such products in the category tree.

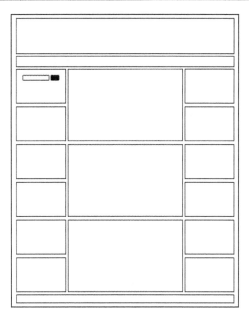

The Quick search box can be placed into the middle area of the website pages, at the very top. This will ensure the search box is one of the first design elements that customers see when they first open the website pages. This can be done to push prospective customers to use the search facility rather than the category tree or other means of navigation.

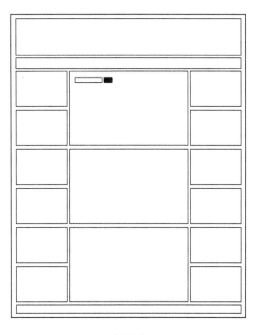

Finally, it can be added to the right side column, either to the top or the middle. This approach will make customers concentrate on using the category tree and other means of navigation rather than using the Quick search box.

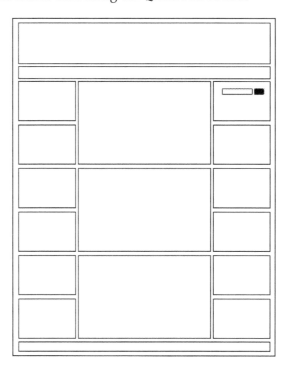

The Quick search box itself should not be put very close to other design elements, so that it can be easily noticed by customers.

It should not be made too short, so that customers can type longer keywords or key phrases consisting of several keywords without losing any part of the search string.

Ideally, the auto-suggest feature should be implemented for keywords, as was described in previous chapters (there are several contributions for osCommerce that allow for this functionality).

Some sources recommend setting auto-focus onto the Quick search box when the page is loaded, though this may not be applicable to a particular online store.

If there are many entries in the product catalog (several thousand entries for example), it will be a good idea to give customers a facility to pre-filter search results by top categories, so along with the search box there will be a drop-down menu with category names, and the search results will be limited by the selected category.

Finally, pressing *Enter* should initiate the search process in the same way as pressing the **Search** button. The search button should always be present there. It's recommended to simply use the "search" as the name of the button, and not a graphic icon. It will make the function of the Quick search box more prominent to customers.

Shopping Cart Box

The shopping cart box is used to display the content of the Shopping Cart to the customer, or to display general information about what's located in the customer's Shopping Cart without actually displaying it in detail there.

The shopping cart box in osCommerce is usually placed in either the header of the page or the right side column. If placed in the header, the Shopping Cart box doesn't usually display the actual content of the Shopping Cart, but only the number of products in the cart and total order amount. There should be a link added there to lead the customer to the Shopping Cart page. There can be also a link for the Checkout page there, which will skip through the Shopping Cart page and redirect the customer directly to the login/checkout pages.

Sometimes an osCommerce online store will display a corresponding icon (shopping trolley) instead of displaying the name of the information box. A better practice would be to display both the icon and the actual name of the shopping cart box. Both the icon and the name should be made clickable and should lead the customer to the Shopping Cart page.

If the shopping cart box is put into a side column (and it makes sense to put it into the right-hand side column, at the very top of it), its look and feel will change slightly.

First of all, the list of products that are currently in the Shopping Cart may be displayed there. Depending on the width of the column and correspondingly the width of the shopping cart box, it may or may not contain a very small thumbnail for each product. It will also contain product name and quantity. In default osCommerce, the link on each product actually leads the customer to the Product Information page. It can be changed and lead the customer to the shopping Cart page instead. Along with each product it's possible to display a small "Remove" icon (as a tiny red cross for example) to make it easier for customers to manage the content of their Shopping Cart.

The current order total can be also displayed in the shopping cart box, or a sub-total (depending on whether the shipping fees and taxes are known).

In the very bottom of the Shopping cart box, it makes sense to display a security seal and/or logos of the payment methods accepted by the online store (credit card logos, PayPal logo, etc.).

If the customers are expected to have a significant number of products in their Shopping Cart, and the rest of the information boxes in the right side column contain some important information, the shopping cart box may have to be shortened. The product listing may be removed from it in exchange of the total number of products and total price if the number of products in the Shopping Cart is greater than a certain predefined value (five for example). In that case the shopping cart box will display the Product Listing of not more than four products, and as soon as the customer adds one more product to the cart, the list of products will be changed to a piece of text that informs the customer about the total number of products in the Shopping Cart and their total price.

Again, both shopping cart box icon and title should be linked to the Shopping Cart page for user convenience.

Currency and Language Boxes

Currency and language selection are implemented as two separate information boxes in osCommerce. They are usually placed in the right side column of an online store.

But quite often, an online store only trades locally, and in that case would only accept one currency and would not have more than one language. Therefore the currency and language boxes would become redundant and could be removed to save the page space for more important information.

If the online store accepts multiple currencies, the currency box can be placed right under the shopping cart box, so that customers could easily switch the currency and see order total values in the preferred currency. The currency box by default contains a drop-down box with the list of all accepted currencies. Selecting any currency from the list causes automatic page reload, and all prices change according to the selected currency. This method seems optimal for changing the current currency of an osCommerce online store. Alternatively, clickable currency icons could be displayed in the Currency box, and clicking an icon would change currency selection in osCommerce and also highlight the clicked icon.

To allow customers to switch between multiple languages, osCommerce has a special Language box. It's usually placed in the right column, and contains flags for all installed and enabled languages. It can be improved further. First of all, it doesn't necessarily have to be put into the right side column, but can be added to the header of pages of the online store. Instead of a drop-down box there will be clickable language icons.

In order to improve usability, it's better to add hint texts with the name of each language to the corresponding language icon. Also, it's better to have the currently selected language highlighted while other language icons are pale, so that the customers can easily see which language is currently selected.

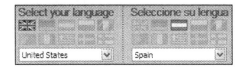

It should be noted that osCommerce can automatically set the default language based on the customer's browser's locale settings. Also, a language in osCommerce can be associated with its default currency. If a corresponding option is enabled in osCommerce, changing the language also automatically changes the currency.

Breadcrumbs and Navigation Panels

The so called "Breadcrumbs" design element is intended to help customers with navigation through the product catalog when they are browsing through sub-categories.

It contains the category path, starting from the very top-level categories down to the currently selected sub-category, plus it may also contain the currently selected product.

This design element is usually present on almost all pages of an osCommerce website, in the header of the page, and is aligned to the left.

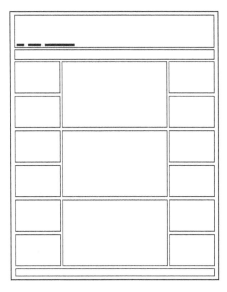

In osCommerce's default design, this element may not be very noticeable. This can be improved by making its colors more contrasting and also by making its font size a little bit bigger than in the default design. It can be also moved to the top part of the middle area of the pages to make it even easier to find if the prospective customers are expected to often go deep into the category tree and then come back to categories of previous levels.

The standard breadcrumbs feature can be improved further by turning it into a fully functional navigation panel. It will be then moved into the top part of the middle area of osCommerce pages, and, besides the trail of categories will contain **Previous** and **Next** links (or control buttons). Those links or buttons will work differently depending on the content of the page:

- On the category details page, they will navigate back and forth between the sister categories of the same level in the category tree.

- On the product details page, they will navigate back and forth either between the sister products of the same parent category, or between the sister products of the same search results.

Along with the links or control buttons, it makes sense to display the actual names of the corresponding previous or next category or product—it will make the navigation easier and more predictable for customers, and will also work well for SEO.

Category Tree

The category tree is one of the key navigation elements of osCommerce design. But before suggesting on how it should look and where to put it on the pages, let's consider the case when the category tree becomes redundant and can be excluded from the design completely.

If there are few products in the product catalog, and if the products are all similar or can be all listed in one page without the need to implement **Previous** and **Next** navigation controls—the category tree is not required, and can be totally excluded from the design to make it look simpler, and to save page space for other design elements.

The category tree, if placed in a box, is usually located in the left side column of an online store based on osCommerce, either at the very top of the column or after the Quick Search box.

Some designs have the tree of categories (or at least the very top categories) replicated in the header of the web pages as tabs, so that the customers can have access to the categories from absolutely every page of an online store. This approach also gives customers a clearer feeling of browsing through departments of the online store, where each department (category) is visually separated from others by a separate category tab.

The regular osCommerce category box contains the tree of categories. Clicking on a category reloads the page and opens its sub-categories in the box and also in the middle area of the page. Each category by default displays the number of products within itself or within its sub-categories. Actually, this number of products is of not much use, and can be disabled to make the category box look more consistent (and much faster—as then the online store will not have to query the database to find out the number of products in each category and its sub-categories every time the category box loads up).

If there are only a few categories in the category tree, and all are top categories, it is possible to show a special graphic representation of each category in the category box. This is not too good for SEO, but can improve the look and feel of the whole website. But in most cases, categories in the category box are displayed as text links.

If there are multiple categories and sub-categories of different levels, several solutions can be used.

First, the category tree can be implemented as a set of pop-up menus that pop up when the customer hovers the mouse cursor over the corresponding menu. Each pop-up menu is a category (with a link to the category details page), and it may contain sub-menus for sub-categories. It should be noted that this approach requires special JavaScript to be embedded into web pages (or a special CSS file), and, although it seems to be a good solution for product catalogs with two or three levels of sub-categories, it may not be suitable for larger product catalogs with more category levels.

It is important to note that the pop-up menu approach is very good for search engine optimization in terms of forwarding search engine bots from the main page of the online store directly to all pages of its categories and sub-categories. It should be noted that to make it search-engine friendly, the menu should not be built using JavaScript, but simple HTML lists and proper CSS instead. This way search engine bots will actually be able to reach Product Listings under each category or sub-category of literally any level directly from the main page. And since the main page usually has the highest page rank, its page rank will help to give higher page ranks to category and sub-category pages, and also, which is the most important, to the pages of individual products!

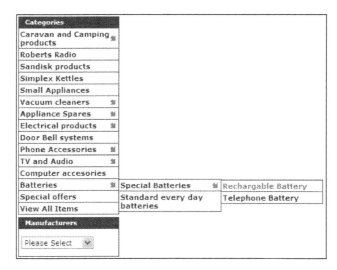

If there are many categories of different levels in the product catalog, the category box may only contain top-level categories in the beginning. Then, when the customer clicks any of the top categories link, the category box may change to only display the "child" categories of the selected top category. When the customer selects one of those "child" categories, the category box changes again, displaying "child" categories of the selected sub-category, and so on. The online store should of course contain links to categories of higher (parent) levels at any moment of time—the breadcrumbs feature can be used.

A variation of the latest approach would be not only to display top categories in the category box from the beginning, but also display one to two of the most popular sub-categories for each top category.

Filter Box

In order to improve navigation, an additional Filter box can be introduced when there are so many products in the catalog that standard navigation and search facilities are not enough.

A typical Filter box would usually contain filters that allow for limiting the current selection of products (either in a category or in the search results page) by product type, manufacturer (brand), price, and other properties.

The Filter box can be displayed in either of the side columns (preferably in the left-hand side column close under the category box if the latter is not too long, or even above the category box if it contains too many categories),

or in the middle area of the page, right over the Product Listing.

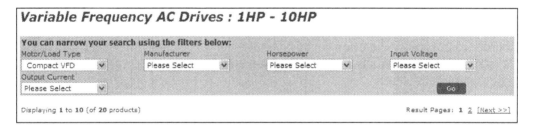

The Filter box may contain drop-downs with filter values and a "Filter" button, or clickable filter values, as links that immediately filter the Product Listing, whether it was a filter by product type, manufacturer, price or a filter by any of the product properties.

Login and Account History Links

Customers should be given a facility to log in to their accounts, or register for a new account in the online store. Corresponding links to "My Account" are usually placed into the header of the online store's pages. They can be also placed into the very top part of the header:

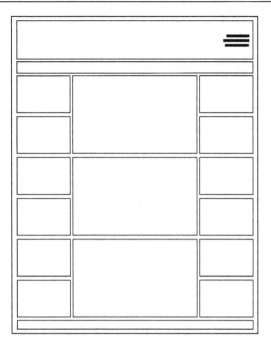

or at the part of page header where other links are located (and where the breadcrumbs are also displayed):

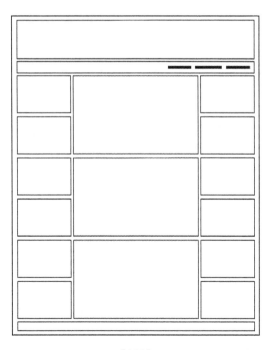

Some online stores display the login facilities in one of the side columns (usually in the right side column).

Once the customer is logged in, a new link should appear called "Log off".

Actually, the link that leads the customer to the account pages should be enough. Even so, some online stores have a special information box, usually in their right column, where they duplicate the links the customer would see on the My Account page—links to the account management pages, to the address book management pages, to order history, and subscription management pages.

Control Button Colors and Positions

Control buttons should be distinct from other design elements on the pages of an online store. They can be split into at least two classes: general control buttons, and buttons that lead customers to the purchase.

Those buttons that lead customers to the purchase should be made brighter with more solid colors to ensure the customers can always easily find them on the pages. Such buttons would be:

- "Buy now" on either Product Listing page or Product Information page
- "Checkout" on the Shopping Cart page
- "Continue" on the checkout pages

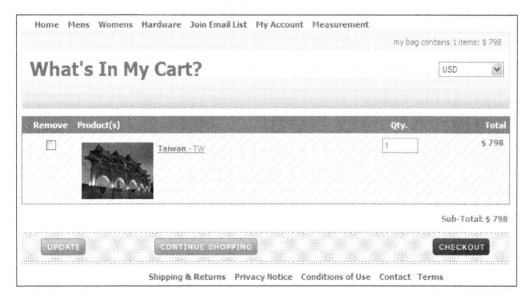

Control buttons in osCommerce are usually located in the bottom of the middle area of the page. However for example in the case of the Product Information page, it makes sense to duplicate control buttons in the header and in the footer of the main area of the page to make it more convenient and easier for customers to add products to the Shopping Cart.

Those buttons that assume further action should be aligned to the right side of the page, and buttons that assume return to the previous page or to the previous level when navigating through the product catalog should be aligned to the left side of the page. Such alignment will make navigation more obvious and comfortable for the customers.

Standard osCommerce Images

osCommerce comes with a number of standard images that are displayed on all sorts of pages, for example on the Main page (the "What's new here?" icon), on the Shopping Cart page (the "What's in my Cart?" icon), the icon on the Login page, and so on.

Actually, those standard images had better be removed from the design of an online store completely; they are unlikely to match any design integrated into an osCommerce online store.

Messages (Information, Warnings, and Errors)

osCommerce generates certain messages (information, warnings, and errors) and those messages are either displayed on the pages of an osCommerce online store, or are displayed in pop-up message windows.

While message windows are displayed in a standard manner for websites, the warning and information and error messages that are displayed in osCommerce pages can be improved.

First, it's the font size of those messages. By default it's too small and should be increased to make it easier to read the messages, and make the messages look more prominent.

The background of the messages can also be changed to make it clearer for customers whether an error has occurred, or if it was a warning or a general information message or a notification.

Also, the tiny icons associated with messages can be improved too, again to make it easier for customers to understand what kind of message they are seeing on the page — whether it is a warning, an error, or a notification.

Fast Design

Design of an online store can affect the page load speed of every page. It can also affect the workload that is put on the web server by the online store. Of course, optimized SQL queries and PHP scripts are very important too, but both the speed of the website and optimized server performance depend a lot on the design.

Why Speed is Important

Page load speed is very important especially for an online store, simply because customers do not like waiting. Customers of an online store may not want to wait more than just a few seconds (about four to eight based on different pieces of research) before they can see the content of the page.

Of course, if the page load time can be minimized to, say, one to two seconds that would be an ideal solution for an online store. But if it takes more than ten seconds to load a web page (irrespective of whether it's the Main page, Product Listing or Product Information page), the customers may choose to leave that online store and try another one.

How to Measure Page Load Speed in osCommerce

Page load speed depends on how fast the database is, how fast the PHP scripts that query the database are, and on how large the resulting HTML page that is sent to the customer's web browser in response to the query is. Here, how large means how large the HTML itself is and how large all images and other objects embedded into HTML are, i.e. how large a total amount of data is to be downloaded to the customer's computer by the web browser over the Internet.

Of course the time required to download one and the same amount of data depends on the customer's Internet connection speed. So it would be of great help to know what is the average Internet connection speed of customers that belong to the targeted audience. Sometimes, the targeted audience are supposed to have only high-speed Internet connections, and the size of web pages will not be that critical.

But in all other cases, it's better to have web pages optimized in terms of their size.

Page load speed can be measured by free tools available in the Internet. Like, for example `http://www.websiteoptimization.com/services/analyze/`. It takes the entered URL and opens it several times, finding the average page load speed and reporting how much time it would take to load the page if the customers had Internet connection of various speeds (from modem to T1 connection). What's more is that the service reports on the size of certain parts of the page, such as pure HTML size, size of images, size of CSS files, etc.

It lists all page objects sorted by size too, so that it's possible to see which page elements cause the page loading to be slow.

How to Optimize Page Load Speed

There are several ways to optimize the page load speed of an osCommerce website (besides optimizing the database and PHP scripts of course):

- osCommerce cache should be used where possible, to allow the web server to simply use cached parts of the page—such as the category tree for example, instead of generating corresponding HTML every time by querying the database.

- Wherever possible included files should be used (JavaScript files, CSS files, just parts of HTML design that are not likely to be created using some data from the database) so that web browsers could use their own cache management facilities.

- GZip compression can be turned on, so that all pages will be automatically archived on the web server before sending them to the web browser; this will decrease the page load time, but will put a certain workload on the customer's local computer (to open archived data) and on the web server.

  Experiments demonstrate that considerably less workload is required to archive web pages than to push complete pages to the web browsers—in the latter case, when a lot of customers are browsing through an online store, the web sever may become overloaded and start responding slowly on further requests.

- Product images should be made "lighter", i.e. thumbnails should be created for all product images and thumbnails should be used on Product Listing pages, and also in the information boxes through the whole online store.

Branding

The brand of an online store should be carried throughout the whole website. Actually from the visual point of view, brand would consist of the online store name (often the same as the domain name), logo, color scheme, and specific style of design elements.

It's an obvious requirement that those elements of the brand would not change when the customers browse from one page of the online store to another. The brand of an online store, the style of design elements through all pages and documents of an online store should be made consistent.

A recognizable brand can help an online store receive more orders from returning customers in the future, and also from new customers referred by existing customers.

A recognizable brand is easier (and cheaper!) to advertise.

Email Templates and Newsletters

Elements of the brand can be also added into emails and newsletters to improve brand awareness.

So the logo can be made a part of the HTML email template, and emails and newsletters can use a color scheme that resembles the online store design.

Email notifications (like customer registration, order confirmation, and order status updates) and also newsletters sent from the Administration panel of an online store can all use the same color scheme as the online store itself, and also use similar design elements.

Downloadable and Printable Documents

All downloadable and printable documents that customers can receive from an online store (such as invoice, order details, packing slip, and receipt) can resemble the look and feel of the online store.

At the very least, those documents should contain the same logo as the online store, and ideally use similar font styles too.

Such documents can be downloaded as PDF files, and also printed directly from pages of the online store, or received along with order confirmation/status change notification emails.

Downloadable Product Catalog and Brochures

It's not only documents related to an order that can be downloaded from an osCommerce online store, but also the entire product catalog or its parts (like information about an individual product) that can be made downloadable (preferably in PDF format) from the website.

By allowing customers to download a product catalog or individual product brochures, and by having those PDF files designed in a similar way to how the online store is designed, the following can be achieved:

- Better brand awareness, affecting the customer who downloaded the product catalog or brochures, and also friends, colleagues, and relatives of the customer to whom the customer may show the downloaded brochure

- Increased number of orders from those customers who were not ready to buy products immediately but needed some time to think and discuss the purchase with their partners or colleagues

What to Include

The following elements should be included into downloadable product brochures:

- Logo
- Online store name
- Color scheme that resembles the one used by the online store
- URL of the online store and of each individual product or category page
- Physical address and contact details (like telephone number, FAX, etc.) of the company behind the online store, ideally along with a map that would help customers find their way (if there is a showroom where the same products as can be ordered from the website, can be purchased by customers)
- For each product or category there should be its name, description, URL on the website, model number (if any), main image and additional images, if any, key properties (if any), variants (if any), and price together with the date of when it was valid—this is very important since the customer may come back to the online store or come to the showroom days, weeks, months after the product brochure was downloaded and of course the price may have changed since then

How to Generate Product Brochures

The best way to generate a downloadable product catalog or product brochures would be to have them generated by a special scheduled script that would update PDF brochures nightly.

At the same time, should any product be changed from the Administration panel, the changes (either in its availability, name, description, price, etc.) need to be reflected in all downloadable content as soon as possible.

Therefore, a special button or menu item can be implemented in the Administration panel that would initiate the update procedure for all affected PDF downloadable documents.

PDF brochures would be linked from pages of an online store. A link to the complete product catalog can be put into the information box of the website, and links to individual product brochures can be added to Product Information pages.

This is not only good for customer confidence and for brand awareness, but also good for SEO, as search engines will index PDF brochures as well as they index other pages of the website, and links to the website and its PDF brochures will more likely appear in the search results, as keyword density in a PDF brochure would be even higher than on an individual Product Information page (because there are other design elements in HTML pages, and nothing but textual content and related product images in downloadable PDF documents).

Banners

Those banners that the online store uses to advertise itself on other websites should also be designed in a way that makes it impossible not to notice its brand. Therefore, ideally the logo of the online store (or at least its name) would appear on such banners, along with the special offer information or new product information.

Updating osCommerce Design

The default osCommerce installation comes with a pre-integrated relatively simple design. Usually, online stores based on osCommerce require redesign before they can be launched and start receiving orders.

But what if after some time the design of an osCommerce online store needs to be changed or updated again?

Why Change a Design

Obviously as an online store develops, its design changes slightly; some design elements are removed, some added, some change position on the pages or change their style.

But there are certain cases when the design of the whole online store should be changed almost at the same time, or when an online store should have several variants of design, each used for its own purpose:

- To test new design ideas it is better to have a copy of the current design where it is possible to add, delete, change design elements, colors, styles, etc.

- To change design promptly in accordance with the latest promotion actions and marketing ideas.

- To run an e-commerce solution consisting of several front ends linked to the same back end, where each front end can have its own design or share the same design template among several front ends.

- To update the design of an online store seasonally (like adding some Christmas characters and snowflakes in winter, adding bunnies and chocolate eggs at Easter, implementing spring, summer, autumn, and winter moods, etc.).

- To support a multi-cultural system where customers who come from different countries or regions are presented with different designs.

Design Templates

Design templates are the best way forward when the task is to be able to change design instantly, or to support several designs at the same time, or test new design ideas without affecting the design of the production online store.

Design templates allow the separating of design from the business logic of an osCommerce online store, where one and the same set of PHP scripts implementing business logic and communication with the database can be connected with one of several different design templates "on the fly".

A freely available contribution called STS allows for having the design templates concept implemented in osCommerce. The contribution can be downloaded from `http://addons.oscommerce.com/info/1524`. Its installation requires quite some modifications of an online store, so it's better to assign a professional osCommerce development company to integrate it. Note that once STS has been installed, installation of other contributions may not be as straightforward as described in installation manuals as STS, in fact, changes the way that osCommerce works from the inside, splitting what can be called "default osCommerce" into two parts: business logic and design.

Summary

Design is an important part of an online store. It not only makes the user's browsing and buying experience pleasant, but also can help improve online sales.

osCommerce comes pre-designed, but most online merchants may find it beneficial for their online business to have their osCommerce online store redesigned so that the site matches the corporate identity design, product catalog, or target audience, or a combination of these.

The design of an online store should be created in a way that it helps customers finding products they are looking for, and making a purchase.

osCommerce design should be made compatible and good looking on any customer's screen, irrespective of the customer's screen resolution or web browser used.

It's the design of an online store that can help to break into international Internet markets, besides of course support for multiple currencies, languages, and payment and shipping options.

Page load speed affects sales, and osCommerce design should be optimized to allow for fast loading pages (of course along with the optimization of the database and PHP scripts).

An online store may benefit a lot from having a design that can be easily changed. Design templates for osCommerce is the right solution that can help change the design easily without changes in business logic, testing new design conceptions, support promotions, and advertisement campaigns.

In the next chapter, we will review how sales can be improved in osCommerce by improving the product catalog.

7

Improving Product Catalog

Products advertised on an online store can be one of the best sell gears themselves. It's what the customers come searching for, and it's website navigation that makes a difference by helping customers find what they want or, instead, by confusing them. And it's Product Information that contains a very clear description of what the product is for and what are its specifications that makes a difference when the customer is about to buy a product.

By improving the product catalog in many ways, from online store navigation to product information, online merchants can significantly improve visitor-to-customer conversion rates.

Making Navigation More Obvious

Simple and obvious (natural) navigation through the product catalog is a key to converting more visitors into customers. If a customer is experiencing difficulties finding products in the catalog, there is a big chance the customer will choose to leave the site and try to find similar products somewhere else.

Category Tree

Products in osCommerce are usually grouped in categories. Categories can have child categories, forming a category tree. Products in osCommerce may belong to one or several categories, making the navigation either easier or, on the contrary, more cumbersome depending on how well the category tree is built.

The category name would usually describe products that belong to that particular category. The category name should not be made too long, otherwise it can break the layout of the osCommerce category tree. Having said that, for the sake of SEO it's better to use related keywords in category names, so that search engines sould associate the keywords from the category name with the corresponding list of products.

Even though it would be enough for customers if each sub-category used its own name, for the sake of SEO it is better to include the name of a category of higher level into the name of a sub-category. For example, a website that sells home appliances would rather have the following categories: *Cookers – Range Cookers – Electric Range Cookers* than *Cookers – Range – Electric*. This approach will make category names look similar to the queries that prospective customers use in search engines to find products sold online on the Internet.

Tree Levels

Categories in the tree are split into levels. There are usually a certain number of top categories, and then each one can have its own child categories, and so on.

It's recommended to have as few levels in the category tree as possible to avoid making the navigation process too long and confusing for customers. At the same time, it should be made easy for customers to find a product within the category; if there are too many products in one category, the product search process will become too complex. The number of levels in the category tree clearly depends on the number of products in the catalog, and of course on how diverse the product range is.

Most customers would prefer only one level of categories in the category tree, but this can only work well for relatively small product catalogs, or for product catalogs with very similar products. Where a bigger list of products is split only into several main categories without any sub-categories, it's suggested to introduce alternative methods of filtering and navigation, because otherwise the customer may be confused with too many products in each category.

On the average, the category tree should contain two or three levels of categories. This is convenient for customers, and also allows for organizing a Product List of up to several thousand items. Of course, it depends on how many products are put into each category, and on how many child categories are in each category. To make the navigation easier, it's not recommended to put more than a dozen sub-categories into a category.

At the same time, the category tree should not have excessive branches, because adding sub-categories just for the sake of it will not make navigation easier; rather it will limit the length of the list of products available to the customer in categories of upper levels and therefore, negatively affect online sales.

Online Sales without the Category Tree

In certain cases, the category tree may not be required at all — this happens either when there are only a few products in the product catalog that can all be displayed on the same page, or when all the products in the product catalog are similar and cannot be split into different categories; but then other filters and navigation elements should be used.

Sometimes the category tree is so long, or has so many levels, that it would bring more confusion into the navigation process rather than make it easier for customers. In those cases, it may make sense to stop using the tree of categories, and offer an alternative filter and navigation facilities to the customers instead.

For example, a properly built Advanced Search facility can do just fine if the tree of categories appears to be too long or too cumbersome.

Products in Multiple Categories

Products in osCommerce can be assigned to more than one category. A complete copy of the product can be created in the Administration panel of osCommerce, or the same product can be linked to more than one category.

Having the same product in more than one category improves its visibility to customers, and improves its chances to be bought. At the same time, having too many products in several categories can make the category tree not so useful, and will mean the current categories do not describe the products that are included into them in the best way.

When does it make sense to include the same product into more than one category?

- When one category actually contains a part of product range from the second category, but doesn't belong to it directly. For example, a website that sells MP3 players may contain a special top-level category "Headphones", but also its "Hard drive players" category may contain a sub-category called "Compatible headphones". In that case, the "Compatible headphones" sub-category would contain products that are also a part of the top level "Headphones" category. This way of building the category tree and organizing products in it will help customers find headphones for a specific type/model of MP3 player, rather than searching directly for headphones in the general category.

- It's also possible to use multiple categories to promote products. Products would belong to certain categories that describe them best, but also to a special category called "Best selling" or "Featured" that would only contain some products and would effectively mark/highlight/promote those products better than the others. For example, an online store that specializes in selling watches can have several top categories like "Running & Sports Watches", "Ladies Leisure Watches", "Men's Leisure Watches", and also two special categories called "Best selling Watches" and "Featured Watches" that would include only some products from all those categories. One has to be very careful when putting the same product into multiple categories because of SEO. If done properly, search engines will only index one, the most important, link to the Product Information page. Effectively, this means those additional categories could be restricted to stop search engines indexing them by mentioning them in, for example, `robots.txt` file.

Alternative Categories

Some online stores may need to use a special alternative category tree to ease the navigation.

This feature doesn't come with the default installation of osCommerce, and would have to be implemented separately. Or instead of adding yet another copy of the category tree, two top categories can be chosen to contain a category tree each. Then, the category tree box in the front end would need to be modified to display only sub-categories of one of the two top categories chosen earlier. So effectively, having both category trees still managed in a regular osCommerce way in the back end, the online store will get two separate category trees in the front end.

Online merchants can get sample code with plenty of useful information in Monika Mathé's book *Deep Inside osCommerce: The Cookbook* published by Packt Publishing (ISBN 978-1-84719-090-1).

Alternative categories can be used in many ways. For example, an online store that sells cakes, pastries, and cookies could have two category trees. One would contain common categories that would split the product catalog by product type, like "Cakes", "Confections", "Cookies", "Deserts", "Dietary", etc.

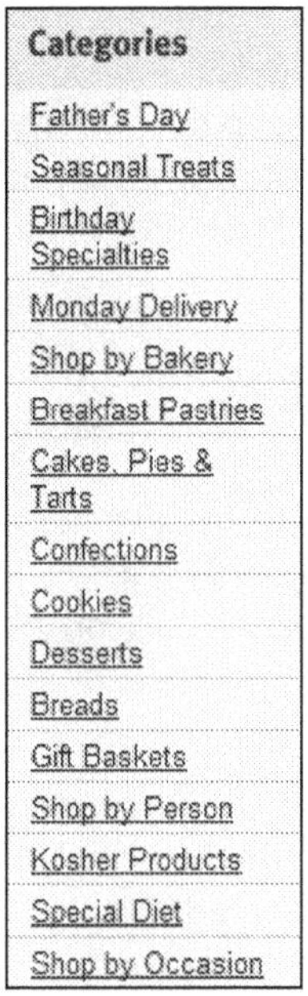

Categories

Father's Day

Seasonal Treats

Birthday
Specialties

Monday Delivery

Shop by Bakery

Breakfast Pastries

Cakes, Pies &
Tarts

Confections

Cookies

Desserts

Breads

Gift Baskets

Shop by Person

Kosher Products

Special Diet

Shop by Occasion

The second category tree would group certain products from various categories by the occasion they are good for, like "Birthday", "Wedding", "Anniversary", "Thanksgiving Day", and so on.

**Shop by
Occasion**

Autumn
Celebrations

Christmas Gifts

Easter Treats

Halloween Treats

July 4th Desserts

Mother's Day
Gifts

St. Patrick's Day

Thanksgiving
Desserts

Valentine Sweets

Shop by Brand

Depending on the nature of products being offered online, brands (or manufacturers) can be more important or better known to prospective customers than categories, and it can be more convenient for customers to navigate through the product catalog using brand filters than categories.

osCommerce has built-in support for product manufacturers (brands), and can display a filter by brand in the front end. This functionality can be extended further by:

- Introducing brand information pages, where brand marketing description is displayed, along with logotypes, and also where all products that belong to that brand are listed; alternatively on such pages there could be links placed to the corresponding product listings (usually to the Advanced Search Results page): http://addons.oscommerce.com/info/4836

- Implementing a combined filter by brand AND category, which is a modification of the default filter on the Product Listing page; when on the category details page, besides sub-categories and products the online store lists all brands of products that belong to that category, and when on the brand information page the online store lists all categories of products that belong to that brand.

The "Shop by brand" feature doesn't only make the navigation and product selection process easier for customers, but is also beneficial for SEO as it associates well known brands with categories and individual products of online store.

In some cases, brand navigation can have more than one level. Then, the top level brands (like for example, "Casio"), will have sub-brands (like for example, "Casio Baby-G" and "Casio Futurist").

If a significant number of products belong to each brand in the online product catalog, the "Shop by brand" feature can evolve into so called "brand stores". Each major brand gets its own front end (or mini-store).

The following osCommerce contribution could be of help when implementing the mini-stores functionality: `http://addons.oscommerce.com/info/1730`.

A special sub-domain or domain name can be given to a brand store to better explain to customers and search engines what sort of products are offered by the brand store. For better brand recognition, even the look and feel of the brand store can be changed to match the look and feel usually associated with the selected brand or with the corresponding products.

Additional Filters

Along with grouping by category or brand, products can be grouped or filtered in several other ways, making it easier for customers to find what exactly they are interested in and what they can afford buying.

Such filters can be used to fine-tune search results, making the selection of products in a category or brand narrower.

Filters by Price

Filter by product price is one of the most popular and obvious to use for customers among additional filters. It allows the Administration of the online store to set up several price levels, and then the customers can choose this or that price level to get the list of products within the price interval.

This helps customers limit their product search results to those products they can afford, or to those products they think are good enough as their price lies in a certain price range.

It's important to note that price intervals can be different depending on the type of products that are sold online. For example, an online store that sells MP3 players and game consoles would most probably have two different price interval sets for those two product types.

Also, to make them look nicer (or as it's sometimes described—friendlier), price filters would very much depend on the currency chosen should the online store support multiple currencies.

Price filters can be added to one of the side columns:

or put in the top of the middle area of the page with te Product Listing—in the latter case it will make sense to make them applicable to the specific product range only. There is an osCommerce contribution that implements price filters functionality: `http://addons.oscommerce.com/info/1276`.

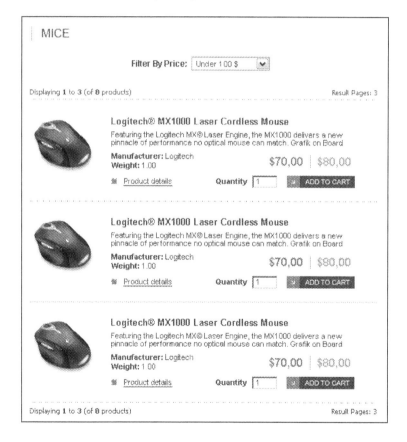

Filter by Free Stock

Customers do not usually want to wait several days until their orders are dispatched. Next-day delivery is the preferred option of most online buyers. If the online store holds its own stock of certain products, the orders can be dispatched quicker if all products in the order are available in stock, and no purchase orders need to be sent to suppliers.

Filter by free stock is a special feature that filters the entire product catalog and only displays products that are available in free stock. Actually, products do not have to be sold from a warehouse that belongs to the online merchant, it can be a supplier's warehouse too; what really matters is how quickly the order can be delivered to the customer and correspondingly, if all ordered products are in stock.

Filter by free stock can be applied to the Product Listing within a certain category, search results, or to the entire product catalog. In the latter case, filter by stock doesn't only filter products out, but also some categories where there is no product in free stock, to avoid the situations where customers browse through empty categories in the category tree.

There is an osCommerce contribution that implements this functionality:

`http://addons.oscommerce.com/info/2805.`

Filters by Additional Properties

Products of many types are very well described by technical specifications, or by a set of properties and property values. Sometimes, it makes it much easier for customers to understand how a product can address their needs to look into its technical specification rather than its marketing description.

Additional properties and their values can be added into the database and assigned to products in order to better describe those products, and highlight the most important features and specifications of the products.

For example, for a website that sells TV sets, one of the main properties of a product will be its size in inches—for example up to 20", up to 29", up to 39", up to 49", and over 50". For a website that sells digital cameras, one of the most important product properties would be the number of megapixels—up to 3, up to 5, 6, 7, 8, 9, and over 9 megapixels. MP3 players may have two key properties that define them (besides other additional properties that each and every product may have). Those would be memory capacity in GB (under 2GB, up to 8GB, up to 30GB, up to 60GB, and over 60GB) and type (music, music + photo, music + photo + video).

Properties (or features) should also be well described themselves, to give the customer an idea what actually this or that feature can be used for, and what this or that value of a parameter means. In the example with MP3 players, the description for the "capacity" property could tell the customers about different types of data storage solutions used to store audio, video files, and images in MP3 players, and description of each particular value of the "capacity" property (like 2GB, 8GB, etc.) could tell customers about how many songs, on the average, could be stored in the memory of such MP3 players.

Therefore, on the Product Information page, in the list of properties (or features), the names of the features can be made clickable, and a specially designed pop-up window with detailed description of the property or property value can be displayed to help customers to make their choice.

Properties and property values can also be used as filters. Such filters would be applied to Product Listings (either category or search results) and the online store would extract properties and their values from all listed products. Filters would be built dynamically depending on the products that are in the listing, and would allow for narrowing the Product Listing to just a few products matching the selected filters.

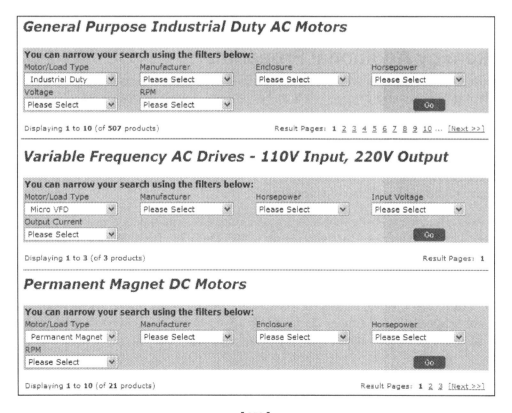

Product Listing

The Product Listing is an important element of an osCommerce-based online store that either lists products or sub-categories of a certain category, or search results. The way products appear in the Product Listing, and also the information given about each product in the listing, can affect the customer's decision to place an order online.

Top Offers

When a Product Listing page first opens to the customer, the customer first of all sees products displayed at the beginning of the listing. The customer will more likely add one of the products displayed in the top of the listing to the Shopping Cart than a product located in the middle of the page or in its very bottom or on one of the following pages of product listing, if all those products are very similar, simply because the customer doesn't need to scroll the page down or switch to another page of the Product Listing to see those top products.

This works very similarly to how search results in search engines work — the top several links in the search results listing have more chances to be explored by users than all the other links because of the way the page is constructed and because of the way the customers look at the page.

Products that are more often displayed in the top of the product listing have more chances to be sold. It is possible to improve the profits generated by an osCommerce online store by manually defining products that will be displayed in the top of the Product Listing.

It makes sense to put products with the highest margin (the difference between the cost price and sale price) that are currently in stock to the top of the product listing. This way customers will be buying such products more often, and even though the turnover of the online store may remain the same, the generated profits will grow higher.

Such products can be also highlighted with a certain color or special icons to make them easier to notice even if the customer changes the sort order from the default one.

There are at least two methods by which products can be selected in the osCommerce Administration panel. First of all, it's possible to install a special contribution that would allow marking certain products as "Featured". Corresponding contributions can be downloaded from osCommerce website at `http://addons.oscommerce.com/info/2283` and `http://addons.oscommerce.com/info/4066`.

Secondly, it is possible to employ a more flexible solution, and instead of having featured and non-featured products, have a special sort order (or importance index) assigned to each product, so that products with higher sort order (or the more important ones) get closer to the top of the Product Listing independent of whether it's the category Product Listing or a search results Product Listing. A special contribution for this can be downloaded from `http://addons.oscommerce.com/info/911`.

The second method is better as it allows for a more accurate and flexible management of the product catalog.

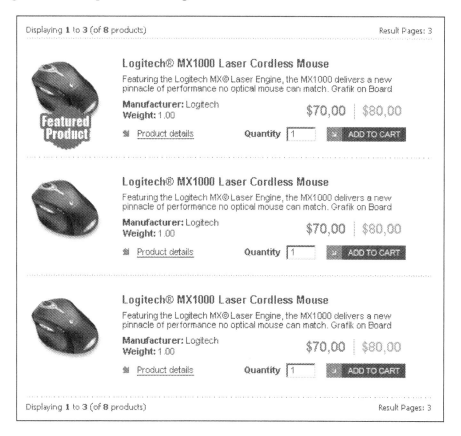

New Products

Some customers may be interested in the latest additions to the product catalog, especially if the online store sells some very tangible products or products where updates to the product range happen often.

Products recently added to the product catalog can be highlighted as "New products" either with a color and/or a special icon. This highlighting can be preserved in any Product Listing so that newly added products would be easy to find on all pages.

Sometimes an online merchant would like to have some of the previously added products highlighted as "New" either because those products sell very well, or there have been many additions to the catalog recently, but not all of them were so important compared to the products added to the catalog just before the latest additions.

In such cases the "New" flag can be made editable at the product level in the osCommerce Administration panel, so that the online merchant has full control over the new products. Sample code and more information on how to implement this and other useful features can be found in Monika Mathé's *Deep Inside osCommerce: The Cookbook* published by Packt Publishing (ISBN 978-1-84719-090-1).

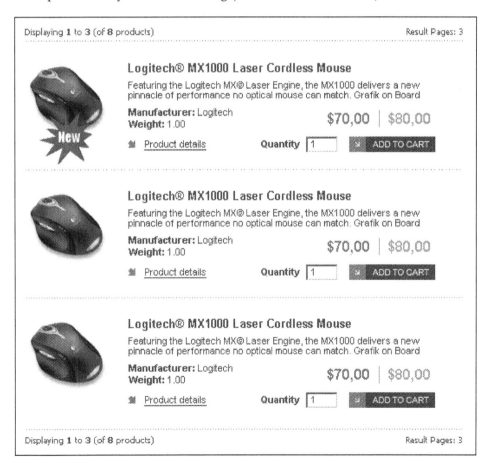

Expected Products and Pre-Order

Products do not necessarily have to be in stock when the customer goes through the Product Listings. Some products may not even have been introduced to the market by the time the customer sees them in the Product Listing and wants to buy/pre-order them.

Instead of "Buy now" or "Add to cart" such products should have the "Pre-order" facility.

Also, the customers should be told if some products are currently out of stock, and, if it's possible to say, when the products are likely to be back in stock.

Sorting Options

The osCommerce Product Listing is sorted by name by default. Products can also be sorted manually by the Administration of the online store if the corresponding feature is implemented.

osCommerce allows for the sorting option to be set by customers. A customer can click the header of one of the columns (product name, price, date added to the product catalog, etc.) and the product listing will be re-ordered accordingly.

But what if the product listing page doesn't have any columns, or if the customer wants to see, for example, the best selling products first in the Product Listing?

In that case, a special drop-down box with sort options can be placed on the Product Listing page to make it easier for customers to re-arrange the Product Listing in a way that makes it easier for them to find the product they are interested in.

Special sorting options may include:

- Default sorting (either by product number assigned automatically in the database, or by the default sort order set manually in the Administration panel)
- Best selling first
- Newest first
- Oldest first

- Cheapest first
- Cheapest last
- Name A-Z
- Name Z-A
- Brands A-Z
- Brands Z-A

Although there are contributions like `http://addons.oscommerce.com/info/4312` that implement some of the sorting options mentioned above, certain sorting options may require extensive modifications in the database queries and scripts to bring up Product Listings.

Search

The search facility is one of the crucial features of an online store that can either help the online merchant improve the turnover, or, should it be implemented in a way that doesn't bring the expected results in response to customers' queries, cause frustration and negatively affect sale figures.

Search is especially important when an online store has a large number of products in the catalog, and/or products cannot be easily sorted by categories and the search feature takes the place of navigation by categories.

Quick Search and Advanced Search

The osCommerce solution supports Quick Search and Advanced Search features.

The Quick Search feature usually allows for searching by one or several keywords. The search is against product name or description database fields.

Those keywords can be entered in the Quick Search edit box in the front end, and the search results are returned in the format of a Product Listing page where each product matches the search criteria. This is very much like the Advanced Search results page (which actually is the same for both Advanced Search and Quick Search), except that when using the Advanced Search feature more conditions can be specified, like lowest and highest price, categories and manufacturers of products to be found, and dates when the products were added to the product catalog.

The Quick Search feature can be improved in several ways:

- Filter by category can be added to the Quick Search box, allowing customers to refine their search results in advance `http://addons.oscommerce.com/info/2708`. The keyword edit box can be made to accept not only keywords and key phrases, but also expressions with logical operators: AND, OR, NOT; this can be extended further by making the keyword edit box accept key phrases enclosed in quotes, effectively enabling the feature of searching products by the whole key phrase (and not its parts) in product names and descriptions. While the search help window suggests it, the search doesn't really work as expected for the AND/OR logical operators.

- The auto-suggest feature can be implemented (as was described in the previous chapters) to make it easier for customers to specify the correct product names or product model numbers if the customer only knows a part `http://addons.oscommerce.com/info/4144/`.

These manipulations with the keyword edit box are also applicable to the Advanced Search feature. As a matter of fact, search by the date when certain products were added to the catalog is used very rarely by the customers, so it may make sense to remove that filter from the Advanced Search page in order to make it look compact and easier to use. Also, filters that allow for searching by category and manufacturer can be improved to allow multiple selections of both manufacturers and categories.

It can be improved further by adding filters by property values if the product catalog has support for these.

Yet another improvement is related rather to the search results page; if the customer used the Advanced Search feature, it would make further navigation and searching easier for customer if the specified search criteria were displayed (and were made editable) on the search results page and it was possible to change the search criteria in order to refine the search results. This can be achieved by installing the following contribution: `http://addons.oscommerce.com/info/4111`.

It is also possible to highlight the search terms in product names and descriptions to make it easier for customers to locate the most suitable products in search results. The following osCommerce contribution could be used: `http://addons.oscommerce.com/info/1086`. Interestingly enough, there also exists a special contribution that highlights keywords on your online store page when the user comes from search engines, such as Google or Yahoo!: `http://addons.oscommerce.com/info/3820`.

SEARCH

Search: [   ] 🔍 SEARCH

☐ Search In Product Descriptions

Categories: [All Categories ▼]   Manufacturers: [Logitech ▼]

☑ Include Subcategories

Price From: [70.00]   Price To: [80.00]

Date From: [10/15/2006]   Date To: [11/18/2006]

Displaying 1 to 2 (of 8 products)   Result Pages: 4

Logitech® MX1000 Laser Cordless Mouse

Featuring the Logitech MX® Laser Engine, the MX1000 delivers a new
pinnacle of performance no optical mouse can match. Grafik on Board

Manufacturer: Logitech
Weight: 1.00 $70,00 $80,00

🗶 Product details   Quantity [1]   ↴ ADD TO CART

Logitech® MX1000 Laser Cordless Mouse

Featuring the Logitech MX® Laser Engine, the MX1000 delivers a new
pinnacle of performance no optical mouse can match. Grafik on Board

Manufacturer: Logitech
Weight: 1.00 $70,00 $80,00

🗶 Product details   Quantity [1]   ↴ ADD TO CART

Displaying 1 to 2 (of 8 products)   Result Pages: 4

Relevancy of Search Results

Relevancy of the search results to the search criteria is one of the keys to customer satisfaction with the search feature of an online store. The customer is more likely to buy products if they are relevant to the specified search criteria. The customer is more likely to notice such products if they are brought up to the very top of the Product Listing on the search results page.

Therefore, the Product Listing on the search results page can be improved by ordering it according to the relevancy of products to the specified search criteria, by default.

In a very simple situation, a more relevant product will be considered as one that has more occurrences of the specified search terms in product name, and then product description. Product name here is more important than product description, similarly to how this works in popular search engines.

The search feature of an osCommerce online store has to be extensively modified in order to have Product Listing sorted by relevancy on the search results page.

Found Nothing—What Should We Do?

If there are no matching products in the product catalog, osCommerce displays a default and quite an unfriendly message telling the customer about that and suggesting trying different search criteria.

It is still possible to improve this default functionality though, to make it more helpful to customers:

- Search criteria can be displayed on the search results page to make it easier for the customer to change them and try searching for products again: http://addons.oscommerce.com/info/4111

- A special text message can be displayed on the search results page to inform the customer about successful searches performed by other customers that contained similar keywords: http://addons.oscommerce.com/info/1266

- A short list of best selling (or featured) products can be displayed on the search results page, in case the customer would be interested in them.

- Product information in the database can be extended by an additional keywords field that would contain certain keywords that the customers are likely to use when searching for that particular product (additional keywords that can describe the product, incorrectly spelled product name, model, or most significant keywords, etc.); the standard osCommerce search feature can be changed to use product name, product description, AND the additional keywords field; this will increase the probability of finding products desired by customer in the product catalog: http://addons.oscommerce.com/info/4685

- Sometimes customers make a mistake while typing in a keyword or product name or model number. There is a special facility in MySQL that allows for matching two strings of text (or rather two words) if they sound similar. This feature of the MySQL database can be used in osCommerce to bring up products that have a product name or model number similar to the entered keyword, even though its not possible to establish a direct match between the keyword and product name or model number.

Product Information

Information about individual products is what customers pay most attention to when they choose which product to buy online. The more complete that information is, and the more attractive it looks to the customer, the more the chances are that the customer would place an online order.

Product Name and Description

The product's name is what most customers would be looking for in their searches; it's what describes and identifies a product in most cases.

The product name should be descriptive enough to give customers an idea about the functions of the product or about its features. It may also contain category name and /or manufacturer/brand name if it's a suitable product to use the brand name as one of the selling features.

However, there are some products (like printer cartridges for example) that may be better described by their model numbers, and then these should be also included into product name.

There are products that are very well described by their features. For example computer products, like laptops may have their manufacturer, model number, CPU, RAM, and HDD characteristics included into the product name to make it easier for customers to choose the product they want.

The product catalog benefits from introducing short descriptions for products. Short descriptions can be used in the Product Listing and on the Product Information page, and would usually contain a very short description of the reason why this or that product is ideal to address customer's needs.

It would usually contain description of the most important "selling points". If the online store sells MP3 player, the short description may contain weight and dimensions information, amount of memory included, and supported formats. If the online store sells natural cosmetics, the product's short description may tell the customers what exactly the product does, what it improves, and how it can be used. An online store selling home appliances would put information about the product's dimensions, energy consumption level, noise, warranty, and some main/unique features into the short description.

The product's long description is usually displayed on the Product Information page only, and contains the so called "marketing text"—i.e. besides the fact that it should describe the product in detail, it should also contain certain parts that will be calling customers to action, to buy the product online. When the customer is looking for a product, the customer is often looking for a solution to address certain needs. Therefore, not only features of the product should be placed into long description, but also information about how these or those needs of the customer can be satisfied if the customer was to purchase the product.

If properly prepared, the product's long description can become one of the strongest salling points. HTML tags can be used in the product's long description to highlight certain parts of it. It's not only useful to draw customer's attention to the most important features or solutions provided by the product, but also for SEO, as search engines would also look for highlighted parts of the product description in the first turn.

Technical specifications are important for certain types of products as they describe the very features or ingredients of the product better than anything else. Computer parts or complete computer systems, mobile phones, audio and video equipment, machinery, even nutrition products, etc.—products where the customer may be very well educated about technical characteristics or ingredients of the desired product, can be very well described by the product's technical specification/ingredients (of course along with more marketing-oriented long description). Those specifications can be displayed on a special tab of the Product Information page, and can also be even used to compare two or more products, or to filter products in Product Listings.

Additional Images and Image Galleries

Product images should be big and sharp enough to give the customer the best impression about the look and feel and features of each product. When using images of different sizes, each thumbnail or bigger image ideally should be checked to ensure the maximum possible quality of the picture.

Of course, the proportions of the original image should be kept when creating a thumbnail of a bigger image.

Additional product images can be used either to demonstrate some very specific features or details of the product, or to demonstrate different ways in which the product can be used.

Because the customer cannot just explore the product as in a regular shop, additional product pictures that let the customer see the full details of the product can help the customer make the decision to buy the product. Also, seeing different ways in which the product can be used (similar to the "serving suggestions" that one can see on boxes with food products in the supermarkets) can help the customer to decide whether the product could be used to address some of the customer's needs.

These contributions allow for multiple product images, and also for full size images and thumbnails associated with a product: `http://addons.oscommerce.com/info/1611` and `http://addons.oscommerce.com/info/1289`.

Image galleries with slide show, where the images either change automatically, or the main image can be easily changed by moving the mouse cursor over the thumbnails, are an efficient way to demonstrate a product's additional images, especially if the customer is not yet aware of all the features of the product or of how the product could be used.

Image galleries could be implemented using a script called "lightbox". More information about lighbox and how to use it to gain the best presentation effect can be found at `http://www.huddletogether.com/projects/lightbox2/`. There is a contribution for osCommerce available from `http://addons.oscommerce.com/info/5236` that also implements a lightbox feature for enlarged product images. The lightbox solution makes the most of it when it's employed to display a set of several images, so it may make sense to combine it with any of the contributions or custom-built solutions used to allow for several additional images per osCommerce product.

Associated Video Clips

Sometimes the most efficient way to describe some products, especially the ones that contain plenty of features that are supposedly new to the target audience, is to include links to the related video clips into product description.

Such video clips can be provided by the product manufacturer, by independent reviewers, or created "in-house". They can be hosted on the same server where the online store is hosted, or on any other web server to spare web traffic and reduce the workload of the main web server. Video format should be the most common one, so that all customers could watch the video clips. It is recommended to include an embedded video player into the web page so that even those customers who do not have compatible video player software installed on their computer could watch the clip. The following contribution will allow for displaying embedded video clips on the product information page: `http://addons.oscommerce.com/info/4415`.

Manufacturer Information (Brochures) and Category Information (Buying Guides)

As with video clips, some manufacturers supply detailed product information, marketing description, technical specification, warranty description, and even product manuals as downloadable brochures (most often in PDF format).

Links to those brochures can be added to the Product Information page, so that customers could download brochures to their local computers and read all the information about products offline, and also show to their friends, partners, etc.

Buying guides can be created for product categories. Those buying guides can not only be made available for download from a special page, but also be added to the Product Information pages of corresponding individual products. Like brochures supplied by manufacturers, buying guides will often come in PDF format.

It is considered to be useful to place a link to a website where users can download special viewer software for PDF files on a web page that contains links to PDF files to ensure that all customers can read manufacturer brochures and buying guides.

Product Reviews

Product ratings may not be very useful to the customers as they do not really describe other customers' experience with the product. Reviews given by other customers to the product often play an important role in affecting a customer's decision to buy or not to buy a particular product.

Product reviews can be also given by third-party experts in that type of products, or simply by the online store team itself, but in such cases, the reviews should be marked accordingly to clearly identify the reviewer.

Reviews are easier to notice if placed on the Product Information page. If there are several reviews and/or some of them are relatively large, a brief summary of such reviews can be placed on the Product Information page along with the link to the page where the customer can read those reviews in detail. Of course, it should be possible for the customer to add the product to the Shopping Cart from the dedicated reviews page.

To display reviews on the Product Information page, online merchants may want to use this osCommerce contribution: `http://addons.oscommerce.com/info/3340`.

If there are no reviews for products given by the customers of an online store yet, it is possible to use one of the external review databases and extract reviews given by customers who bought the same products elsewhere.

Product Price

Product price is one of the most important bits of information about the product that most often affects a customer's decision to buy or not to buy the product online.

But, interestingly enough, some online stores would prefer to hide the price of certain products for various reasons. Sometimes it is done to make the customer call the sales team and let the sales team give the customer a quote according to customer's exact requirements (for example, in the case of having products that come in various configurations). Sometimes it is done because the supplier (or manufacturer of certain products) would not like the price to be available in the online stores and would simply forbid the retailers to disclose the price to customers on the website.

An osCommerce contribution could be installed to allow for this functionality. It can be found at http://addons.oscommerce.com/info/2500.

Either way, it is recommended to put a free phone number that customers could dial to check the price and delivery terms with the sales team. One obvious inconvenience for customers, besides the necessity to dial the phone number, is that one of the main functions of an online store, to be open to the customers 24/7, ceases to exist in that case as only a few online stores would have a sale team available 24/7.

Product price may or may not contain tax. For selling to the public, it's recommended to display price with tax in larger font, and below price without tax with the corresponding note. But online stores that mostly sell to businesses would rather display price without tax first, and price with tax second, using smaller font size.

Often to make the price look attractive to customers, online merchants display the recommended retail price (RRP) (or it is sometimes called Manufacturer's suggested sale price i.e. SRP or MSRP) and then the actual price the customer would be paying followed by the amount of savings compared to RRP. Adding an RRP price in osCommerce is relatively easy; there are contributions available to download (for example http://addons.oscommerce.com/info/3574) that can make it possible to enter RRP and current price for each product. Savings are better displayed in percent, so that if the store price is $8 and the actual saving is only $2, it may still be a significant savings of 20% of a $10 RRP. The special price feature can made to work in the same way, displaying the savings in percent.

If the online store provides quantity-based discounts on certain products, it makes sense to highlight such products in the Product Listing, and also put information about quantity-based prices on the Product Information page. Again, the percent savings will make a difference and more clearly demonstrate how much the customer can save when buying several products at once. A special table with quantities and corresponding prices can be displayed on the Product Information page.

There are at least two osCommerce contributions that could be used to allow for this functionality. Those are `http://addons.oscommerce.com/info/4658` and `http://addons.oscommerce.com/info/2269`.

In order to reward the customer for buying several different products at once, the online store can give the customer a discount based on current special offer. Special offer prices can be entered for certain products, and can replace the normal store price for those products when the order total exceeds a certain amount. Information about special offers and promotions and also about the required order total for special offers and promotions to be activated can be displayed on corresponding product pages, and also can be gathered together on a special dedicated page where all currently available offers are listed.

Stock Levels

Product stock levels can be displayed on the Product Listing and Product Information pages. It's especially important to give customers a clear picture of the current stock levels if the business model of the online store assumes dispatching orders from its own warehouse or ordering products from suppliers first and then sending them directly to the customers, or first receiving them in its own warehouse and dispatching to the customers thereafter.

For business customers, stock levels would ideally be displayed as the exact numbers of items in stock, as business customers tend to buy multiple products at a time.

For consumers, exact stock levels do not have to be displayed. Instead, icons indicating stock status (for example, green for when there's enough quantity in stock, yellow for products with limited/critical stock levels, and red for products out of stock) can be used on Product Listing and Product Information pages.

A special contribution can be downloaded from `http://addons.oscommerce.com/info/968` and installed to allow for this functionality.

The date when products are likely to be back in stock can be displayed alongside the corresponding icon/zero stock level, so customers can see it and come back to the online store on that date to purchase the desired products. Or if the customer is ready to pre-order the product, this will give the customer an idea of when it's possible to expect the product to be actually delivered. In that case, the date when products are likely to be back in stock should be included into the order confirmation email and into printed/downloadable documents, such as the invoice.

Additional Features

Besides improving Product Information and Product Listings, product catalog can be improved further by implementing several additional features. Those features are related to product in this or that way, and can be used to make it easier for customers to order products online.

Recently Viewed Products

The list of recently viewed products can be displayed in one of the side columns. Five to ten recently viewed product names can be displayed in an information box, with links to the corresponding Product Information pages.

If the product catalog contains a number of similar products, customers would often like to be able to choose between them. Also, this feature gives customers an opportunity to easily go back to the previously viewed products no matter how many different clicks "ago" the customer was actually viewing the Product Information page.

Also, to increase the turnover, the online store can list several products from the most recently viewed categories. Products that belong to the categories the customer expressed interest in are more likely to be sold than other ones.

osCommerce contributions that provide this sort of functionality can be found at: `http://addons.oscommerce.com/info/3204` and `http://addons.oscommerce.com/info/1567`.

There are marketing solutions that analyze customers' browsing history before the customers get to the purchase, and arranges products accordingly for further customers.

These solutions determine similarities in products viewed by customers who placed online orders. Then products bought by customers are associated with products customers viewed before the purchase. And products bought can be automatically suggested by the online store to those customers who currently view products viewed before the purchase by other customers.

Report Better Price

Many online stores are willing to accept the challenge of the discounted prices of their competitors. In order to demonstrate to customers that most of their competitor's prices can be beaten, a corresponding banner or text message can be displayed on one of the pages of the online store.

A special form can be displayed once a customer clicks the Report Better Price banner. That form would collect customer's details (or would take current customer account details if the customer is logged in), and ask the customer to confirm the name of the competitor and the lower price.

Online merchants may want to install the following osCommerce contribution to have this functionality implemented in their online stores:
`http://addons.oscommerce.com/info/4278`.

Price Monitoring Feature

Sometimes a customer can't afford to pay the product's price, even if the product is exactly what this customer is looking for. As product price changes from time to time — there's still a way to sell the product to the customer.

The customer can be invited to leave an email address (or other contact information) and specify the maximum affordable price the customer is ready to pay for the product. In that case, the online store could monitor product's price, and as soon as it reaches the level specified by the customer, the online store would notify the customer about that by sending an automatic email, or by notifying the Administration of the online store so that the customer could be given a phone call.

Depending on the margin set on that particular product, the online store may want to sell the product to the customer for a discounted price right away.

Going International

International online trading requires certain modifications and improvements in the online store in general, and in the product catalog in particular.

Auto-Detection

First of all, the online store should be able to detect automatically where the customer is opening the website pages from, and either propose to the customer switching to a separate front end dedicated to the region the customer is located in, or switch the language and currency settings automatically.

It's good to know that default osCommerce installation already has this facility built in. It tries to automatically select the most appropriate language based on the browser locale settings, which sometimes leads to improper presentation of the online store, as osCommerce may determine the customer's default language and find the same language registered in the database, so when the customer opens the online store, osCommerce selects the language according to the customer's default locale even if osCommerce texts have never been properly translated into the selected language. The customer may then see categories and products without names and descriptions, pages without textual content or with strange system variables instead, etc.

Therefore, it's recommended to remove all extra languages from osCommerce database during the set up, to ensure that customers can only see the website and product catalog in one of the maintained languages.

Descriptions

Product descriptions should be provided in the supported languages. Descriptions in default language can be also used, but then not all international customers would be able to buy products online from the website.

Product descriptions should be professionally translated into other languages. It's not acceptable to use any auto-translation tools, because instead of the properly prepared marketing and features description, international customers will see very unprofessionally looking texts. It's not only bad for the image of the online store, but also leads to mistakes and misunderstandings about the features of certain products.

Currencies and Prices

Product price is usually specified in the default currency in osCommerce, and then, should the customer switch to another currency, the osCommerce online store would take the current conversion rates and calculate the new price in the new currency accordingly.

Depending on the marketing strategy, currency exchange rate can be specified manually by the online store owner, or updated automatically from a website that publishes this information.

osCommerce has support for both manual currency exchange rate correction and for automatic download of currency exchange rates from such websites.

To avoid manual interaction, the update of currency exchange rate can be scheduled to be performed on a daily basis.

Yet another way to manage prices in different currencies would be to set up a special feature that would allow for setting prices in different currencies on the per product basis. This feature would allow for having "friendly" prices for products in all currencies, not depending on the currency exchange rate.

For example, a product that costs $9.99 might normally cost £5.01. In the case of "friendly" prices, its price in British Pounds would be set to £4.99. "Friendly" prices help selling products to international customers. The corresponding contribution is available at `http://addons.oscommerce.com/info/4445`.

Shipping and Payment Methods

Shipping and payment methods can be different for different countries and regions.

Therefore, the online store needs to be configured to avoid any confusion with this or that payment or shipping method not available in certain regions but still displayed during the checkout process as one of the options. For example, ground shipping methods should not be available for deliveries to Europe when the online store delivers products from its warehouse in the USA. As shipping methods in osCommerce can be linked to corresponding zones, this becomes a matter of proper configuration of zones and shipping and payment methods in the back end of the online store.

Also, depending on the product characteristics (price, weight, dimensions), certain products may not be available for delivery in certain countries or regions. Information about whether there are any restrictions on selling certain products in certain countries should be made available to the customers on the Product Information page to avoid further confusion and frustration when the product is added to the Shopping Cart and the customer finds out only on the Checkout pages that the order can not be delivered because of certain products being a part of it.

Summary

In this chapter, we have reviewed various ways to improve online sales by improving the product catalog. We concentrated on improving navigation and making it more obvious to the customers, and enhancing search facilities by introducing additional filters. We considered various ways to improve the Product Listing and Product Information pages.

In the next chapter, we will discuss how and why order values can be increased, and what effect it has on the turnover and profit figures.

8

Increasing Order Value

Increasing the values of online orders automatically increases the turnover of an online store, because the number of customers remains the same but the average order amount increases. Profit figures also increase, though the profitability of the business may drop, and the margin the online store makes on orders with increased value may drop because incentive discounts are often offered to customers to make them buy more.

But increasing order values doesn't necessarily have to negatively affect the margins at the same time. Because the value of the order can be increased not only by providing discounts to customers who buy many products simultaneously, but also by making the customers aware of related products that are likely to be of interest to them, or by selling extra services to customers. Then, the margin that the online store makes on an average order doesn't have to change as customers will be just buying more products and services at regular prices.

While dealing with the website, the customer should not feel too much pressure to buy several units of the same product, several different but related products, or some more expensive products, because otherwise the customer may just leave the online store.

Just as in the real-life situation at, for example, a farm market, the seller needs to know when to stop bombarding a customer with more options and more products and concentrate on making a sale.

There can be different reasons why the customer would choose to buy more than planned from the beginning, but in any case the customer should be left happy about the purchase made. Increasing order values should put both the customer and the online merchant in a win-win situation.

Increasing Order Values for Customers

For a customer, the value of the order is increased if the customer gets more than anticipated and also gets products or services that can be of use in the future. The customer should never be sold products or services that will not be of use or will not make the customer happy about spending money with the online store—because otherwise the customer will not buy from the same online store again in the future, and will not recommend the online store to any friends or colleagues.

The order value is increased if the customer gets certain products in addition to the products originally added to the shopping basket, maybe with a certain discount. Or if some additional services (like free extra warranty for specific products or special—free, faster, etc.—delivery terms) become available to the customer once the order total exceeds certain amount.

If an online store offers some products related to the products already added to the shopping basket, and the customer was not aware of existence of such products in the product catalog, the customer may gladly add those products to the order. The customer will consider the order to be of an increased value when the originally added products and the newly added ones complement each other. Effectively, the customer gets a better solution to address his or her needs and will be happier to buy and use such products together.

Increasing Order Values for Store Owners

For online merchants, each order makes turnover and profit. Obviously, the more is the order total amount (value), the better are the turnover and profit figures in general. However, it should be noted that profit often varies from product to product, and two orders with the same or similar total amounts can bring the online merchant completely different profit figures. Sometimes an order with less total amount brings more profit than another order with larger total amount.

So the increased value of an order will not mean the increased order total, but rather the increased value that the order brings to the online store's total profit figures.

Sometimes certain individual products in orders with increased total value can even be sold with negative profit (i.e. when individual product's price is below the cost of the product), but as soon as the product is a "deal breaker" and makes the customer complete the online purchase such that total order's value is still much higher than total order's cost, it makes sense to go for it and allow some products to be bought below their cost level, together with other products on orders with increased value.

Offers Being Reasonable

In most cases, the customer has certain interests/needs and is looking for products capable of addressing those needs. Therefore, the customer is usually pretty determined to choose products from a certain range. The customer is focused on products from a certain range, on products that have certain features, on products that can address certain needs.

The online store should never let the customer lose that focus, but rather help the customer to find the most appropriate products.

Also, some customers have certain figures in mind that they are ready to spend to address their needs/satisfy certain interests. Those figures are not necessarily clearly defined by customers, but there is always a certain limit that a customer cannot afford to overspend.

Even if all the products in the Shopping Cart (those originally selected and the ones added later in attempt to increase order value) are of interest to the customer, the customer may still leave the online store if total order value goes over the maximum amount the customer can afford to spend at the moment. Customers will not necessarily go to remove less important products from the Shopping Cart in that case; they may just choose to close the web browser or navigate to another online store.

The website should constantly remind the customer how the value of the order for the customer is increased when more products/services are added. The more the customer is told about all the features and possibilities that become available with all the products included into an order, the less the customer will feel unhappy about spending more money on the order.

This means that the value of the order should grow on both sides, for the online store and for the customer at the same time. Only a win-win deal brings the best results, with both the customer and the online merchant being happy about the deal. In its own turn, this leads to further business between the customer and the online store.

Increasing Profits and Not Necessarily Order Totals

Working on increasing order value for an online store means not just increasing order value and turnover generated by online sales, but rather increasing generated profits. If turnover figures remain the same and the profit figures grow, this means the optimization is performed correctly. If profit figures remain the same and the turnover figures grow, in a short term perspective, this just puts more workload on the online store, but can still result in more profits in the future from returning customers and customers referred by other customers.

Determine the most Profitable Products

At first sight, the most profitable products are those where the product's margin is the best. But actually, it's a bit more complicated than that, since some products may be more difficult to deliver to customers than some other ones, and even though the difference between the cost and the sale price is high for a certain product, packing and delivery costs may "eat out" the margin and eventually such products will not help to achieve better profit figures.

When determining the most profitable products, the online store owner should take into account all aspects of the whole process, from receiving an online order to delivering the product to the customer's door.

The most profitable products can be highlighted in the product catalog, advertised on the website and other websites, and be suggested.

Such offers could include a special discount that would be applicable only if the total order value exceeds a certain amount. This could, on the one hand, make the customer happier because of the discount received on certain products, and on the other hand, increase the number of orders with increased value.

Determine the Best-Selling Products

Best-selling products are easy to determine based on the customers' order history.

osCommerce has certain built-in facilities to compile the list of best-selling products and display it on either the main page, or a special Best-selling Products page, or in one of the information boxes in a side column.

It's also possible to improve that functionality further, and instead of dealing with the list of best-selling products, create a special list of best-selling categories and pick up the most profitable products from the best-selling categories.

Customers can be offered a choice of best-selling products to stimulate their interest in buying, but it is also possible to sort the list of best-selling products by profitability so that the customers first see the best-selling products that are, at the same time, the most profitable ones. There's no support for profits in the default installation of osCommerce; online merchants would need to add the supplier (or "buy") price to their products and fill those values in for each product. Then, gross profit can be calculated for each product, and those products with the highest gross profits could be positioned first in the list of "best-selling" products.

This way the online store recommends products to the customers based on the choice of other customers, and at the same time, can receive greater profits by selling the most profitable of the best-selling products online.

Selling Related Products Together

Related (or complementary) products are easier to sell together. The customer may be looking for a particular product only, but along with that product the customer may be interested in products that are in some way related to the original one. The customer may not even have that interest before the online store informs the customer about an offer of products related to the product of original interest.

The online store can stimulate customers' interest in more advanced offers, either by:

- Decreasing total price of the offer if products are bought together
- Leaving price the same but adding value to the order by recommending related products that the customer was not aware of or didn't think about before

It's easier to sell related products when the promotion materials contain information about how those products can be used together.

For example, a website that sells bedclothes will sell its products better if it demonstrates to the customers how duvet and pillow sets, sheets, and other products will look when put together on a fully prepared bed. Or when buying an MP3 player, the customer may be interested in buying headphones and also vouchers to be spent in online music stores. Or if buying a cowboy hat online, the customer may be interested in purchasing a pair of boots of the same style to accompany the hat, even if the customer was not interested in such boots in particular originally.

Cross-Selling Products and Categories

Offering complementary products together, or after the customer has already purchased one of the related products, is called cross-selling. It not only increases order value, but also decreases the likelihood of the customer buying such products from competitors.

It's possible to cross-sell either different but complementary products, or accessories for certain products. When an online store is able to offer both complementary products and accessories for a single product, those should be visually separated on the website pages to make the web pages easier to use for customers.

There's no built-in support for cross-selling in osCommerce, but fortunately there are a couple of contributions that can be downloaded from: `http://addons.oscommerce.com/info/4408` and `http://addons.oscommerce.com/info/1415`.

Cross-Selling Product to Product

There may be one or more products complementary to a single product that the online store would like to cross-sell.

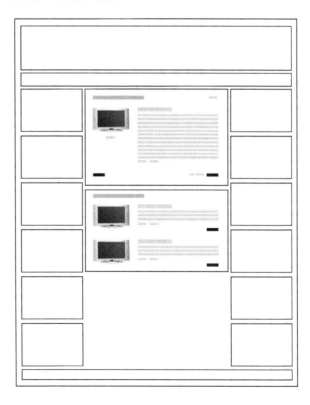

Such complementary products can be put in a list on the product information page for the corresponding product, under Product Description. It's not recommended to put a long list of such products, as it can make it difficult for customers to use it. If design of the product information page supports information tabs, complementary products can be put into a separate tab. The same goes with accessories for a product, which can be put into yet another information tab on the Product Information page (if design of the product information page allows for this).

The online store should be built in a way that on the one hand helps the customer to keep focus on the product of original interest, but on the other hand allows the customer to buy or open detailed information pages about complementary products. This can be achieved by:

- Opening the product information pages of complementary products in a new browser window when the customer clicks on them.

- Allowing the customer to add complementary products into the Shopping Cart directly from the original product's page (by providing "Add to Cart" buttons for each complementary product, or by having one "Add to Cart" button and multiple "Quantity" boxes — one for each product).

- Displaying the list of complementary products not on the product information page, but on a special page placed "in between" the product information page and the Shopping Cart page, meaning that when the customer adds a product to the Shopping Cart, the website would check if it has any related products, and list those on a page giving the customer a choice to select one or several of the listed products, and have those added to the Shopping Cart along with the original product.

Cross-Selling Categories

Sometimes, a single product can be complementary to all products of a certain category. In this case, it may make sense to link a product or several as cross-sell items to category.

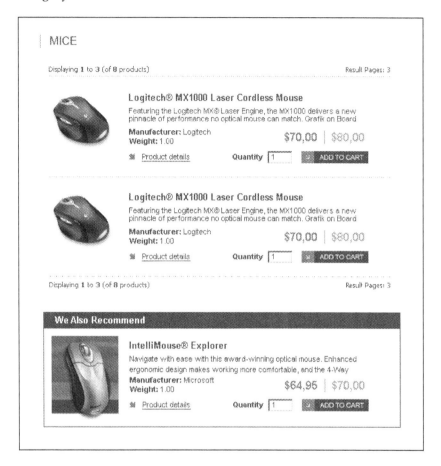

Vice versa, a whole category of products can be complementary to a product, and in that case, by linking the category as cross-sell to a single product, all that category's products become related to that single product and will be displayed as cross-sell products on the corresponding Product Information page. (Of course, it's better to display only a limited number of cross-sell products on the Product Information page, and use some sort of random rotation if the number of cross-sell products is too large).

Finally, categories can be cross-linked together, so that all products of one category will become linked to the products of another category.

Cross-Selling Based on Customers' Choices

We have discussed several ways to link related products together manually. It is also possible to cross-sell related products based only on customers' choices.

In that case, previous order history would be analyzed by a special script, and certain products that were bought together with the original product will be listed on that product's details page. This feature is already built into osCommerce, but sometimes it needs to be fine-tuned because the database tables it uses are not optimized for large number of orders and this analysis can affect the performance of the website.

Cross-Sell by Email

An online store can be pro-active in terms of selling related products to its customers.

Several days after a customer's order has been delivered, the online store may send an automated email to the customer asking to confirm whether the he or she is happy about the delivered goods, and if they have any comments about the products and/or the whole service that could help to improve customer's experience with this online store, and if the feedback about the products and services could be published as testimonials on the website.

But along with that information, the email can contain a special section that would recommend to the customer products related to ones the customer has just bought. Such products could be either linked to the original product manually by the online store Administration, or determined by a special algorithm/script based on other customers' order history. If the customer had purchased several products together, the list of related products could be split by the products purchased on the customer's original order.

The tone of the email of course should not be insistent; it should inform the customer about the possibility of buying related products online, and explain the benefits of buying this or that related product alongside the original one.

Also, related products can be added simply to any email the customer receives from an online store, like an order status update notification, for example.

Minimum Order Amount Strategy

To motivate customers placing large online orders, the minimum order strategy can be used. This method enables certain benefits for customers only when their order total reaches a certain minimum level.

Some online stores have this as a rule that the online order amount should not be less than a certain value, or that the number of products in the order should be, again, not less than a certain number. The reason for this is in the business model of the online store, in how the orders are processed and delivered.

For example, an online store that sells various materials for crafts (paper, cards, stickers, paints, stamps, and other products) may set the minimum order amount to, say, $5 as otherwise processing an order may not be profitable.

Or an online store that sells wine may set the minimum number of products in an order to 6 (bottles), as otherwise delivery of the order will not be possible at the desired margin level.

But the minimum order amount strategy should not be used only to protect the interests of the online store owner; it can also be used to motivate customers placing larger orders online by providing them with additional benefits and rewards.

The online store should promote all benefits that the customer can get by placing an order online with an order total greater than the minimum order amount. Information about the minimum order amount and corresponding benefits for customers can be either placed on a special page, or added directly to the Product Information, Shopping Cart, or Checkout pages.

It is useful to not only display currently available offers according to the current order total, but also display the list of offers that would be available if the customer had more products in the order. This will further motivate customers to increase the value of their orders to get access to special offers.

For Payment Methods

Certain payment methods, usually not available to customers, can be enabled when a customer places an order with a total greater than the minimum order amount for those payment methods.

Such payment methods may include, for example, bank transfer and credit account. Or an online finance option can become available for customers who place orders with an order total greater than a certain amount.

Also, payment terms may be different when customers place larger orders. For example, instead of 100% prepayment, the customer can be charged 50% in advance and 50% on dispatch of the order. Or the whole order amount can be split into several installments.

On the Checkout Payment page, the list of special payment methods can be enabled for the customer if the order total exceeds the minimum order amount, or such payment methods can be listed there but be disabled for the customer and the corresponding message would contain information about how much the customer should add to the order to qualify for those special payment methods.

For Shipping Methods

Rewarding customers by providing them access to special payment methods and payment terms makes it more convenient for customers to pay for the goods.

But special shipping methods can become a real reward for those customers who place online orders with a total greater than the minimum order amount.

- Free delivery—the shipping fee can be waived completely if a customer places a larger order. To motivate customers adding more goods to the order, the online store can display corresponding message on the Shopping Cart page, notifying the customer about how much more should be added to the order to make that order eligible for free delivery. Also, corresponding information can be put onto the Product Information and Product Listing pages; then some of the more expensive products will be marked with the corresponding Free Delivery icon automatically.

- Next-day free delivery shipping can be made available for the customer if order amount exceeds the specified minimum order amount for next-day free delivery, and the ordered products are in stock or can be delivered by suppliers to the customer next day. The same as in the case with Free delivery, the Next-day free delivery can be advertised on the Product Information, Product Listing, Shopping Cart, and of course Checkout pages.

  Customers do not like waiting for their orders to be delivered, so allowing them to receive ordered goods next day without paying anything extra for that service can become a good selling point, and can really make a great difference compared to the service provided by competitors.

- A fixed time delivery option can be made available to the customer if the order total exceeds a certain minimum amount. In that case, the customer may be able to choose if the delivery should be performed before, for example, 9am, or on Saturday in the morning.

- A split delivery option can be made available for larger orders, when the order contains some items that are in stock and some items that are temporarily out of stock. In such a situation, the customer may be given a choice to either have all products delivered at the same time, or a part of the order delivered now and the rest of the items as soon as they come back in stock. Such options can be advertised on the Shopping Cart page and on the Checkout pages, and can be made available free of charge for customers who place larger orders online.

The same as with special payment methods, special shipping methods should be promoted to the customer even if the customer's order doesn't exceed the minimum order amount for those shipping methods. In such cases, on the Shopping Cart page, and also on the Checkout Shipping page of an osCommerce online store, there can be a message placed explaining to the customer how much should be added to the order to have those special shipping methods available for that order.

Giveaways

Giveaways are products that the online store can literally give away to the customers free of charge under certain circumstances. Giveaways are used as deal breakers, as something the customer can get for free if, for example, the customer orders certain products or if the order total exceeds a specified minimum amount.

osCommerce has a couple of contributions that can handle giveaways. The first is the so called "Get 1 Free" contribution (available from `http://addons.oscommerce.com/info/4990`) that allows promoting a product by giving away a free product when the customer buys a specified number of the promoted product. The other is the so called "Dangling Carrot" contribution (available from `http://addons.oscommerce.com/info/2990`) that allows creating gifts (free or discounted) that appear at various levels of Shopping Cart value.

Giveaways can be just regular products from the product catalog, or, more often, they can be products the online store can't sell on their own or products that occupy certain space in the warehouse that needs to be cleaned up to allocate new products there.

Even though the value of giveaway products for the online store is not critical, for end customers such products must be of non-zero value to make the whole conception of giveaways work.

Obviously, the customers should be made aware of the existence of giveaway products in the product catalog.

Products marked as "giveaway" in the Administration panel of the online store can be all listed on a special page, each with the minimum order amount that would allow a customer to get that product free of charge. Also, corresponding information may appear in the Product Listings and on the Product Information pages.

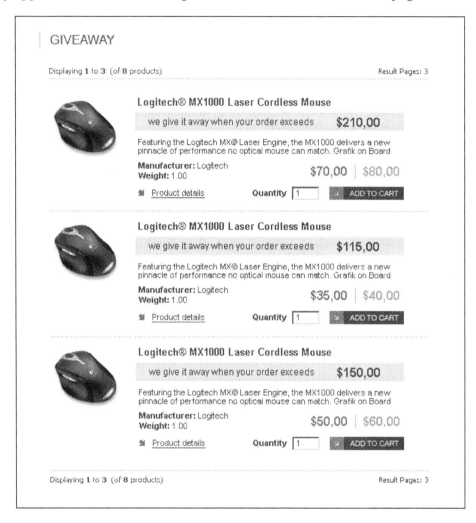

Giveaways can be displayed on the Shopping Cart page of an online store. Those giveaways that the customer has access to because of the order amount should be highlighted as "enabled" and the customer should be able to add those to the Shopping Cart. Giveaways that the customer doesn't have access to because the order amount is not large enough should be displayed as "disabled" but the page should contain information about how much more the customer should add to the order to enable those giveaways.

A slightly different solution can link giveaway products to other specific products, not general order total amount. In that case, the customer becomes eligible to get certain giveaways free of charge only if the order contains certain products.

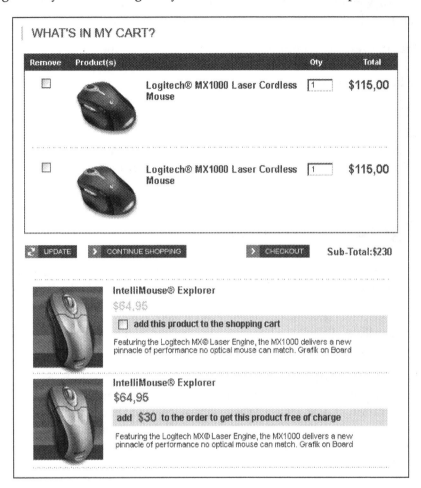

Freebies

Additionally to giveaway products, an osCommerce online store can attract customers to place larger orders by providing customers with free services that are not specifically related to particular items of the product catalog.

For example the customers can be presented with a gift voucher (to be spent either at the very same online shop, or at another shop, not necessarily an online one) if order total exceeds certain minimum amount, or free gift wrapping services can be enabled for the customer, etc.

Complex Products

We will call those products that consist of more than one item from the product catalog complex products. Actually, complex products are also part of the product catalog, and can be bought in the very same way as regular products.

It's just that the value of complex products is greater than the value of regular products as effectively several regular products are bought at once when the customer buys one complex product. Therefore, the online store saves on delivery and advertisement costs compared to the situation when several regular products are bought by different customers. Online merchants may want to check the "2gether" osCommerce contribution that allows for linking of two products together with a money or percentage discount, which is given to the customer during the Checkout process. The contribution can be downloaded from: `http://addons.oscommerce.com/info/3929`.

Configurable Products

Configurable products are those that the Administration of an online store can create based on certain "templates", and then the customers can choose between several options for each element of the template associated with a particular product.

Even this description sounds a little bit complicated, but it works pretty straightforwardly and almost all online store owners and end customers already have experience dealing with such products in the past.

If we take computer products, complete computer systems would be a good example of configurable products. If an online store sells complete computer systems, the Administration may want not to sell only some predefined configurations of hardware, but rather to give customers some flexibility in choosing certain options themselves based on their own requirements and on how much they can afford to pay for such a product.

An osCommerce contribution that implements support for custom computer systems can be downloaded from: `http://addons.oscommerce.com/info/407`.

The Administration of such an online store can prepare several "templates" for each general type of the computer system that is available for purchase online. Such templates can be made different from each other in the total number of pre-selected and configurable elements, and also in the options available within each element of a template.

Templates can be created for, for example, home-based multimedia PC, office PC, game server, graphics processing station, etc. Elements of the templates would include CPU, hard drive, mother board, graphics card, monitor, network adapter, extended warranty, pre-installed software, etc. Each element of each template can be either predefined by the Administration of the online store, or a choice of several options can be given to an element for customers to choose the option they require and can afford.

For example, in the case of an office PC template, the hard drive element can be preselected to the "80GB" value, with possible options "120GB" and "160GB". When the customer chooses an option different from the currently selected one, the web page should recalculate the total price of the configurable product automatically. It's preferable to have this done without the Product Information page being reloaded. AJAX technology or plain JavaScript could be used.

In the example above, the extended warranty element may not have any pre-selected options (so its price by default would be $0), but it can also contain options like "2 years extended warranty (+$50)" and "4 years extended warranty (+$70)".

By providing customers with a default configuration and making it possible to choose different (and often more expensive) options, the online store will increase the value of orders and at the same time, add more value for customers by providing them with more advanced products and solutions.

It's not only computer systems that can be sold online as configurable products. Such products and services as gift baskets, hosting services, machinery products, and many others can also be sold as configurable products with osCommerce.

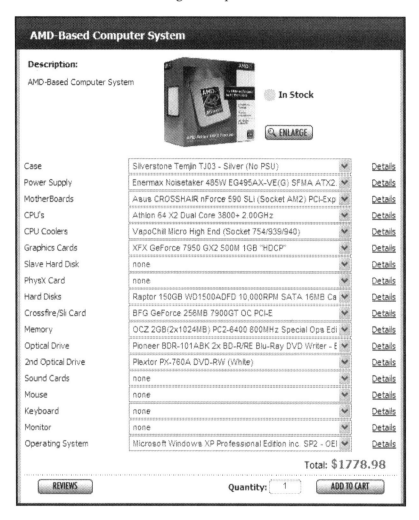

Different elements of a configurable product may allow for different types of selection of options based on the type of the element itself. In the example with computer systems, the CPU element can be displayed as a drop-down with different choices of CPUs available for that system or as a list of options where only one option can be selected at a time. But the Additional Software element can be displayed as a list of available options where different options can be selected at the same time (like, for example, office software, anti-virus software, photo-processing software, etc).

Again, this functionality is applicable not only to computer products, but to all sorts of products where the customer can be given the freedom to choose options and features of the product.

In either case, not depending on the way the products, and elements, and options are displayed on the Product Information page, the total price of the configured product should be changed automatically each time the customer chooses another option to make sure the customer is fully aware of the total price the current configuration of the product costs.

There may be special products included into some templates, which are removed from the product catalog otherwise. Effectively, such products and services become only available as parts of configurable templates. Those can be special fitting services for home appliances, extra warranty for computer systems, etc.

Products that are not configurable themselves can also be used to increase order value. On the Product Information page, it's possible to list all configurations of which such products are an important part of. This will work similarly to the cross-selling feature except that the cross-linking is based on the links between individual products and configurable products.

Product Bundles

Products can be grouped together for various reasons. Often different products are related or complement the functions of each other (like a computer mouse and a keyboard); sometimes products combined together add more value to the offer (an online store that sells souvenirs can offer Swiss army knives and Zippo lighters together, or if an online store sells wine, six different bottles of wine can be gathered together to represent a new offer); or one product can be considered to be an accessory of another (like sunglasses sold separately and also together with cases, or mobile phones can be sold separately and also together with Bluetooth headsets and mobile chargers).

There are two ways to promote product bundles:

First of all, a bundle on its own can represent added value because the Administration of the online store pre-selected those products to be sold together in order to provide customers with the best value. Bundle products are treated as regular products in the online store (i.e. it's possible to search for them, see their Product Information page, buy them, etc.). It is possible to use the idea of a "serving suggestion" to advertise bundled products. This means that on the promotional materials (pictures, downloadable brochures), products that are parts of the bundle should be all combined together as if they were used together. For example an online store that sells bedclothes may advertise bundles that contain sheets, duvet clothes, pillowcases all used together to make a bed.

But this will not always work (or rather will work only rarely) as customers nowadays are buying not only products but also bargains. The customers may not only want to get products for their money, but also get a discount that the online store is willing to give out for selling several products at a time. Only then, will the customers consider the deal to be worthwhile. Therefore, a facility to set a discount on a bundle of products should be present to effectively sell several products together. Such discounts should be broadly advertised through all the pages of the online store where the customer can see the bundled product (Product Listing, Product Information page, Shopping Cart page, and information boxes in the side columns).

An osCommerce contribution called "Bundled Products" implements support for product bundles. It can be downloaded from: `http://addons.oscommerce.com/info/2015`.

Design of the Bundled Product Page

The design of the Product Information page for bundled products can be improved to make the value of the offer more obvious to the customers.

First of all, like every product, a bundled product would have its image(s) and description. The marketing value of buying several products together should be clearly explained in the description, and also the product image would ideally demonstrate how all the products that are a part of the bundle are good together.

The way the website displays the bundle's price should send a clear message to the customer and contain information about the bargain the customer gets when buying bundled products together. For example the normal price of all bundled products can be given, and then struck out, and underneath, in bigger font size, the special bundle price can be given and also the discount in percent can be displayed.

It may make sense to list individual products that are parts of the bundle just below the description to demonstrate to customers in more detail what they actually get when they buy that bundle product.

The design of regular product pages can be improved as well. If a product is sold separately, but is also a part of one or more bundle offers, those offers can all be listed on the Product Information page along with the discount the customer gets if he or she buys that product as a part of the bundle offer.

PANASONIC - 50" FLAT-PANEL PLASMA HDTV $2,429.99

Select Panasonic Plasma TVs with your purchase of a select Panasonic Digital Camera

Lorem ipsum dolor sit amet, consectetuer adipiscing elit, sed diam nonummy nibh euismod tincidunt ut

Weight: 1.00

+ enlarge image

Lorem ipsum dolor sit amet, consectetuer adipiscing elit, sed diam nonummy nibh euismod ut laoreet dolore magna aliquam erat volutpat. Ut wisi enim ad minim veniam, quis nostrud exerci tation ullamcorper suscipit lobortis nisl ut aliquip ex ea commodo consequat. Duis autem vel eum iriure dolor in hendrerit in vulputate velit esse molestie consequat, vel illum dolore eu feugiat nulla facilisis at vero et accumsan et iusto odio dignissim qui blandit praesent luptatum zzril delenit augue duis dolore te feugait

$200 OFF

TH-50PX75U 1366 x 768 resolution; 3 HDMI inputs; black cabinet; 16:9 aspect ratio; Secure Digital media slot $2,299.99
Go to details

Save 20% on PANASONIC - 50" FLAT-PANEL PLASMA HDTV when buying in a bundle

Panasonic - Lumix 7.2MP Digital Camera

DMC-LZ7S. 6x optical/4x digital zoom; 2.5" TFT-LCD; sleek and slim; direct-print capability $2,349.99
Go to details

Save 15% Panasonic - Lumix 7.2MP Digital Camera when buying in a bundle

REVIEWS   Quantity 1   ADD TO CART

Also, all bundle offers can be listed under a special category to make it easier for customers to locate bundled products among other products in the catalog.

Stock Control

It should be noted that complex (configurable or bundle) products do not usually have stock themselves, but instead stock control system should take into account stock levels of individual products that are parts of complex products. If an online store displays stock levels or stock status for products, it should also display stock levels or stock statuses for complex products.

For configurable products, it makes sense to display stock levels/statuses for individual elements when certain options are selected, and the whole product's stock status will become dependent on stock status of individual selected options. For bundle products, stock levels and statuses will also depend on stock levels and statuses of individual products included into the bundle. The lowest stock level of an individual product included into the bundle will automatically become the stock level of the bundle product itself. The same goes for stock status. If some individual products are out of stock, the "back in stock" date of the whole bundle product will be equal to the "back in stock" date of the one of the individual products which is last to be back in stock.

Design of the Shopping Cart Page

The Shopping Cart page may become a little bit "overcrowded" with up-sell and cross-sell products, giveaways and freebies, and other special offers and features that the online store uses to increase order value.

Therefore, a lot of attention should be given to the design of that page, to ensure that its main function — displaying the selected products and inviting the customer to proceed to the Checkout pages — has not been hidden from the customers in favor of other, additional functions.

Summary

By increasing order value, the online store can increase its turnover and profits. Even if the turnover is not increased, profits can be made higher as the online store saves on shipping and advertising costs.

The value of the order should be also increased for customers, so that the customer is happy about a fair deal. Related products are easier to sell together, as it's easier for customers to see how such products could be used together, and how using such products together can better address their particular needs. Related products can be cross-linked, or combined together into more complex products (either configurable or fixed product bundles). Minimum order strategy can be used to encourage customers to place larger orders online and in return receive extra services, not available on other orders.

In the next chapter, we concentrate on numerous ways to make the most of osCommerce by using various discount strategies.

9

Increasing the Turnover via Promotions and Special Offers

Advertising promotions and discount offers may seem like the most obvious and easiest way to increase the number of customers and orders to increase the turnover of an online store.

This is because even though the customers may get a better price on certain products or services during the promotion period, or buy products at a discounted price, it doesn't mean the online store will start losing profits if it runs a promotion campaign or allows customers to buy certain products at a discounted rate. The profitability level may be affected of course, and the relative amount of profit compared to the turnover per period might get decreased, but profit figures will most probably go up when running a properly planned promotion campaign.

A promotion campaign can be run for a product or group of products, and usually provides certain special options when making a purchase, like for example discounted product price, special delivery options, or additional products and services that come free of charge along with the products being promoted.

Therefore, a discount given on certain products doesn't necessarily have to decrease profit figures. How it affects profit figures depends purely on the conditions set by the Administration of the online store.

A promotion campaign not only increases the number of sales of promoted products or services, but may also increase the number of visitors to the online store, who might register as customers and place online orders. Even if the newly attracted customers do not buy at the first visit, they may still leave their email addresses and other contact details in the database, and those contact details could be used in further advertising campaigns (with the customer's permission, of course).

Promotions can be made available for all customers of an online store, or only for a limited number of customers. For example if the online store sells to retail and trade customers, it may have certain special offers available only to its trade (business) customers. It may also have special prices for almost every product, giving a discount to the trade customer based on their purchase history.

Another way to increase the number of visitors and, effectively, customers of the online store is obviously to keep winning market share. To do it, and also for the sake of search engine optimization, the online merchant may choose to run an e-commerce system consisting of several front ends and one and the same back end. We will consider this approach in more detail later in this chapter.

An alternative to that approach would be to get other websites to promote products sold by the online store by inviting them to participate in an affiliate program.

Which Products to Promote

Products can be promoted in many ways. It is extremely important to know which products to promote, so that the business works with its maximum efficiency, and the turnover and profit figures grow further.

New Products

Certain products could be advertised and promoted simply because they are new products to the market and their existence and availability in stock is a good promotion reason on its own. Promotion of such products differs from other promotions because it doesn't necessarily require any discounts or special offers to be applied—customers would be happy to buy new well advertised products as soon as those products become available in the online store.

Best-Selling Products

The best-selling products are also easier to promote than others, and they too do not really require a discount to be applied to be promoted because customers are already interested a great deal in such products and are ready to buy them. However, a little discount or special delivery options can make the deal look even more luxurious for customers.

Best-selling products should be determined based on the sale statistics for a certain time period. For an online store with about 100 or 1,000 products on offer, it would always make sense to determine up to 10-20 best-selling products in all categories and promote them heavily in various media and on the website itself. Having too many products on special offer can be confusing to customers, and may not be profitable to the online merchant. The value of the special offer itself will become less important if there are too many special offers available in the product catalog. A separate page with special offers and promotions, banners on other pages of the online store, banner advertising on the main page of the website — all that can make a difference and highlight the importance of listed special offers.

Of course, it is possible to add more best-selling products to the promotion campaign and advertise those within their corresponding categories in the online store to make the campaign even more effective.

It is not only the best-selling products that could be promoted, but also the best-selling categories. A best selling category is one that contains the largest number of sales of its own products, or of products related to its sub-categories. Having best-selling products and categories promoted through the online store makes it especially convenient for customers when the online store has a large number of products on offer.

The Most Profitable Products

It is possible to promote the most profitable products by providing time-limited price discounts. The most profitable products are very easy to define by calculating the difference between the cost price and the sale price. If the profit margin that the online stores makes on such a product is good enough, or is even better than what can be called good compared to other products, the sale price can be discounted so that the online store still makes profit on selling the product, but at the same time, customers are given a valuable discount compared to the product's default sale price.

For example, if a product costs $75 to purchase from suppliers, and its normal sale price is $150, the online store can promote that product and assign a time-limited discounted price of $119 to motivate customers placing more orders for that particular product. The online store still makes good margin on the discounted price of $119 (up to 37%!), and at the same time, the price for the end customers is discounted, so the product is more affordable for customers, and also, the difference between the discounted and normal sale price makes the product more attractive.

Also, the larger number of products bought by customers of an online store, the cheaper the online store can buy those products from its own suppliers; so discounting the price of the most profitable products and selling more of them will most probably make those products even more profitable.

Of course, the Administration of an online store should always maintain an acceptable level of profitability, and manage sale prices accordingly. If the purchase price for products goes down as the online store buys products cheaper, having the same level of profitability will result in the sale price also going down, though the proportion may not be maintained here. Having a margin of, say, 35% on two products, one with $100 purchase price, and the other one with $50 purchase price gives two different amounts of gross profit, one two times greater than the other. But there are other costs involved in fulfillment of a customer's order that can make the sale price not profitable at a certain level, so even though the margin may be still the same when the purchase price goes down, there could be some "lowest sale price" figure specified on a per-product basis that guarantees the online store a certain level of profit even if the product is sold at the lowest sale price.

It makes sense to update the database and scripts of your osCommerce online store, add the "supplier price" and "lowest sale price" fields, and allow for changing those fields in the back-end for each product. When a customer places an order, the current values of those fields could be also copied from the corresponding record in the "products" table into the "order items" table.

This will allow for running reports on both current product range, finding the most (or least) profitable products, and also on the historical data—getting some more or less realistic profitability figures.

There is an osCommerce contribution that does a part of this update, but in order to get reports based on order items rather than only on currently present products one would have to modify it. This module can be downloaded from `http://addons.oscommerce.com/info/1594`.

All Clearance Stock Must Go!

Almost any business that has products stocked in a warehouse faces a situation from time to time when the warehouse is full of products ordered earlier from suppliers, and so new products can't be accomodated. And if the online merchant is sure the new products will sell better, the decision can be made to clear the warehouse of older products by advertising a special clearance sale on such products.

In that case, the price of such products can be decreased to either make at least a very little profit or no profit at all—it can be even lowered down to the original purchase price—in order to free up the space for new products.

The list of such clearance products can be put on a separate page in osCommerce, which will always list the best special/clearance offers.

It is important to indicate the number of items in stock that can be sold at the special price in that case, as the possible number of sales is limited to the number of products available in stock. Such products cannot be re-ordered from suppliers, or even if they can be ordered again, the price will most probably be different then.

Special Purchase Price

The most profitable products are also those that were bought at a special purchase price.

Sometimes suppliers reward retailers with certain special offers and discount deals themselves, or they may need to clean up space in their own warehouses for new products and this makes them give out older products much cheaper to clean up the warehouse space faster.

In this way a washing machine that would normally cost the online merchant around $400 could be offered by the supplier for only $1. This may or may not affect the sale price that the Administration of the online store has set for that product, but if it does, a special message (like "while stock lasts") should appear along with the special sale price to warn customers about it being a limited offer.

Product Bundles

Bundles of products can include products with different margin levels. But it's the total margin level of the whole product bundle that the online merchant is interested in keeping reasonably high.

Therefore, the most profitable products could be added to a bundle along with not-so-profitable products to make the whole deal look better for customers, still having it reasonably profitable for the online merchant.

Also, the most popular (or best-selling) products could be bundled with products with higher sale price or less popular ones to move stock of those other products faster.

Products That are Too Expensive

There may be some products in the online store catalog that are too expensive for customers to buy them online, even though the customers would like to buy such products if they were offered them at a cheaper price.

It's not difficult to determine such products even if the product catalog is large.

The online merchant should compare the list of products sorted by the number of impressions of each product page with the list of best-selling products.

When the same product takes reasonably high positions in both lists, the price is right for customers, and it's a popular product.

But when a product is positioned reasonably high in the impressions list, and has fewer sales according to the product sale report, this may mean the price is too high for customers who belong to the target audience of the online store.

If the sale price can be lowered without losing much of the profit, it makes sense to run a special promotion campaign for such products, lower the price, and massively advertise that special offer on the website. Then compare the two lists again in some time at the future to see if the situation with sales (and correspondingly profits!) has improved.

Recommended Retail Price and Purchase Price

Recommended retail price can be set either by the manufacturer or the supplier. Unfortunately, there is no built-in support for Recommended Retail Price (RRP) in osCommerce, but it could be added to an online store relatively easily, by modifying several `.PHP` files and altering the database a little. In fact, a contribution that allows for that functionality is available from `http://addons.oscommerce.com/info/3574`.

One may find it interesting to know that RRP itself is sometimes referred to as Suggested Retail Price (SRP) or even Manufacturer's Suggested Retail Price (MSRP). But regardless of what it's called, it is just a nice figure that not so many retailers use as the current price nowadays.

It's the end customer who is mostly interested in RRP, as this price is used to demonstrate the difference between the recommended and current sale price offered by the online store. RRP should only be displayed in the front end of an osCommerce online store when it differs a lot from the current product's sale price. If the difference is not much for a certain product, it is better not to display it for that particular product. Usually, along with the RRP price (struck out) the online store would display the percentage of savings the customer makes when he or she buys that product from the online store at the current price.

RRP works similarly to how the special price feature works, and it affects the customer's decision to buy or not to buy products in a similar manner.

Purchase or cost price (again, not supported by osCommerce by default) is the price the online store pays to buy the product from its supplier (or directly from the manufacturer). Purchase price may change depending on how many products the online merchant buys from the suppliers, and how much the online merchant spends with that supplier per certain period of time. Therefore, it's important to keep it up to date in the osCommerce database, so that profit figures and sale price could be updated accordingly.

If the online store gets the same products from more than one supplier, a system that selects the cheapest purchase price should be implemented. Correspondingly, in that case, the current supplier for a particular product may change all the time, as the stock levels and purchase prices set by suppliers also change.

Purchase price, being set in the Administration panel of an osCommerce online store, may affect the sale price, and also obviously affects the profit margin of each product.

Purchase price and RRP may change from time to time. In order to make it possible for the online merchant to check profit levels made on previous orders, it is recommended to store current purchase price and, optionally, RRP, along with the rest of the product information in the "order" record in the database. Then, it will be possible to calculate profits in orders received at any time in the past.

Special Prices

Promotions and discounted offers assume the sale price of a product will be decreased. Additional options can be used to optimize the promotion campaign besides affecting the price.

The special (discounted) price could be limited by date, for example it could be valid for a period of 1 month from the date when the campaign starts.

The special product price can be limited by stock levels, and then the discount will only last while stock lasts.

An alternative to the special price offer limited by date is the so called "count down" sale. This is when there is a special "expiry" date AND time set on an individual product basis, besides the special price, to make customers aware of how much time is left before the special offer ends. The countdown clock can be displayed on the product page to stimulate customers buying the product at the special price, and also, a dedicated additional page can be implemented in osCommerce to list all such products.

The default installation of osCommerce supports special product prices either limited or not limited by the expiry date. It has no built-in support for countdown sales, nor does it have support for promotions limited by stock quantity. Such features would usually have to be added to an osCommerce online store. There is an osCommerce contribution called "Happy Hour" that could be further modified to allow for "count down" sales. It can be downloaded from `http://addons.oscommerce.com/info/3568`, and the countdown script could be downloaded from `http://addons.oscommerce.com/info/3710`.

Sale Manager Contribution

There is a contribution available for download from `www.oscommerce.com` that makes it easier for online merchants to set special prices for multiple products at once and run promotion campaigns.

The module can be downloaded from the following link:
`http://addons.oscommerce.com/info/1340`.

Several sales can be managed at the same time. This solution provides online merchants with tools to define, manage, and exploit sale campaigns.

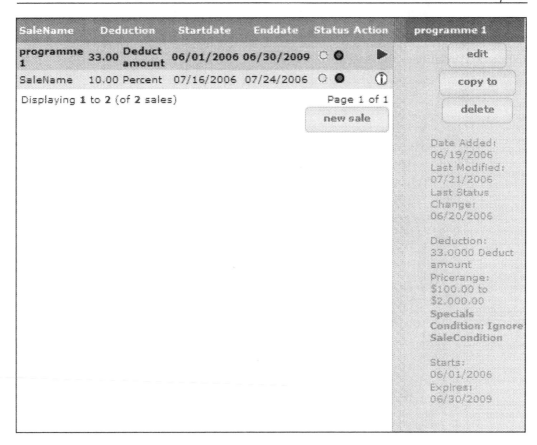

Special price discounts and promotions can be applied on either the complete product catalog, or only on product items that belong to specific categories.

Products that are to be included into the sale can be filtered out by their prices. This, for example, gives an online merchant the facility to lower the price on the most expensive products without altering the prices of all other ones.

Quantity Discounts

To increase the value of sale orders online, merchants can try to motivate customers to buy more products at once. Even by providing the customer with a discount, the online merchant may still increase the order's profitability if the customer buys several products at once, as the online store saves money on delivery and order processing costs.

We will consider several types of discounts in this chapter, and we will start with so called "quantity discounts".

Quantity discounts can be of two similar types.

First of all, the online store can have a special price per product when the customer wants to buy several of the same product in one go. For example, an online store that sells nutrition products can have a default price of $20 set for some product. But if the client wants to buy two of absolutely the same product at once (and it's quite a realistic situation as many customers of such an online store would require more and more of such products at some point of time in the future), the price for each product could be lowered and set to only $18, so that two of the product would cost the customer $36 instead of $40. Then if the customer decides to buy seven such products at the same time, the price per product for cases when customers buy more than five products at a time can be set to $15 — so instead of paying $140 (7 x $20), the customer would end up paying only $105, having saved $35 on the deal!

The second type of discount can be applied on a per product basis when the total number of products in an order exceeds a certain level. Of course, it makes sense to enable that sort of discount only if the online store sells all products at the same or a very similar price. Then, irrespective of the customer buying the same product several times or buying different products, each individual product's price in the Shopping Cart would be calculated according to the discount level set per product per the specified quantity of products in the order.

The discount level should be set in a way that the discount looks attractive to clients and makes the clients want to buy more products, but at the same time, it should leave enough room for delivery costs to be compensated irrespective of how many products the customer is buying, and for profit received by the online store to keep increasing as the number of products in the customer's order increases.

If quantity discounts are available for certain products, it is suggested to mark such products with a corresponding icon or text mark in the product listing, and also display a corresponding table with quantities and discounted prices on the product information page, like for example:

Quantity	Price
1	$30
2-5	$27
6-10	$25
11-	$23

There is a contribution called "Simple Price Break" that could be used to implement quantity discounts. It can be downloaded from http://addons.oscommerce.com/info/4658. There is yet another contribution of similar nature called "Quantity Price Breaks Per Product" that can be downloaded from http://addons.oscommerce.com/info/1242.

"Buy One Get One Free" Discounts

Yet another discount that can be implemented is somewhat similar to quantity discounts, and is called a "Buy one get one free" discount. Or, in a more general case, "Buy X, get Y free".

Such a promotion allows the customers to get free or highly discounted products when buying a certain number of other products at the same time. An example of this offer, when selling kitchen appliances, may sound like: "Buy American Foodstores and get a free mixer", or, when selling IT hardware: "Buy 2 monitors and get free wireless headphones".

Product(s) "Y" in the definition of the discount above should be either related to product(s) "X", or be a very popular/best-selling add-on that can drive up the sale of less popular (worse selling) product(s) "X". Having product(s) "Y" added to the order free of charge or highly discounted if bought together with product(s) "X" can make a real difference to some customers and can make up their mind in regards to placing an online order.

Of course, that discount needs to be set up in a way that it generates profit on every online order, therefore the cost price of product(s) "Y" would be usually significantly less than the profit made on product(s) "X".

Information about the availability of such a discount can be displayed on the Product page, on the Product Listing page (in both cases, under each product, of either group "X" or group "Y"), on a separate page with other discounts and special offers, and on the Shopping Cart page. It should only be displayed on the Shopping Cart page when corresponding products of either group "X" or "Y" have been added to the Shopping Cart by the client.

Two osCommerce contributions could be utilized to allow for "buy one get one free" type discounts. Those are the "2gether discount" (can be downloaded from `http://addons.oscommerce.com/info/3929`) and the "Dangling Carrot" module (can be downloaded form `http://addons.oscommerce.com/info/2990`).

Discounts Based on Order Value

Customers can be eligible for certain discounts based on the values of orders they are placing online. Simply enough, the more is the order value (or rather the profit that can be made on that order), the more the amount of the discount can be.

A special message can be displayed on the Shopping Cart page informing the customers about any available discount/special offer if order value (or profit) has reached a certain amount, or indicating how much the order value should be increased to make the discount/special offer available to the customer. Also, a similar message can be displayed on the Product Information page.

Discounts based on order value help selling more expensive products, and make it easier to sell multiple products at once.

Such discounts can either be enabled for any order based on order value, or only for orders with certain products.

Discounts become applicable only starting from a certain order value (or rather profit value).

Technical implementation of this feature can be based on two price levels per each product, where one price is the product's default price and another is the product's price when order total reaches a specific amount. This critical order total amount can be set different for different products, so that order value-based discount may change as the customer adds more products to the order.

The discount itself will be calculated as a difference between the two price levels, and a corresponding amount will be subtracted from order total value according to the content of the Shopping Cart and to the corresponding price levels set on a per-product basis.

This approach works especially well when an online store sells mostly relatively expensive products.

For example, product A's price can be set to $300, and as soon as order total value reaches $700, that product's price could drop to $270 for the customer. Effectively, if the customer already has an order total of $500, including product A, and adds another product worth $250 to that order, order total value will be calculated as $720 instead of $750, as product A's price will be changed accordingly ($270 instead of $300 for orders with total value greater than $700).

Special Shipping Offers

It's not only product price that can be changed if order total value reaches or exceeds a certain amount. Customers can be motivated to order more products or more expensive products by enabling special delivery methods on orders with a higher value.

For example, free delivery or next day delivery, or Saturday delivery, or "after hours" delivery, or precise time slot delivery could be made available to the customer whose order total reaches or exceeds a certain amount.

The customer should be made aware of special delivery methods that are available depending on order amount, or that could be made available to the customer if the order total reaches a certain amount. A corresponding message can be placed on the Shopping Cart page, and also on the Checkout Shipping page. It may look like: "Add only $66.50 to the order and have your products delivered Next Day free of charge!"

Giveaways

Similar to special delivery methods, an online store may have certain products on offer to be "sold" to the customer for free if the order total value reaches a certain amount. We discussed giveaways in the previous chapter in detail, so here we will just remind that giveaway products can be displayed on the Shopping Cart page with a special text message motivating the customer to increase the value of the order, to have certain products added to the order free of charge.

Discount Coupons and Gift Vouchers

Discount coupons functionality provides the Administration of an online store with the facility to set up targeted discounts available to individual customers or specific customer groups only. Discount coupons can stimulate customers to buy more products at the same time, and can also be used to track the success of advertising campaigns. Also, discount coupons could be used to reward customers of the online store for referring more new customers to the website.

Gift vouchers allow customers to have a credit balance linked to their account in an osCommerce-based online store. That credit balance can be used to pay for orders. A customer can redeem a gift voucher and add money to the credit balance. Customers can buy gift vouchers from the online store itself, or receive them from the Administration of online store or other customers as a gift.

Gift vouchers should not be considered as a way to promote certain products, but rather as a way to let some customers of the online store pre-pay the vouchers and give the vouchers to their friends or close ones as a gift; so that the recipient of the gift voucher could come to the online store and use the received voucher to pay (in full or partially) for the order.

Gift vouchers can be also sent by the Administration of the online store to some of its very loyal customers as a gift on some occasion (like Christmas, or customer's birthday if the online store has information about customer's day of birth) to thank the customer for being loyal.

Once a gift voucher has been purchased by a customer (or generated by the Administration of the online store), it can be sent either as a special code via email, or printed as a gift certificate and sent to the recipient by post.

There is a contribution for osCommerce called Credit Class & Gift Voucher (which can be downloaded from `http://addons.oscommerce.com/info/4135/`) that implements functionality of discount coupons and gift vouchers at the same time.

A discount coupon is actually a special code that the end customer either receives from the online store, or sees in some advertisement and uses when placing an online order to get a certain discount. The administration of the online store can send a special email to its customers with the discount coupon code in it.

The code for each discount coupon can either be entered manually by the online merchant, or generated by the module, automatically.

A coupon can be configured to discount order total price by certain percent, or by a fixed amount. It can also be configured to allow for free shipping on a customer's order. The customer enters the coupon code during the checkout procedure, and redeems the coupon to claim the discount.

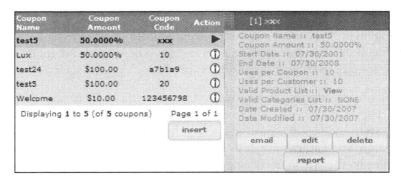

The administration of the online store can limit usage of certain discount coupon by:

- Number of usages per customer
- Total number of usages
- Product category or specific products only
- Minimum order total amount
- Time period

Effective Use of Discount Coupons

A discount coupon created by the Administration of an online store should have a purpose. There could be several reasons why it makes sense to create a discount coupon and send it to the customers.

First of all, a discount coupon can be used as a way to promote the online store itself or some of its specific products. Therefore, the coupon can be made applicable to any product or only to specific products or a product group (category) that needs to be promoted.

It's possible to use discount coupons to promote specific products because those products need to be sold from stock to clear out the warehouse for new products. It is possible to use discount coupons to promote some more expensive products that bring good profit to the online merchant, so that the discount given to the customers will not affect the profitability of such products too much but may increase the total profits made online.

Discount coupons can be used to reward repeat customers, or to turn first or second time customers into repeat customers. In that case, the more times the customer has bought from the online store, the larger is the amount of discount that could be provided to the customer on further orders.

Discount coupons can be used to make customers interested in referring their friends, relatives, colleagues, or partners to the online store—a special discount coupon can be sent to existing customers with an explanation text about how they or anybody else to whom they send that coupon code could use it, to get a discount when placing an online order. Discount coupons could be used as a method to make customers feel they are a part of an exclusive club, where only club members have access to the specific exclusive discounts on products.

Secondly, discount coupons can be used to track the efficiency of advertising campaigns. This is a very easy and straightforward method, as it allows for inclusion of an individual discount coupon code into all advertisements within an ad campaign, and for tracking orders by discount coupon code afterwards. Correspondingly, the efficiency of this or that advertising campaign is very easy to monitor as soon as the Administration panel of an online store provides a sale report with filters by discount coupons.

Finally, a discount coupon sent to a customer could be just a good way to say "sorry" for an issue with the product, or any provided service. If delivery of the customer's order was delayed, or the customer was sent a wrong product, a coupon that guarantees a discount on the next order will not only say "sorry" to the customer, but may also motivate the customer to place yet another order in the future.

Making Customers Aware of Discounts

Before the customer can use a discount coupon, the customer of course needs to be made aware of its existence and receive the special coupon code to redeem it later when placing an online order.

So how can an online store make new and existing customers aware of discount coupon offers?

First of all, for customers who have already placed an order in the past, a special electronic newsletter can be emailed featuring the discount coupon. Or the letters could be sent by post, each containing a special discount coupon code that the customer could use when buying online again. Customers can even be sent a printed catalog of products with the discount coupon promotion in it, so that the customers could actually see what they can get a discount on, even before they log into their account on the website.

Developing further the idea of sending customers an email or a letter, a special email or a special letter could be sent to each customer who placed at least one online order in the past with a discount coupon promotion on products of brands or types purchased earlier. Brand and product type can be determined by studying the customer's history of purchases. If the customer has bought products of a certain brand/manufacturer online in the past, there are good chances the customer would like to do it again in the future, and by sending a discount coupon to that customer, the online store actually motivates the customer to place a new order now (especially if the discount coupon promotion is time or stock limited!).

Some new customers may learn about discounts from their friends who received an email or a letter from the online store.

There are special websites that work as discount and special offer directories. Effectively, they try to list discount offers provided by different websites (including online stores) and make those available to their own customers. Advertising in such directories can bring a lot of new sales to an online store, though the online merchant should clearly understand that customers who came from such discount offers directories will most probably be very price-sensitive and may not buy again (i.e. turn into repeat customers) unless they are given a discount again.

Interestingly enough, the online store itself can advertise some of its discount coupon promotions. It can be a banner or a text message on its pages telling the website visitors about the promotion and also informing them about which discount coupon code to use to get a discount. Usually, the amount of discount would not be too big in this case. This method can be used to push customers into making up their minds about buying online in that particular online store. Such discount coupons will be often limited by date and stock.

Information about existing and upcoming promotions, including discount coupon codes, can be printed in local newspapers (or included into their online versions) in the regions where the target audience of the online store is supposed to be present. Marketing specialists suggest choosing Thursday and Friday issues of newspapers to achieve better effect in weekend sales.

Similar to the newspapers, advertising materials containing a discount coupon code could be included into magazines (printed and their online version).

Especially interesting is a discount deal that an online merchant can propose to a magazine to be available to its readers only. According to the deal, the magazine would publish the advertisement either in its printed or online version, and the online store will give all customers who used a corresponding coupon code a special discount. A prospective customer would not have any other way to get a discount than to read about it in the magazine, or be advised by another reader. The magazine itself would be interested in advertising the discount offer as exclusively available to its readers, and making as many of its readers as possible, aware of the offer.

Rebates

A rebate as advertised by an online store is effectively a promise to give the customer a certain amount of money back after the customer has placed an order, has fully paid for the order, and filled in a special rebate claiming form (which can also be used to ask clients some questions about the their satisfaction with the product or service provided, and about their plans to buy certain brands or product types in the future) and sent it to the online store by post or in an electronic format (via email).

Rebates can "trigger" a customer's decision to place an order as they are promised a discount (or a certain amount of money back) once the order is complete. But rebates do not work exactly like simple discount coupons or other discounts. Rebates work better for online merchants and they are actually more profitable than any of the other discounts discussed earlier.

There are two reasons for that:

- First of all, not all customers of an online store would be looking for a discount. There are price-sensitive customers who would very seriously consider the price, and a rebate would make a great difference to their decision to place an order with that particular online store. But there are also less price-sensitive customers, who can be attracted by the fact of the existence of a rebate offer, but may not consider actually claiming a rebate once the order has been placed and the goods received.

- Secondly, a rebate claim form can be used by the Administration of the online store to get important information about how satisfied the customer is with purchased products and provided services, and also to learn about customer's preferences on product brands and about the customer's intention to buy products of certain brands and types in the future. That information can be processed and entered into a database that can be further used to send some customers (who indicated that would not mind receiving promotional materials from the online store!) information about ongoing promotions and special discount coupons.

Also, some studies say that the "pain" of buying a product can be eased by offering the customer rebate if the customer is price-sensitive. But once the order is placed, it becomes less important for some customers to actually claim the rebate back. Also, some customers won't be bothered to fill in the claim rebate form; it just doesn't seem worth the effort for them.

Avoiding an Addiction to Discounts

A common problem that may result in losses in business for an online merchant can be the so called "addiction" to discounts.

Customers of an online store should see the value in the products they buy. If it is only the discount that affects their decision to buy online, as soon as the discount is not offered anymore the customers will stop buying. Correspondingly, the turnover of the online store will drop and this will affect the profits. Unless of course, the discounts are combined with many other ways to market and promote the online store itself and its products.

Also, online merchants, seeing the turnover figures improving when providing their customers with discounts may miss something very important—the way in which the profit figures change along with the turnover. As more discounts are applied, the less profitable is the business, the smaller the profit that can be made on each single order.

Also, the more the turnover, the greater are the costs of running the business. Really, the greater the number of orders placed online, the more the personnel and efforts required to process those orders, the more the cost for delivery services, etc. Operational costs may also grow up, and the online merchant should be very careful when making decisions to hire more staff, or move into new premises if the turnover growth is based on the strategy of offering discounts to customers. Strategic business decisions should be based on the growth of actual profit figures, not the turnover!

We are of course not saying discounts are bad for business—they are good as they help attract more customers who can become repeat customers in the future and also discounts can increase sales and profit figures at the same time. What we are saying here is that an online merchant should be very careful when choosing the type of discount to advertise on the website and how to set products' prices in order to not only increase turnover but, most importantly, profit.

Winning Market Share

The bigger the share of the market covered by an online store, the more is the turnover of that online store as more and more customers get to the online store directly or indirectly when searching for products that the online store has to offer. Before considering the expansion and winning a bigger share of the market, the online store should consider if it will still be possible to provide the increased number of customers with at least the same level of quality service as is maintained by the online store at the moment.

The market share can be won by using advertising, PR, and marketing efforts. It can be won by:

- Implementing a successful search engine optimization of the online store
- Expanding the product range offered online
- Translating an online store into multiple languages and starting international trading.

But there are some more ways to win market share, more customers, and effectively increase the turnover of an online store than that.

Affiliate Program

Running an affiliate program allows an online store to establish its very own network of resellers, have its affiliates (resellers) refer customers to the online store, and have affiliates do promotion of products and services sold online. The more active affiliates an online store has in its network, the more are the chances that the potential customer will end up on either the website of the online store or one of its affiliates' websites when searching for products and services offered by the online store.

It makes sense to start establishing a reseller network when the online store itself already has a good record of sales, or when at least the products have some strong potential, as potential resellers would need to see their chance to make profit on becoming an affiliate to that particular online store.

We looked at the technical solutions available to an osCommerce online store to run an affiliate program in Chapter 2. There are solutions that can be integrated directly into osCommerce to establish a store's very own affiliate program, or an online store can participate in popular third-party affiliate programs to get a better exposure among the potential resellers.

In either case, support for multiple tiers of affiliate program can be beneficial for an online store in order to win a bigger market share by increasing the total number of affiliates of different tiers. It also builds a network for each affiliate, which if configured and promoted right, can expand very quickly among multiple website owners.

Two things should be done by the online store in order to maintain the affiliate network and expand it further:

- Provide affiliates with proper marketing materials to advertise products and services on their own sites.
- Provide affiliates with proper and up-to-date statistics and prompt payments of their commissions.

B2B Program for Trade Customers

Trade (or business) customers are usually smaller businesses who would like to buy their inventory from the online store, and either re-sell it further or use it as they deem appropriate.

For example, an online store that sells nutrition products may have smaller resellers set up as its business customers who would place relatively big orders online or offline, and would then resell purchased products to their own customers (often to their local customers). Another example would be about an online store that sells white goods. Development companies may place relatively big online or offline orders for certain types of white goods to use those products in their newly developed properties—i.e. even though there's no direct sale to the end customers here, products sold by the online store reach the end customers in the future anyway.

By having a special B2B (wholesale) program for its trade customers, an online store not only effectively wins more market (as orders placed by end customers are effectively fulfilled by the online store) but also increases its turnover directly by selling more products at a time to fulfill purchase orders placed by its trade customers.

It should be noted that a B2B program may help to increase profits of an online store, but can negatively affect growth of its profitability as trade customers would usually ask for better terms than the end customers.

By better terms, here we would understand special payment terms, special delivery methods, and of course special product pricing.

If an online store has multiple business customers, they can be split into several groups. Criteria for inclusion into this or that trade customer group would usually depend on the total amount of orders placed by the trade customer in the past.

Different trade customer groups may have different payment and shipping terms, and different prices too.

In order to become a registered trade customer, a business would normally be asked to provide a proof of its trade history for a certain period of time, and sometimes to place its first order of a specific amount. After that, the business customer can be added to one of the business customer groups where special payment and shipping conditions, product range, and prices will be made available.

Online merchant can either hire a qualified osCommerce developer to implement a B2B program precisely according to the specific requirements of that online merchant, or purchase one of the already existing osCommerce-based solutions with B2B program already implemented.

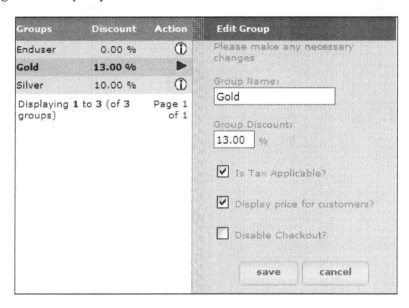

Each group of users could have its default discount in percent. This discount is applied to each and every product if a special price setting is not in force.

It is possible to enable and disable tax depending on the customer group.

A special setting is responsible for displaying product price to customers of the group. This feature is useful when an online store shouldn't display product prices to its visitors, but only to registered customers.

The Disable Checkout option can be used to turn the online store into an online catalog or online brochure, and encourage customers to get in contact with the Administration or the sales team of the online store to place orders or get quotes. A customer can be assigned to one of the existing customer groups. There is always at least one default customer group. Visitors to the online store are treated as customers who belong to the default customer group.

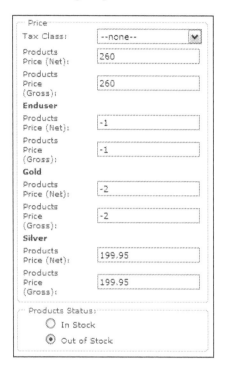

Product price can be specified per each customer group. Price can be specified in several different ways.

"-2" in the price edit box means the online store will use default customer group's discount.

"-1" in the price edit box means the online store will disable the product for customers of that group completely.

Any other value in the price edit box means the online store should use the specified price when displaying the product to customers of that specific customer group.

Of course, the system requires the default (retail) price to be set up in the back end of the online store for each product.

Making a Difference for Trade Customers

Trade customers would expect the online store to treat them differently than retail customers.

This may result in a different product range. Some products may not be of interest to trade customers at all, and those will most likely be excluded from the product range available to trade customers to make it easier for them to find the products of interest in the product catalog.

It may also result into different shipping methods available to trade customers. First of all, the amount of orders placed by trade customers will be different from the amount of orders placed by retail customers. Total order weight will likely be different too. Online merchants can expect the trade customers to place larger orders than retail customers, and correspondingly delivery charges may be calculated in a different way for trade customers than for retail customers' orders.

Of course, trade customers would expect certain discounts and special promotions to be made available by the Administration of the online store. The price of each product offered to trade customers can be set depending on which customer group the trade customer belongs to. Usually, customers who belong to a certain customer group expect to get at least a given discount percent, plus discounted product prices for some groups can be set to make the deal even sweeter for trade customers of those customer groups. Special promotions and discounts (like, for example, when buying products in bulk or while the stock lasts) can be made available solely for trade customers, or even for trade customers who belong to a certain customer group only.

To make the ordering process easier for trade customers, the online merchant may consider building a special front end where trade customers could log into their account and see the product range and prices according to their customer group. Also, the very way in which products are added to the Shopping Cart may be made different, easier to use for trade customers who usually order multiple products at once. Therefore, a quantity field can be added to any Product Listing or Product Information page. Also, when adding a product to the shopping cart, the shopping cart page may be skipped to save the customer's time on clicking the "Continue shopping" button. Instead, the Shopping Cart total can be displayed either in the header of the site or in one of its side columns. A special page can be developed for trade customers to make it even simpler and more straightforward to order multiple products at once. The page would consist of several edit boxes where trade customer could put in the desired product model number and corresponding quantity required. By pressing only one "Add to Cart" button, a trade customer would make the website add all the products and all quantities into the shopping cart without losing the time on one-by-one product selection, which is suitable for retail customers but is not suitable for trade customers.

Trade customers often expect special payment terms on their purchases. Like, for example, the so called "net 30 terms"—a 30 days delay in paying the full amount for purchase orders placed online or offline. Such payment terms could be provided to specific customer groups only.

Also, additional payment methods can be enabled for certain customer groups, like bank transfer, which may not be available for retail customers at all, or a Credit Account payment method, which may only be available for trade customers.

A credit account payment method allows customers to buy products without actually paying for them until their credit balance with the online store reaches a certain amount called the "credit limit". The credit limit can be set on either a per-group or per-customer basis. The customer is usually given a period of time when the credit balance should reach zero, but as soon as the customer makes the first payment, the credit account payment method again becomes available to that particular trade customer, and the customer can continue shopping for products online, though of course, the customer can only buy products that will not cause the current balance to exceed that customer's credit limit.

Multiple Front Ends (Online Mall Solution)

Almost every other big osCommerce project nowadays turns into a complex system where the store owner wishes to have multiple online stores (front ends) linked to the same back end and the same osCommerce database.

There are several reasons to consider this approach for online business.

First, having multiple front ends all linked to the same back end allows for having different (from the buyer's point of view) online stores. Correspondingly, approaching various niche markets becomes possible. Each front end may have its own design, products, and even domain names. Each front end can be marketed separately, depending on the best approach to reach its target audience in order to win a larger market share.

Second, managing several online stores using the same back end is way easier than managing several separate online stores. The online store management team can be the same for all front ends, all orders are stored in one place, and all dispatches can be also managed more easily. Finally, reports and statistics will show the status of the whole business and not just some of its parts. If properly implemented, the system should allow for very easy catalog management. Changes in the product catalog will be automatically distributed among all front ends. This approach also allows for selling franchise licenses to other businesses, where each franchise has its own domain, similar design, and the same or very similar product range. A franchise business will be promoted and managed by each licensee, but it's the Top Administrator of the e-commerce system who will have full control over all franchised online stores and will be able to help licensees if required.

Third, having the product catalog split into several front ends may improve SEO of the whole system. Each front end can be given its specific product range, so keyword density within a particular front end can be higher than for a website that has all the products. Also, all front ends can point to each other, improving page ranks. One fairly important note here is that it's preferable to have different descriptions per product per each individual front end, as otherwise the problem of duplicate content may ruin SEO efforts.

Fourth, having a system with multiple front ends in place, the online store management team can launch a much featured affiliate program. Front ends are hosted on the same server where the back end of the system is located. Naturally, a front end of an online store with its list of products, with its own design, is an ideal solution for an affiliate business. The store management team would just need to assign a certain commission percent on all orders received from an affiliate's front end, and the system is ready to go live! All received orders will be stored in the database as orders received from a certain front end, and commission percent will be really easy to calculate.

There is a contribution available for free download at `http://addons.oscommerce.com/info/1730/` that helps to turn an osCommerce-based online store into a multiple front ends solution. It should be noted that to turn osCommerce into a truly multiple front end system, a significant amount of development and marketing efforts should be invested into the business, but a multiple front end system can pay for itself very soon if properly marketed.

Summary

The turnover of an online store can be increased in many ways. Two of them that we considered in this chapter are by using discounts and by winning larger market share.

There may be various types of discounts applied to product prices, but an online merchant should never forget to monitor the profitability of the business and apply such discounts as will increase the turnover while at the same time the profit figures will continue to grow, even if at a reduced speed.

Also, increased turnover may result into a significant increase of operational costs, so the online store's profitability may be significantly affected by the increased turnover, and the online merchant should not only work on increasing the turnover, but also on reducing operational costs and making order processing and dispatching as fast as possible and of the highest quality.

Of course, the turnover of an online store can be increased by increasing its market share. Again, it can be achieved in many ways, where the main principle is to make the end customer come to the online store even if the customer is dealing with another player in the market and would prefer to buy products from them. An affiliate program, and a B2B program for trade customers, will direct end an customer's order to the online store even if the end customer bought from an affiliate (reseller), or if a B2B customer buys products online to fulfill either a single order or orders multiple products at a better price to supply future sales with products directly from stock.

The multiple front ends solution allows for winning niche markets easily and promoting parts of product catalog of the main online store elsewhere, having customer's orders gathered together in one place to make online store management easier for its Administration.

In the next chapter, we will talk about how the ordering (Checkout) process can be improved in osCommerce, and how a customer's personal account could be used to increase the number of sales, the turnover, and profits.

10

Improving Conversion Rates and Customer Experience

Having dedicated previous chapters to various aspects of running an online business powered by osCommerce, it makes sense to look back and see how the efficiency of an online store can be measured and improved, and how that efficiency affects the business as a whole.

There are not many ways to measure the efficiency of any business. One can say the business is efficient if it regularly achieves its targets. But what is important is not only if the targets are achieved, but also how much effort it took to achieve them.

For example, the same amount of profits could be achieved by an online store with different turnover figures, depending on the effectiveness and profitability of the business.

By improving the efficiency of the business, the online merchant makes it possible to achieve the same targets investing less effort and less funds; hence more effort and money could be invested into further business development.

Why Improve Conversion Rates?

The conversion rate represents the efficiency of an e-commerce-based online business—to some degree. Several conversion rates could be measured, from how many impressions of an advertisement on other websites convert into clicks to the online store, to how many visitors to the online store later become its customers (i.e. place online orders) and later repeat customers.

Improving conversion rates actually means improving the efficiency of the business, and its profitability. This is because it may cost a significant amount of money and effort to attract visitors to the online store, and converting so many of those visitors into customers simply pays off for the money spent on PR, advertising, etc. A simple business model could be built that demonstrates how the profit produced by an online store depends on the cost of advertising and PR—in fact, how the business's profitability depends on Return on Investment (ROI). Correspondingly, the more visitors of online store place online orders, the less each individual order costs to the online merchant (the so called cost per acquisition becomes cheaper), the higher is ROI, and the more efficient is that particular online business.

Visitors to an online store convert into customers (place online orders) when they have had a positive experience with the online store. The best experience a customer can get is when the online store offers the customer exactly what the customer desires, within the customer's budget, and the order placement process is easy and secure. A mixture of all that, sometimes in a different order, usually ensures good visitor-to-customer conversion rates.

Therefore, the online store should help the customer find the desired product (even if the customer doesn't know exactly what it is), provide the customer with price options if the product's price is out of that customer's budget, and provide the customer with a straightforward and secure facility to place an online order. Positive customer experience with an online store results in improved conversion rates, and correspondingly, improved efficiency and profitability of an online business.

Conversion Rates in osCommerce

Before conversion rates can be improved, they should be measured.

But how can they be measured in osCommerce? And which conversion rates are to be measured?

There are different types of conversion rates that indicate how efficient and successful the online business is.

Visitors to Customers Conversion Rate

The conversion rate that is used often is the ratio of the number of buyers to the number of visitors to the online store. To measure this conversion rate, the online merchant needs to know how many visitors visited the store in a certain period of time, and how many of those have placed orders.

It should be mentioned that whatever method is used to measure those figures, it should make a clear difference between all orders placed online in a certain period of time, and those orders that have been placed by new visitors/customers during the same period.

It should also be noted that a number of new visitors may not be ready to place an online order straight away, so when they come back later to place an order, that order should be counted accordingly, along with other orders placed by the customers during that past time period. This means that figures for past time periods might change a bit in the future. The longer the period of measurements, the more precise those measurements will be, and the less likely they are to change significantly in the future.

This conversion rate shows how good the online store is in terms of selling products to very new visitors, how good it is in terms of converting visitors into customers who placed at least one online order. This will also show how many visitors were converted into buyers.

Any statistical package could be used to get approximate values of the conversion rate like Google Analytics (former Urchin) or the less complex Webalizer. Dividing the number of orders placed by new visitors by the number of those visits gives the online merchant an approximate value of the conversion rate during a certain period of time.

Let's assume the number of unique visitors to an online store per month is 15,000, and the number of online orders placed by those new unique visitors is 570. This means that the online store has a general conversion rate of 3.8% for new visitors.

For most online stores that rate would be less than 10%, which in the best-case scenario means that the online store needs to attract at least 100 new unique visitors to get 10 online orders. If the general conversion rate is just 1%, the online store would have to attract at least 1,000 new unique visitors to get 10 online orders, which obviously makes a big difference! Assuming each new unique visitor has seen the online store's paid advertisement on another website or in a search engine, and clicked the link, we can calculate how different the so called "cost of acquisition" of each new visitor will be for online stores with different conversion rates.

Let's assume that on the average each click on the advertisement displayed on another website or in a search engine costs the online merchant $0.40.

In the first case, where we have a 10% conversion rate, the online store needs to spend:

100   x $0.40   = $40

to get 10 online orders. Each order "costs" $4, which is spent on acquiring the customer.

In the second case, where we have a 1% conversion rate, the online store needs to spend:

1,000   x $0.40   = $400

to get 10 online orders. In that case, each order's cost is already $40, and this is to attract only one new customer!

That's a huge difference, and it demonstrates how important it is to work on improving the general conversion rate from new visitors to customers.

Customers to Repeat Customers Conversion Rate

Yet another rate can be calculated when measuring the number of customers who place their second, third, and so on orders. It can be calculated by dividing the number of customers with more than one order on the account by the total number of registered customers who placed at least one online order.

This rate is also very important, as it demonstrates how much the online store actually saves on not paying for acquiring multiple orders from already registered customers.

Let's suppose at least one of seven registered customers places at least one order during a certain period of time. This means that the return customers conversion rate is at least 14.28%.

As soon as customers order more than once, it starts to improve the general conversion rate — because now, instead of getting all orders from new customers and paying a certain amount for attracting new customers, the online merchant gets 14.28% of orders "free" — i.e. without paying for acquiring the customer on such orders.

So even if the general conversion rate is 1%, but one of each seven customers will place at least one more order with the online store in the future, the actual conversion rate for that period of time is about 1.14%.

This makes a significant difference in the actual cost of acquiring new customers; instead of $400 to get 10 new customers/orders, the online merchant would actually pay 877 x $0.40 =$350.8, where 877 is the required number of new visitors, who, along with customers who ordered previously, would place 10 orders in total.

Of course, the more orders placed by customers who have already bought from the online store at least once, the "cheaper" are those orders to the online merchant. Therefore, online merchants are very much interested in converting customers into repeat customers.

Conversion of Referring Sources, Media Types, and Advertising Campaigns

The above conversion rates show how the online store performs in general, whereas conversion rates by specific referring sources (such as other websites, search engines, magazines, TV ads, etc.) demonstrate more specifically how visitors referred by those referring sources convert into customers.

Knowing specific referring sources' conversion rates helps to identify those referring sources that generate most of the customer traffic. Also, it's possible to see which referring sources do not produce a traffic of visitors who later convert into customers.

This usually means that visitors who come from those not-converting referring sources:

- Cannot find the products they are looking for on the website easily enough.
- Find the price is not right for them.
- There are some other reasons that stop them from placing online orders.

This may be because.

- The online store's presence in the referring source is not right, in which case then it should be changed.
- The main page or landing pages may be confusing for most of the visitors who were referred by those specific referring sources, in which case the content of landing pages (or even the main page of the online store if it's where most of the visitors get to) should be reworked.

- The price of products offered by the online store is not right for visitors referred by those specific referring sources. In that case, if it's not possible to lower the price because of tight margins, it may make sense to terminate the online store's presence in those referring sources with lower conversion rate from visitors to customers and invest that saved money into other referring sources with higher conversion rates.

Each visitor who comes to the website via some paid advertisement and leaves the website without placing an order is a loss of money spent on advertising in the corresponding referring source. The loss of the money spent on attracting one visitor obviously does not affect the whole business, but if the conversion rate is too small, the total figures spent on attracting non-buying visitors grow high and become quite noticeable.

As with referring sources, it's possible to calculate some more general conversion rates, like by media type. Usually, an online store would be advertised in media of several different types, including the Internet, printed magazines, newspapers, classifieds, exterior advertisements, TV, radio, etc.

The costs of advertising usually differs depending on the media type. Correspondingly, knowing conversion rates by media type helps to identify those that refer visitors who better convert into customers, and those that refer visitors who do not often convert into customers later on.

As with referring sources, the cause of lower conversion rate should be carefully examined, and corresponding measures taken. The online merchant should consider the case when the target audience of the online store prefers certain media types over others.

If it's impossible to improve the low conversion rate of a certain media type, and the costs of referring visitors by that media type are significant, the online merchant should consider ending the presence of the online store in that media type, and investing those funds into advertising in other media types with better conversion rates.

Most of the statistical packages (such as Google Analytics) allow for monitoring conversion rates of referring sources and media types, but mostly the online ones. In order to track conversion rates of all referring sources and media types, including those offline (i.e. printed, aired, etc.), the online store should use some more advanced methods.

For example, a special landing page could be developed for a specific referring source (like some magazine, or radio), and then statistics could be gathered on how many visitors were referred to that page, and how many of those visitors later placed at least one online order.

To record which landing page the customer has first come to, it's possible to use cookies that are stored on the customer's computer for a certain number of days. During the checkout process, osCommerce can check the value of a special cookie and store its value into the database, along with the order. The conversion rate of a referring source or media type could be easily calculated by dividing the number of orders placed by visitors to the landing page related to the referring source or whole media type by the total number of visitors to that page.

Usually, the conversion rate of an advertising campaign depends on:

- Whether it reaches the target audience of the online store
- If the content of the advertisement is right for that target audience
- If visitors who reach the online store can easily find products they are or might be interested in
- If the price of the advertised products is within the budget of customers who belong to the target audience

As with referring sources, it's possible to set up a special landing page for each advertising campaign, and use special cookies to track how many of the visitors who "land" on that page actually place online orders later on.

With an advertising campaign, it's also possible to use some sort of a discount coupon code that would either give customers a discount, free delivery option, or, for example, register the customer as a participant in a lottery where the prize is, again, one of the products being offered by the online store. This method can help an online merchant to track the conversion rates of offline advertising campaigns.

Actually, the same methods can help the online merchant to track conversion of not only advertising campaigns, but also referring sources — as one and the same landing page or discount coupon code could become a unique identifier of a certain advertising campaign AND referring source at the same time.

Conversion of Certain Categories, Brands, and Individual Products

Product catalog and product information of course affect the online store's conversion rates a lot.

Visitors to an online store will become customers if products that the online store has on offer are the products that those visitors are looking for, or see as a way to address their needs even if they do not have an exact picture of the desired products in their minds yet.

Conversion rates calculated by category, brand, or individual product may demonstrate:

- Which parts of the product catalog actually generate orders and which parts do not

- Where there's room for improvement, of either product information, category information, brand information, or simply product sale price

- Which categories or brands or individual products convert most of visitors into customers — it makes sense to promote such parts of the product catalog extensively

- Which categories, brands, or individual products do not convert visitors into customers at all, and therefore should be either improved, reworked, or removed from the online store completely to concentrate visitors' attention on those products that do actually convert visitors into customers

It is relatively easy to calculate the number of unique visitors that some category page, or brand (manufacturer) page, or product page has received per certain period of time. It is also possible to use the cookie method and store a certain value into that cookie on visitor's computer as soon as the visitor opens a certain category, brand, or product page. Then, when some visitors place online orders, osCommerce can read the cookie value and put it along with the customer's order into the database. By dividing the number of orders produced by a certain category, brand, or product page by the number of unique visitors who opened the corresponding page, the online merchant gets the corresponding conversion rates.

Interestingly enough, there could be products, "referrals" that do not convert visitors into customers very well themselves, but motivate visitors to order other products that are somehow related to those "referral" ones. In that situation, statistics on conversion rate will highlight products that act as referrals.

Lower conversion rates on certain categories may call for reconsidering the structure of the product catalog, and re-organizing products in different categories. Lower conversion rates on certain brands may be caused by the target audience not being interested in such brands, or by a non-competitive pricing policy. In that case, it makes sense to ensure that those brands are of interest to the target audience of the online store, and may be rework the prices on products of those brands.

If improvement of conversion rates on some categories and brands is not possible because of tight margins or other reasons, it may make sense to drop certain brands or categories completely from the product catalog to let visitors concentrate on those brands and categories that actually convert visitors into customers, i.e. sell well.

This will not only increase general conversion rates of the online store, but will positively affect the return on investment figures, as less funds will be invested into promotion and support of products that do not bring enough sales and profits.

Conversion of Pages and Page Elements

Conversion rates from visitors to customers often depend on how certain pages of the site are designed, on the information displayed on them, and even on the location and appearance of certain page elements.

Later on in the chapter, we will see how pages and page elements affect conversion rates, how this effect can be measured, and how conversion rates could be improved when measurement procedures are in place and constantly used.

Conversion of Website Navigation and Search Facility

General conversion rate depends a lot on if the visitor to the online store can easily find the desired product or service offered online. Ideally, an online store would be able to suggest to the visitor this or that product even if the visitor doesn't have an exact idea about the desired product yet, but just has some general needs.

Of course, it would be easiest for the client to see the needed products directly on the landing page of the website. In fact, it's possible to realize such a situation by putting in place special landing pages for specific products or groups of products, and advertising those specific products or product groups in different media and putting links to the specific landing pages into advertising materials.

Pointing the visitor to an online store to desired products in an instant dramatically increases the chances of the same visitor placing an order with that online store, i.e. it increases conversion rates, and profitability of the online store.

Understanding how website navigation helps to convert more visitors into customers requires being able to calculate how many steps an average customer makes before he or she adds a product to the shopping basket. It is possible to calculate in osCommerce how many clicks on different category, brand (manufacturer), and product pages an average visitor makes before adding at least one product into the shopping cart.

It is also possible to calculate the relation between the number of clicks and the number of orders placed by visitors to an online store, which will be the conversion rate by clicks (or navigation).

The relation between the number of times the average visitor uses the search facility and the number of products added to the shopping cart or ordered directly from the search results page demonstrates the conversion rate (efficiency) of the search feature of the online store.

Of course, the more optimized the search feature is, the more relevant results (products) it brings to the visitors, the more are the chances for those relevant products to be ordered.

Lower search facility conversion rates mean that the search feature needs to be improved as visitors to the online store are not finding what they are looking for. Or that the visitors to an online store are not entirely sure about what they are looking for, and need some help—in that case it's possible to implement a special wizard or filtering system that could help website visitors in finding exact products even if the visitors are not sure about what they are looking for, and have certain needs but do not know the exact names or models of products.

Paths that Convert Visitors into Customers

An average osCommerce-based online store may have many paths that convert visitors into customers, but they all end up in the same way—with the Checkout Success page, with the order confirmation page. So it is easier to start discovering those paths from the end rather than from the beginning, as we know for sure what's at their end and can start our research from the Checkout Success page.

Which is the page that a visitor to an osCommerce online store would see before the Checkout Success page? It's the Checkout Confirmation page, where the order summary is displayed along with the customer's details and the customer (yes, already a customer since the visitor has already gone through the registration or login process to reach the Checkout Confirmation page) is required to confirm the order.

It is not possible to get to the Checkout Success page without having seen the Checkout Confirmation page earlier.

Which is the page one usually deals with prior to Checkout Confirmation page in osCommerce? It's the Checkout Payment and Checkout Shipping pages, where the customer chooses preferred shipping and payment methods. And it's not possible to get to the Checkout Confirmation page without passing through the Checkout Shipping and then Checkout Payment pages in standard osCommerce.

The customer comes to the Checkout Shipping page from either the New Customer registration pages, or from the Login page — here, for the first time we see how the path that converts visitors into customers splits in two. Actually, the customer may have been already logged in and then clicked one of the Checkout links (in the breadcrumbs, in the Shopping Cart page, etc.), which made the online store display the Checkout Shipping page of the checkout process.

Before that the visitor to an online store might have either pressed the Checkout button on the Shopping Cart page, or clicked the Checkout link in the header being on any page at all, or pressed the Buy Now button on the product listing page or product information page — there are multiple possibilities out there, and it all depends on how a particular osCommerce online store is built.

All the steps described above are more or less obvious and obligatory in standard osCommerce if the visitor to the online store wants to place an order.

But the true interest lies in the paths different visitors choose BEFORE they enter the checkout route. The path from the main/landing page to the checkout page is what should be examined by online merchants, and what should be the target for optimization. Those paths could be determined by statistical packages (like Google Analytics) or tracked by osCommerce online store itself.

In the latter case, a special addition to a script generally used (like for example the `application_top.php` file, which is usually located in the `/includes/` subfolder of the online store) can make it possible to store the names or IDs of all pages opened by the visitor to an online store before the checkout pages, and store them into the database along with the order for further analysis.

It seems obvious that the shorter the path is, the more efficient is the navigation of the online store, and the easier it is for visitors to the site to find what they are looking for. It may be discovered that certain paths end up with the Checkout Success page more often than other paths—in that case, the online merchant may want to study why other paths are not so successful by comparing them to the paths that convert more visitors into customers, and also consider using the pages of successful paths in order to promote complementary products to the ones regularly bought by customers who choose this or that path through the online store.

Conversion Rate Drop during the Checkout Process

Let's go back for a while and concentrate on the checkout process, and on how conversion rate changes from one step to another.

Let's consider the following to be the steps of the checkout process: Shopping Cart, New Customer Registration page/Login page, Checkout Shipping, Checkout Payment, Checkout Confirmation, and Checkout Success pages.

Let's remember that the general conversion rate of an osCommerce-based online store would be the number of customers who actually reach the Checkout Success page divided by the number of unique visitors who come to the online store during a certain period of time.

If the general conversion rate of an online store is 3.8%, this means that of each 1,000 unique visitors only 38 place online orders, only 38 reach the Checkout Success page. But what does it mean for other pages of the online store, and of the checkout process in particular?

For the checkout process pages, this means that their individual conversion rates, figures that show how many visitors or customers have actually reached those pages, will be higher or equal to the general conversion rate of the online store. Talking about the checkout pages, as they are mandatory to visit before an order can be recorded in the database, the individual conversion rate of each previous page will always be higher than or equal to (for the sake of correct theoretical argument, as in most cases, it will be simply higher all the time) the conversion rate of each further page/step of the checkout process.

This means that from a number of visitors who reach the Shopping Cart page, only some get to the New Customer registration/Login page. Of those, only a part would actually go through the registration or login process and end up on the Checkout Shipping page. Of those, only some would go further to the Checkout Payment page. And only a part of those would reach the Checkout Confirmation page. And finally, only a part of those will actually confirm the order and place it online and reach the Checkout Success page.

On each of those steps, the number of visitors and customers who reach further steps usually drops.

It is a task of utmost importance to measure the conversion rates of each page that is a part of the checkout process, see how the individual conversion rate of each page differs from the conversion rates of other pages, understand reasons why the conversion rate differs between the pages of the checkout process, and seek for ways to improve the individual conversion rate of each and every page.

There is a natural drop of conversion rate for checkout process pages, as not all visitors and customers are actually ready to place an online order even though they may have added products to the Shopping Cart, and even registered and created an account, or have already chosen payment and shipping method.

If the individual conversion rate of some page is unexpectedly low, this may be caused by some problem with the previous page, that prevents visitors or customers from moving forward, and results in more visitors or customers leaving the page/ the online store than one would normally expect. Pages can be confusing, too complex, look uncomfortable or not secure enough to continue with the checkout process. The task of an online merchant is to ensure such problems are dealt with promptly to allow for improved general conversion rates of an online store.

As an example, conversion rate could be dropping on each step of the checkout process. It could be 60% on the Shopping Cart page, 32% on the Registration/Login page, 15% on the Checkout Shipping page, 10% on the Checkout Payment page, 6% on the Checkout Confirmation page, and only 3% on the Checkout Success page. The online merchant can work on improving all parts of the online store and checkout process in particular to improve conversion rates.

As with improved conversion rate of ANY page of the checkout process, the online store actually improves its general conversion rate. If all relations between pages and conversion rates stay the same, but instead of 15% of total visitors, 20% reach the Checkout Shipping page after certain improvements of the Shopping Cart and New Customer Registration pages, the online store can count on a 3% x 20 / 15 = 4% general conversion rate! It's a 33% increase in turnover (compared to 3% conversion rate) and most probably an increase in profit figures as well!

Conversion Based on Browsing History

Checking the paths that converted website visitors into customers, one can sometimes find that before certain products were added to the Shopping Cart and bought later on, the visitor to the online store had visited other product pages, or just some other pages of the online store.

If by analyzing multiple orders it's possible to locate certain dependencies, it makes sense to start using those dependencies to convert even more visitors into customers.

For example, the browsing history may show that a number of customers bought product B after they have seen product A. In that case, product B could be featured as something the customer might be interested in while on the product A page, or positioned alongside product A on the product listing page.

Even more than that could be done. Depending on what were the last several pages of the online store seen by the visitor or customer (pages like products, categories, etc.), the online store can list certain products related to those pages and promote them to the customer.

Although it sounds a little bit complicated, it is definitely something that could be achieved with osCommerce.

It's possible to build a custom solution based entirely on osCommerce technology to allow for such "prediction" feature, or use third-party solutions that are very easy to integrate into the online store. That software tracks visits and purchases, and then does all the math on its side, linking products to the browsing history that led to their purchase.

Page Elements that Improve Conversion Rates

Sometimes conversion from visitor to customer starts with an almost unnoticeable page element, like a button or a link, an information box, or an icon. Almost any visible page element can make a difference, affect a customer's decision on placing an order.

In this chapter, we will see how various page elements and web pages themselves affect conversion rates, and how to improve conversion rates by improving the pages.

But before we go any deeper into that topic, let us consider a situation where a decision should be made whether or not and how to put this or that element of design on the page—and the entire element is very important for conversion rates. Let's assume it's the decision of whether to put either the "Add to Cart" button or the "More Info" button on the Product Listing page. So how do we make that decision? Which button would go on the Product Listing page, or maybe both buttons should be placed there?

The answer is very simple and elegant: give no answer yourself. Better let your customers decide. By putting different customers into different situations, by showing two different groups of customers a different design element each, the online merchant can compare conversion rates that are specific to when this or that button was shown on the Product Listing page.

Technically, the implementation of this can be done using cookies. Each time a new visitor comes to an online store, a randomized procedure would virtually put the visitor into one of the two test groups. The value of a special cookie would be set accordingly, so each time that user comes back to the website, the website would only display that button on the Product Listing page to that particular user. And each time the visitor later on places an order and converts into a customer, the value of that cookie would be stored in the database along with the order, so that it would be possible to see which approach, which button actually converts more visitors into customers.

This approach in general could be called "A & B testing" and represents the idea that customers are better given the chance to advise an online merchant on which solution (either A or B) they prefer and which solution would convert more visitors to the online store into its customers.

Main Page/Landing Page

When the customer first gets to an osCommerce-based online store, the customer "lands" on either the main page of the site, or any other page of the site. It can be either a Product Information page, Product listing page, or some specially designed page, which is often referred to as a "landing page".

Specifically built landing pages are often used in advertising campaigns. Customers who saw certain advertising are referred to the corresponding landing page, which not only contains appropriate content, but also records visits so that it will be possible to track the conversion rate and success of particular advertising campaigns.

As already said, it makes sense to put specific content on the landing pages that is related to advertising campaigns, to give the visitor the feeling of the "right place" to be. Quite often, online merchants make a mistake of referring their prospective customers to the main page of their website in each of their ad campaigns. The user may be disoriented and confused as the content of the main page quite often is not related to a particular ad campaign or advertising material the user might have just seen elsewhere. In many cases, the user then has to search for products or special offers on the website, which can further confuse that user and increase the chances of losing a prospective order.

So the rule of the thumb, when designing ad campaigns, is to create appropriate landing pages for those campaigns, and put appropriate content on those pages. Ideally, the landing page would confirm the message (some marketing action, promotion, special offer, etc.) the user has just seen elsewhere, and list some products related to that campaign too. It would also contain a link to the list of other products that are either related to that campaign, or to products listed on the landing page. This way the user will not get too much information at the very same time, but, if really interested in the offer, will be able to easily see (and possibly buy!) products directly on the landing page.

But what if the user comes to the main page of the online store, or to any other page from a search engine? Will the user always be able to see that the content of the page is actually what the user has just searched for?

Most web browsers nowadays send various parameters to the web server when requesting a web page. Among those parameters is the referral string. The referral string is what the user had in the address bar of the web browser before the link leading to the online store (in our particular case) was clicked. So, if the user searched for a certain key phrase in a search engine, the phrase itself and many other parameters including the URL of the search engine would likely be forwarded to the web server where the online store is hosted when the web browser sends a request for the page.

It's possible to create a relatively simple routine to extract the key phrase from the referral URL and display it on the pages of the online store to help the prospective customer to find desired products in the product catalog of the online store. That routine could be placed into the `/includes/application_top.php` script to ensure that every page of the online store is improved accordingly.

Once the routine is in place, the result of its work would look like:

"Thank you for visiting <online store name>! You searched for <key phrase> in <search engine URL>. <Click here> to run the search against our product catalog to let our online store find the best matching results for you" — where the <Click here> link would obviously lead the prospective customer to the Advanced Search results page.

Such an approach helps the user to find what he or she is actually looking for; therefore general conversion rates improve too.

Banners, Special Offers, and Featured Products Announcements

There are some page elements that can be present on any page of the online store, whether it's the main page or one of secondary pages. Those are various banners, special offers, featured products, promotions announcements, etc.

It makes sense to track conversion rates of each such banner, or featured product by recording the number of clicks on any of them, and also by recording the number of orders placed by customers who ever clicked on the banner or a featured product link. Of course, it's possible to record the number of sales of featured products and products on offer, but that measure would not be very accurate on its own, as those products can be bought in a more standard way by customers going through the product catalog.

To track whether the customer who placed an online order actually did click one of the banners or featured product announcements, online merchants could use cookies again. Using cookies in that case is really straightforward; as soon as the user clicks the banner, the corresponding cookie is saved onto the user's computer, and is then picked up by the online store during the checkout process.

The ratio between the number of clicks and the number of orders produced by a banner or featured product would be its conversion rate.

Many aspects may affect the individual conversion rates of design elements. The appearance of those design elements, and their position on the page are very important. Online merchants can experiment both with the look and feel of those elements of page design and of course with their position to find the optimal solution for their business. This gets back to the "A & B testing" method, where some prospective customers are presented with one version of the page, and other customers with another version. But the only difference is the appearance of certain page design element, like a banner or featured product announcement. Comparing the conversion rates of different versions of the same design elements, the online merchant can make an educated decision on how this or that design element or the whole page should look.

Product Listing Page

Wherever the user can see products, where it's any page of the online store, and especially the Product Listing page, it should be made very simple for that user to locate the following crucial information about the product on the page:

- Product name
- Product image
- Product price
- Short description or the main feature or two (often combined with product name)

It's also crucial that prospective customers are given a clear choice of either getting more information about the product, or buying the product straight away (or rather adding it to the Shopping Cart).

It's important to remember that users come to the online store looking for products, more often in the "buy" mood. Therefore, it's essential to give users a facility to buy products, and make it very prominent and unmistakable. The easier it is for prospective customer to buy a product online, the more often those prospective customers who are ready to buy will do so.

Product Information Page

Customers buy products for many reasons, but among those one of the most important is that the customer expects the product to address some specific needs, and make him/her happier.

Selling benefits and not only features demonstrates to prospective customers how a particular product can actually help to make them happier and/or ease their life. By letting the customer know about exactly how the product could be used, and what affect it will make on the customer—i.e. by selling a product as a bundle of benefits and solutions—an online store can actually increase its conversion rates.

For example, describing an electric kettle along with its basic characteristic like capacity, an online merchant could add several words about the number of people (size of family) that kettle would be able to boil the water for in one turn.

Or in the product description of a laptop, weight and size information could be followed by several words about how the customer could take the laptop anywhere, in almost any bag, and enjoy the day being able to work or watch movies or play games in the mean time.

A fridge freezer would be better described not only by its measurements of width, height, and depth, but rather by the size of the family that fridge would suit best, and also the size of the kitchen (whether it's got to be large or not).

Mobile phones could be better described by the lifestyle associated with them — whether it's a mobile phone for business needs, for family and chatting with friends, for outdoor activities, etc.

By associating a product in the customer's mind with some event or place where the customer feels or would feel happier, the online store improves the customer's reassurance in the product, and makes the product look and sound more familiar to the customer. The customer can easily imagine using the product, and also how using the product will positively affect the customer's life.

Hence the conversion rates will be increased and customers will be more likely to order products online.

Shopping Cart and Checkout Pages

Even if the customer is determined to buy a product, if the price is right, and the customer has added the product into the Shopping Cart, there may be some obstacles and distraction that could affect the customer's decision to place an online order, and of course affect the conversion rates.

The Shopping Cart and Checkout pages of an online store need to be made as simple, straightforward, but at the same time confident and secure looking as possible. We already considered how to build the customer's confidence by adding security certificates to the checkout pages, and more product information to the Shopping Cart (product image, description, etc.). Besides that, the Shopping Cart and Checkout pages could be simplified by disabling certain design elements, so that the customer's attention would not get drawn away to anything else on the page that doesn't lead to completing the order placement process.

It is recommended to remove all banners and promotion announcements from the Shopping Cart and Checkout pages if they are not directly related to product(s) currently located in the customer's Shopping Cart. This includes those banners usually displayed in the side columns, header, or footer on all other pages of the online store.

Adding the feeling of security and confidence to the Shopping Cart and Checkout pages by putting the company's contact details can repay in the increased conversion rates.

Simplification of the Checkout pages can be continued by reducing the number of them, and combining some of them together (like putting Login, Customer Registration, Billing, and Shipping options all on one page).

The simpler and quicker the Checkout process is, the more the chances are it won't cause any difficulties and confusion to the site's visitor, and the more the chances that the visitor will convert into a customer.

Checkout Confirmation Page

This page is the most important one as this is exactly the place where customers make their final decision on whether or not to place an order. The same as on the Shopping Cart and Checkout pages, it's recommended to remove all excessive design elements that may distract customers' attention.

In order to improve customer's experience, and give the customer that feeling of having full control over the Checkout process, the customer can be given an opportunity to pay online only on that page, the Checkout Confirmation page, and not earlier while being on other pages of the Checkout process. This method requires a number of serious modifications in the standard osCommerce Checkout process, and often it is better to seek a professional developer's help to change the osCommerce Checkout process in that way.

Once the customer has placed an order by pressing the **Confirm** or **Continue** or **Order** button, that very button could be disabled. It will then not let the customer to accidentally place another, identical order by pressing the button again. The button can be disabled using JavaScript. Also, a special routine could be added into the checkout process that would not accept an order from the same customer for the same products within a period of, say, five minutes after the first order has been received.

Checkout without an Account

Some online stores allow their customers to place online orders without creating an account. As a number of customers may get concerned about an online store having their account information, giving the customer an option to place an online order without creating an account may sound like a good idea! It increases conversion rates by making the whole checkout process simpler, and more secure for such customers.

Google Checkout and PayPal PRO are good examples of that approach, as the customer can switch to either Google Checkout or PayPal PRO directly from the Shopping Cart page of an osCommerce online store, without even getting to the point of creating an account with it. The Google Checkout contribution can be downloaded from `http://addons.oscommerce.com/info/4556` and the PayPal PRO (or PayPal Direct) contribution can be downloaded directly from PayPal at `http://paypaltech.com/content/index.php?option=com_remository&Itemid=64&func=select&id=20` or from `http://addons.oscommerce.com/info/3647`.

Another solution, which is especially useful with websites where customers are likely to place repeat orders, is account information being stored on the customer's computer (in the cookies) and not in the database of the online store.

A customer first fills in the registration form, and answers the question if the account information should be stored on the local computer or on the database. If the customer's choice is the local computer, every time that customer gets back to the online store, adds products to the Shopping Cart, and presses the Checkout button, the online store checks if account information already exists in cookies on the customer computer, retrieves that information, and pre-fills the registration forms accordingly.

This makes it so much easier for end customers to place repeat orders without creating an account with the online store!

Wish Lists and Quotations

Customer experience improves a lot by allowing the customer to save certain products into the Wish List without having to actually place an order for those products.

osCommerce supports storing of the customer's Shopping Cart contents into the customer's account by default. Also, every time the customer logs in, the current Shopping Cart is merged with the customer's saved Shopping Cart contents.

But some prospective customers are not ready to buy products at all! They would like to think about this or that offer and maybe come back later—therefore, the Wish List feature could be used in osCommerce to convert at least some of such prospective customers into actual ones.

A Wish List can be practically the same as the Shopping Cart, except that the Shopping Cart is used for purchasing products whereas the Wish List helps the customer to store products the customer likes or would like to buy at some time in the future.

There is an osCommerce contribution that implements support for the Wish List feature. It can be downloaded from `http://addons.oscommerce.com/info/1682`.

The existing solution allows customers who are logged into their accounts to add products not only into their shopping carts, but also into Wish Lists. A special "Add to Wish List" button then appears on the product information page along with the "Add to Cart" button.

A Wish List is to some degree very similar to a Shopping Cart, but at the same time, it allows customers to add any number of products there without any concerns or doubts. As products can be easily excluded from the Wish List, the Wish List can be saved until the next time the customer logs in, and products from the Wish List can be easily copied into the Shopping Cart.

Wish List could be also used to save products that are currently out of stock there, and come back to the saved products later on when they are likely to be back in stock to purchase them.

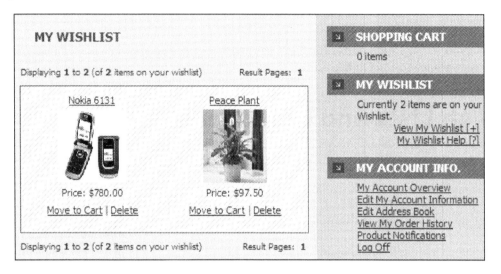

A better solution would be to allow others to have access to one's Wish List. This would then allow customers to create their Wish Lists and share them with their friends, relatives, colleagues, and so on. Therefore, it would be possible to create solutions for wedding gift lists, newborn baby gift lists, and all other special occasions when people are likely to receive presents but would like those presents to be of a certain range.

Besides orders and Wish Lists, online merchants who run osCommerce online stores may allow their customers to request a quotation based on the content of their Shopping Carts. Requesting a quotation makes sense when either the price of products that the customer would like to buy is negotiable, or if the price is not known as along with certain products the customer would also like to order some services. For example, along with laminate floors (where the price can be calculated on a per square meter basis) the customer would also like to order some fitting services.

As an example, a quotation request could be submitted by the prospective customer who wishes to buy several products at the same time and would expect a slightly improved price because of the total order amount and total quantity of items being ordered together. Or if the prospective customer would like to order, say, kitchen furniture, and, along with the products, and possibly appliances, would also like all furniture and appliances to be assembled and installed.

Quotations are regularly based on the content of the Shopping Cart or a Wish List. But since the customers may require some additional services (hence the quotation request), it should be possible for the customer to submit comments or description of the service required in a free-text field.

Ideally, to attract more visitors to submit their requests for quotations, the online store would not require the visitor to pass through the full registration process, and would only collect essential contact details (name, email address, and phone number, and possibly a ZIP code if it's critical to submit a quotation).

Of course, if an existing and logged in customer would like to submit a request for a quotation, the website would simply pre-fill the contact details of the Quotation form with the data extracted from the database.

The administration of the online store receives a request for a quotation in one of several ways. It can be a simple email containing the customer's contact details. This assumes the sales team will simply either give the customer a call or send an email. Or it can be a more advanced solution that would record each request for quotation in the database and allow for further communication via the website between the sales team and the prospective customer.

In the latter case, as soon as the price and scope of the quotation are agreed, the system may even allow the customer to place an online order using content of the request for quotation submitted earlier.

By enabling the functionality of requests for quotes, online merchants make their websites more flexible, and more responsive to the needs of their customers. This improves customers' experience with the online store, and may convert more prospective customers into actual customers by providing them with more flexible options to choose from.

Discontinued Products and Changed Prices

To convert more wish lists and requests for quotations into orders, the online store should be pro-active in communications with the customers.

A special automated email could be sent to prospective customers who saved their Wish Lists or submitted requests for quotations some time ago and never responded to an offer provided by the sales team. It will remind those prospective customers about their requests and invite them to place an order online or by phone or using other means of communication before, for example, the price changes and while the wished or quoted products are still in stock.

Sometimes, if the product range of the online store changes periodically and quite often (say, once a month), content of the Wish Lists, saved Shopping Carts, or submitted requests for quotes may expire. In that case, the online store may send an automated email to prospective customers notifying them about the fact that certain products are to be excluded from product range, and suggest either similar products or simply contacting the sales team to find substitutes.

The price of certain products may increase or decrease, and again, the online store may send an automated notification email to the customer with a suggestion to either place the order now, or contact the sales team to find the best solution.

Payment Methods

The customer's experience and feeling of safety and security while placing online orders very much depends on how the payment facilities are implemented in the online store.

Some customers would not mind placing an online order and submitting their card details. Other customers would rather prefer to call and place a phone order, even though they started the order placement process over the Internet. Yet some other customers would rather submit their card details on the website of the payment processing gateway, which they trust more than the site of the online store.

Therefore, in order to improve overall customer experience, an online store should have solutions suitable for as many customers as possible. Usually, this results in the online store having several payment methods that different customers would find most convenient and secure to use.

Sometimes it's enough to have two payment methods, one being the main method, and another—the backup one. Some online stores do not give the customer a choice between the main and backup payment methods unless the customer fails to submit a payment using the main payment method—then, after displaying an error or warning message the online store would display the main payment method along with the backup one. On the one hand, this reduces confusion as normally it gives the customer a choice of only one payment method. And on the other hand, it makes the online store more flexible by introducing the backup payment method if the customer can't use the main one for any reason.

It makes sense to add the phone number of the sales team to the page of the checkout process where the customer actually submits payment details, just in case the customer would like to continue placing an order by phone.

If the online store implements a payment method where the customer enters card information directly on the website (of course usage of SSL certificate is a MUST in that case!), and yet another payment method where the customer is redirected to the website of the payment gateway — it makes sense to show corresponding information about details of the payment submission process for each supported payment method to let the customer choose the most suitable one.

By being flexible, by listening to the customers' needs and requests, online stores can make a real difference, improve customer experience and of course improve its conversion rates.

Error Handling and Confirmations

Improving error handing is an important part of improving general customer experience.

The standard osCommerce error handling solution is sometimes not enough to ensure the customer has understood what the error is all about, and knows how to fix it to continue the registration or order placement process.

To make it easy to understand the problems and provide immediate solutions, do not disappoint or scare the customer, make it an easy, secure, and safe experience for the customer — these are the main principles of a successful Checkout process. These principles ensure positive customer experience.

Customer Registration

During the registration process, the customer can make all sorts of mistakes. The customer may miss certain fields, mistype dates and other information, etc. Warning and error messages should very clearly explain why the registration process can't be continued until the customer fills in all required information properly, and indicate where on the registration page the customer can find those fields that should be corrected. Such fields could be highlighted with some bright color, or their titles could be highlighted and made to look bolder than the titles of other fields. In either case, the customer should not experience any difficulties in locating such fields on the registration page, and in understanding why those fields need to be filled in, and in which way, and how that information will be used by the online store.

As a very simple example, the standard osCommerce installation asks for customer's date of birth.

First of all, not all customers would like to disclose that information since it's sometimes used to confirm their identity in, for example, their banks. Secondly, most online stores would not be really using that information either, even though they have it in the database.

So really there's not much need for insisting on that field to be filled in by the customer. And moreover, date format changes from country to country, and not all osCommerce-based online stores ensure that the date format on the website has been changed properly and according to the local format of the country where most of the prospective customers are likely to be from.

Payment and Shipping

Error messages that relate to payment processing should contain as little technical information as possible. It's quite often that error messages returned by payment gateways are displayed directly to the customer. But they are sometimes not so easy to understand for the customer, so a better solution would be to handle all error messages returned by payment gateways and display custom/reworked error messages to the customer.

Error messages should clearly explain the reason for the issue (if it's possible at all) and, more importantly, propose a solution. They should encourage the customer to try to pay for the order again and not just leave the site after the first attempt has failed. For example, if the payment gateway has failed to process the transaction because the billing address entered by the customer doesn't match the one registered for the entered credit card, the online store should not only inform the customer about that issue, but of course also advise checking the address in a very polite way, or using another card.

It is the same with the shipping methods in osCommerce. If for some reason the order cannot be delivered to the customer's shipping address by certain shipping carriers, it makes sense to ask the customer to either call the sales team to try to find a solution, or to request a call and then the sales team will give the customer a call to discuss possible delivery options.

If the online store uses several shipping carriers to deliver goods to customers, there could be situations when some shipping methods would be available and some not available to that particular customer, depending of course on the entered delivery address. It doesn't make sense to display information containing any negative message on the pages of the Checkout process. Therefore, it may make sense to simply not list those shipping methods that are not available to that particular customer, based on the customer's delivery address.

Order Confirmation

The order confirmation page should contain all information related to the order, including the list of products, payment and shipping information, customer details, links to the legal terms, refunds and cancellations policies, delivery policy, sales and customer service contact details.

It is important to reassure the customer that the order has actually been received by the online store, so as soon as the customer actually places an order, all that information from the order confirmation/summary page could be sent to the customer in an email confirming the fact of order placement and advising on further steps to be undertaken by the online store to deliver customer's order.

Customer Account

osCommerce implements support for customer accounts. As soon as the customer registers (even before the order gets stored in the database) new customers create an account in standard installation of osCommerce.

The default implementation of customer accounts allows the customer to manage an address book, see previous order history, and change personal information.

- The customer account can be further improved in osCommerce to improve overall customer experience with it. First of all, for previously placed orders the customer account can allow for tracking the status of the order. This feature is implemented in the standard installation of osCommerce, but can be enhanced by providing the customer with not only the status of the order, but also the status of the delivery (or location of the parcel) if the order has already been dispatched. Most shipping carriers provide the facility to track the location of the parcel nowadays; therefore, by implementing special links that open the shipping carrier's delivery tracking page and by inputting delivery tracking numbers into the orders, the online merchant gives customers the facility to monitor delivery without the necessity to contact the Administration of the online store every time. It becomes easier for customers, and also saves the time of the Customer Services department of the online store.

- Special news and announcements available to customers of the website can be made available as soon as an existing customer logs in. They can be implemented as a part of the customer account pages, or as separate pages of the online store that require registration or login to be viewed. That information may relate to the service available to customers of the online store, or to the previously purchased products. It may also contain discount coupons that the customers could use to order more products from the online store with a discount.

- For online stores where customers are likely to order similar or the same products periodically, it makes sense to implement the re-order feature. It may be useful for online stores that sell certain supplements, like printer cartridges, coffee, tea, products for body builders, etc. If the customer would like to order the very same product(s) once again, a special Re-Order link or button could be added to each order in customer's personal order history. As soon as the customer presses that button, the online store would add the products from the selected previous order into customer's shopping basket (if such products are still available in the product catalog). It can make the re-ordering experience really straightforward for online customers.

Back End Improvements

The back end (the Administration Panel) of an online store could be also improved to ensure improved customer service experience. The easier it is to use it, the faster it works, and the more efficient the solutions that can be provided to the customer service team to manage customer accounts and orders—the better the pre-sale, sale, and post-sale experience customers will get, and the more likely they will buy from the same online store once again in the future.

Search Features

When a customer calls the customer service team, it's crucial to be able to promptly find that customer's account, and all associated orders in the database. Customer and order search should be made possible by customer name, address, ZIP, email address, products ordered, and of course order ID.

To speed up the search process, it may make sense to implement a special auto-suggest feature using the AJAX technology, which would be suggesting possible customer details while the customer service representative types them in the search form.

Of course, the database of the online store should be optimized to allow for quick search by one or several fields, as customers would not enjoy having to wait while on the phone and often expect an almost immediate response.

Order Management

Order management, besides standard features like changing order status, and printing the invoice and packing slip, may include some additional activities.

For example, it may be required to re-send the customer the order confirmation email. Or export the invoice into PDF format and send it to the customer via email as a proof of order (sometimes it's required by manufacturers to provide the customer with warranty services).

Some online stores allow their customers to change an order even after it has been already placed, as the actual payment transaction is not processed until the order reaches a certain status. There is a contribution in osCommerce that allows for order creation and order editing.

This solution can be downloaded from `http://addons.oscommerce.com/info/1435`.

It allows for creating new customer accounts, new orders, and also editing existing orders in the back end of the online store. It is possible to perform some sort of advanced search by category, product name, or model when adding a new product to the order.

The newest versions of that solution allow for almost real-time updating of order information in the database using the AJAX technology.

Shipping fee quotes are calculated immediately according to the changed shipping address or ordered products list using the same shipping modules that are used in the front end of the online store, during the Checkout process.

Live Chat Support and Answer Phone

Web-based chat with a live person can be of great help to prospective customers, and can help customers to find the best suitable products, confirm the delivery terms, warranty promise, etc. Web-based chat with a member of the sales or customer service team can eventually result into the customer placing an online order. It makes sense to implement the live chat facility on the online store for pre-sales, sales, and after sales (customer service) support.

There are multiple solutions that allow for web-based chat. Usually, it would be possible to either buy a full version of the live chat system, or rent it from a manufacturer using a hosted version of the system.

It's important to set up live chat departments and operators correctly, so that the customers could be given professional help and advice depending on which question or issue they have.

There are paid and free solutions that could be utilized by an osCommerce store owner to implement live chat and allow customers to ask real person for help and advice. A good example of a paid solution is phpLiveSupport, which is available from `http://www.phplivesupport.com`. It is very easy to integrate it into osCommerce, and all integration instructions are supplied with the installation package.

`http://www.helpcenterlive.com` is a good example of Live chat solution that is available at no cost to the online store owner. The installation manual is available online. Also, the installation routine is built into the package, so in fact after un-packing the files on the web server, the webmaster or the online merchant simply goes through a wizard consisting of several pages and configures the system.

A link, or a button, or corresponding image can be either put in one of the side columns of osCommerce, or added to product pages and checkout pages to make this facility available to the customers when they are more likely to need it.

Answer phone service is important if the online store doesn't operate 24/7 as many customers may still prefer to call first before placing an order. Therefore, the answer phone should be properly configured to help the customers and not disappoint them.

For example, if the customer calls during non-business hours, the answer phone service can ask the customer if it's about one of the previously placed orders or about placing a new order.

If it's about some previously placed order, the answer phone service can ask the customer to leave a message including name, call back phone, and order ID, so that the customer service team could call the customer back next business day. Of course, it is VERY important to always call customers back if they left a message!

If it's about placing a new order, the answer phone service may suggest to the customer either calling next business day, or visiting the website, which is available 24/7.

In either case, the answer phone service needs to clearly tell the name of the company, names of the websites operated by the company (as sometimes the name of the website the customer knows would be different from the company name), and business hours when the sales and customer services teams are available to help the customer.

No complex menus, only a positive attitude towards the customer, and professionalism will ensure positive customer experience with the live chat and answer phone services of an online store. It will result in improved conversion rates from visitors to customers and from customers to repeat customers.

Summary

In this chapter, we reviewed how important it is to monitor and constantly improve conversion rates of online business, and how conversion rates affect the profitability of the business. Conversion rates in osCommerce can be separated into conversion from visitors to customers, and from customers to repeat customers. Also, conversion rates can be monitored by referring source, or type of media. Conversion rates can be different for different products, categories, and manufacturers.

Conversion rates in osCommerce may depend on the content of certain pages of the online store, and even on particular page design elements. The conversion rates of certain pages obviously affect general conversion rates of the online store. It is especially easy to see this on an example of the Checkout pages of an osCommerce-based online store.

We also reviewed how conversion rates could be monitored and further improved in osCommerce, and how positive customer experience affects conversion rates.

In the next chapter, we will further explore monitoring of the performance of the website by creating various reports, and of course understanding those reports and using statistical information to improve the efficiency of an osCommerce-based online business.

11
Understanding and Using Reports

In osCommerce, an online merchant has access to several built-in reports in the default installation of the system. Although some are useful (like Bestselling products report), it's definitely not enough to give the online merchant a clear and detailed picture of the overall status of the business, and more information about whether it's possible to improve the business further, make it more profitable, and more efficient.

In fact, one of the main reasons to run and use reports in osCommerce is to constantly consider opportunities to improve the online business.

The good news is that all (or almost all) the information that is required to build extra reports already exists in the database of an osCommerce-based online store. Some data would have to be taken from third-party tracking solutions (like the ones used to calculate the number of visitors to a website).

Creating new reports is a complex task, but, as soon as they are ready, the online merchant will have all the required information to make educated executive decisions regarding the online business.

In this chapter, we will review different groups of reports, how to create them in osCommerce or using third-party solutions, and, most importantly, how to understand and use those reports to produce the maximum positive benefit for the business. Our goals are to make the business more profitable, and more efficient.

Some of the reports we will be talking about require minor updates to the standard osCommerce database (such as adding the Cost field to the products). We will assume those updates have already been done and also that all products already have their costs set in the database.

Tracking Visitors

The number of visitors to an online store usually changes on a day-to-day basis, even on an hour-to-hour basis. Other parameters that change include the regions the visitors come from, the time they spend on the website, and the pages they view.

For an online merchant, or for an e-commerce manager, it's crucial to have access to that information, be able to understand it, and act accordingly, to increase conversions from visitors to customers, and make the business more efficient and profitable.

Using Day-of-Week and Time-of-Day Statistics

The number of visitors that the website has daily depends on many factors. But quite often, website owners are able to detect a certain pattern in how the number of visitors changes depending on the month of the year, day of the week, or hour of the day. There will be some times when most of the orders are made, and there will be some quieter times, when the website doesn't receive many visits.

Of course, if the online store sells locally or nationwide, the online merchant would not normally expect the customers to buy during the night hours. If the online store sells internationally, and a number of prospective customers live in countries with different time zones, the online store may truly work (i.e. sell) 24 hours a day!

If the statistics show certain ups and downs in the number of visitors every week, the online merchant should try to minimize the number of "downs" or at least minimize the difference between the number of visitors in the "up" day and "down" day.

For example, a day before the "down" day of the week, the online store can send a newsletter to its subscribers, attracting them to come to the site to see new hot offers and products. Also, some special offers providing customers with a really good discount could be put up during the "down" days of the week to attract as many prospective customers as possible, and ensure higher conversion rates on those days.

The same approach can work when checking the hours when the online store sells most of its products, and when there's a quieter period. Time-limited special offers could be introduced then to stimulate more customers. A special price countdown timer can be displayed alongside the product to hasten the customers in making their decisions.

Using Statistics by Page Popularity

Many solutions that track the behavior of website visitors can identified the most popular pages that many customers visit (or that they spend a significant amount of their time browsing).

No matter why those pages attract the visitors to the website, it's important to be able to track if they eventually convert visitors into customers. If a page of an online store is very popular and receives a significant number of visitors daily, but doesn't convert visitors into customers, it's a clear sign the page needs to be redesigned, improved, and its content changed, so that it more actively "sells" products to effectively convert visitors into customers. It may be that the page looks confusing to prospective customers, or they may not be finding enough information on the page to place an online order. All those possibilities need to be explored and decisions made on how to improve popular, but non-converting, pages.

On the other hand, if a web page of an online store converts a good number of visitors into customers, it may make sense to use that page to advertise more products in order to increase sales. It also makes sense to ensure that the products that appear on that page (if any) are the ones with the greatest possible difference between the sale price and the cost, to ensure that each sale brings maximum profit to the online merchant.

Using Third-Party Solutions to Track Visitors

Except for the "Who is Online?" tool, osCommerce doesn't have built-in tools for monitoring visitors to the website. Therefore, it makes sense to use third-party tools to track visitors and monitor their activity on the website.

It should be noted that different third-party solutions use different techniques to calculate the number of visitors and monitor their activity, so results gathered by different solutions will also be different.

Some third-party solutions (like, for example, Google Analytics) require further integration into the online store. There is a contribution for osCommerce that integrates Google Analytics into the site. Not only visitors, even customers can be monitored by Google Analytics as it has a special e-commerce add-on to track down online orders.

Other third-party solutions (like, for example, WebAlizer) do not require integration into online store as they fetch data directly from the web server's log files.

This latter approach doesn't slow down the page loading speed unlike the former ones, but doesn't allow for such comprehensive statistics as can be provided by integrated solutions.

It should be noted that the difference between the "Who is Online?" and tools such as Google Analytics or WebAlizer is that the "Who is Online?" feature allows for real-time tracking to website visitors, whereas other solutions provide information about past visitors of the website.

Monitoring Day-to-Day Conversion Rates

Knowing the number of unique visitors and also the number of online orders received during the day, it's very easy to calculate the general conversion rate of an online store.

Solutions like Google Analytics can do it automatically. If corresponding goals are set then the conversion rate for each goal can be calculated. A goal is actually a web page of the online store. As soon as the customer reaches a certain page of the website, the goal is fulfilled. Additional filters can also be applied. For example, a goal can be considered fulfilled only if a visitor or a customer has reached the goal coming from or through certain other web pages of the online store.

By knowing the online store's day-to-day conversion rates, it's possible to calculate the average conversion rate during a certain time period. It's also possible to see how conversion rates change in time, and what factors (like the start or end of advertising campaigns in certain media or referring sources, season of the year, day of the month, etc.) affect the conversion rates.

Knowing the average conversion rate in the industry is a requirement when creating a business plan for an online store. The minimum number of visitors to the online store to supply the minimum turnover and the minimum profits required to run the business depend on the average conversion rate. Also dependent on the average conversion rate is the advertising cost required to attract that minimum number of visitors effectively.

Reports on Referring Sources

Online stores often advertise in different media and correspondingly have different referring sources for their prospective customers. It's essential to be able to see how each individual referring source performs during a certain period of time, and what is the conversion rate per referring source.

Conversion rate per referring source shows how efficient a certain referring source is, and tells the online merchant or e-commerce manager how to spread the advertising budget among the referring sources with the maximum efficiency.

Of course, it's sometimes not only about the efficiency but also about the volume—there could be some referring sources that are not that efficient in converting visitors into customers, but which supply higher volumes of sales than others. Also, there could be some referring sources that are free to use (nowadays it's natural/organic search results in search engines), and so their conversion rates do not really affect the advertising budgets of the online store.

For each referring source, it's required to know for a certain period of time:

- Number of visitors referred
- Number of visitors converted into customers
- Conversion rate per referring source
- Number of orders placed
- Volume of sales generated
- Volume of profits generated
- Average spend by every referred visitor
- Average spend by every referred customer (i.e. average order amount)
- Bestselling products
- Bestselling categories of products
- Bestselling product brands/manufacturers

Knowing the amount of profits referred by a certain referring source, for a certain period of time, it is possible to calculate its average return on investment by dividing the amount of profits by the amount of advertising costs for that period of time.

If ROI is greater than 1, it means the referring source actually produces certain gross profits. If ROI is 1 or less than that, it may mean the referring source is not worth investing money into, as it doesn't produce any gross profit at all. Every time we use the word "profit" in this chapter, except for special occasions, it's the gross profit, i.e. profit based on margin without any other business costs taken into account.

There could be an exception here. It's when the online store uses some referring sources more for brand awareness and less for attracting customers. If that's the case, ROI on such referring sources will not make any difference, as those referring sources serve another purpose.

By knowing the ROI of a referring source, the online merchant or e-commerce manager can plan gross profits by planning the advertising budget for that referring source ahead, assuming of course, that the ROI will not change.

If ROI is well greater than 1, and the generated gross profits turn into net profits, it makes sense to increase the advertising budget for such a referring source. If ROI is 1 or even less than that it makes sense to try to negotiate a better advertisement rate based on the fact the online store actually loses money by putting advertising into the referring source, re-consider the advertising budget for such referring source, and reconsider the content of the advertisement published there. And if none of those measures helps to improve the situation, it makes sense to cease advertising in that particular referring source and invest the money saved into more profitable ones.

Various referring sources may supply different types of visitors to the online store.

It is important to be able to see what sort of visitors are provided by each referring source, as it allows adjusting the content of the advertisement used to attract visitors from the corresponding referring source. The average spend, by visitor, and by customer, will show the online merchant or e-commerce manager if those visitors who are usually referred by that referring source are ready to buy products online, and if they are ready to buy more expensive products/several products at a time.

Looking into the report by bestselling products, brands, and categories of products by referring source, the online merchant may decide to reconsider the content of the advertisement put into that referring source. If bestselling products sell well because of their price, considering the profile of the average visitor referred by that referring source, it may make sense to highlight that fact in the advertisement. If the online store has exclusive rights to offer some products (or even brands!) online, it may make sense to highlight this fact as well in the advertisement.

Of course, besides the current figures, it's always important to be able to monitor the trends, i.e. how certain figures change in time. For example, what the conversion rate of the referring source was the very same month a year ago, or last month, or last quarter. Or what was the average spend by customers and visitors referred by that referring source. Knowing trends also helps to predict how this or that referring source is likely to perform in the future, and plan advertising budget and sales figures accordingly.

It is possible to improve an osCommerce online store and save statistics by visitors and customers referred by referring sources using the "Referred by" parameter of the HTTP request. This parameter is sent to the online store when a visitor clicks the advertisement link in the referring source. Information about the visit can be stored in the database. It would include the name of the referring source, the date and time of the visit, and certain special keywords or parameters provided in the HTTP request. Also, the name of the referral source could be stored on the user's local computer in a special cookie. Later on, when the user decides to place an order, the online store would extract the name of the referral source from the cookie from the user's computer and save it into the database along with the order. In this way it will be possible to calculate the number of visitors and customers referred by each individual referring source.

Using third party solutions (like Google Analytics) may make this process easier, and will allow the online merchant or e-commerce manager to do without the need to modify the online store.

Reports on Keywords

Some visitors to an online store would either know the URL and type it directly in their web browser, or would see the link to the online store on another website and click it.

But many visitors would search for products or services, the same as or similar to the ones promoted by the online store in search engines, and would then click the link to the online store that appears either in the natural search results section, or in the paid search results section on the search engine's website.

It's very important to know what keywords and key phrases these visitors search for to find the link to the online store.

Search engines, of course, should be considered referring sources too in that situation.

The list of columns in this report would usually be identical to the list of columns in the Report by Referring Source. Of course, instead of referring sources all figures would be calculated on a per keyword/key phrase basis.

Knowing which keyword or key phrase performs better than others allows for adjusting the advertising budget, and investing into those better performing keywords and key phrases.

Sometimes, it makes sense to stop paid advertising on certain keywords if they do not perform well enough to produce gross profit, and spend that part of the budget on better performing keywords. Alternatively, it may make sense to increase the advertising budget on poorly performing keywords as the competition may be too strong and the current budget may simply not be enough to start winning more visitors.

Also, having that information filtered by a referring source may be of a great help to the online merchant or e-commerce manager of the online store. It will then allow monitoring how one and the same keyword or key phrase performs in different referring sources. If performance (i.e. the number or amount or sales, amount of profits, ROI) differs a lot, this is a signal to check advertising budgets as competition on certain keywords may be too strong in some referring sources.

As with the referring sources, the report on keywords is probably easier to run using such third-party tools such as Google Analytics. But it's possible to modify osCommerce (in the same way as modifying it for tracking referring sources) to store keywords used by visitors and customers of the site in the database, and retrieve that stored information later on for the report.

Tracking Sales

Sales in osCommerce can be monitored in different ways. We will consider those later in this chapter, and in the mean time review how sales can be tracked more generally.

Interestingly, the general sales statistics of an online store are not available in the default installation of osCommerce. A number of solutions and contributions have been developed that make this information available to the online merchant. Like for example a contribution that makes it possible to see sale statistics grouped by months and years, including taxes, net prices, shipping, and of course totals, which is available from `http://addons.oscommerce.com/info/539`.

It gives statistics per time periods (like months and years) and demonstrates changes in gross income, product sales, taxable, and tax exempt sales.

Month	Year	Gross Income	Product sales	Exempt sales	Taxable sales	Tax paid	Shpg & Hndlg	Gift Vouchers
Aug	2007	8,779.69	8,530.99	8,530.99	0.00	0.00	248.70	0.00
Jul	2007	5,423.35	5,374.35	5,189.85	184.50	3.75	45.25	11.75
Jun	2007	14,968.53	14,344.16	9,705.16	12,717.00	594.12	30.25	0.00
YTD	2007	29,183.32	28,249.50	23,426.00	12,901.50	597.87	324.20	11.75

It is possible to run a slightly different report that helps to not only understand how the general sale figures tend to change with time, but also allows for applying filters by order status or time, and also splits sales into net sale, tax, shipping fee, discount coupons, and gift vouchers (if corresponding functionality is a part of the online store).

It is fairly important to be able to see statistics of sales by certain time patterns like for example, sales by day of week or sales by hour of a day. Repeating each week or each day (or each month, or each year!), such a report helps the online merchant to understand when the number of orders needs to be improved, and also find out when the target customer audience is in a mood to buy products and services offered by the online store.

For example, if based on that report Monday is not a very good day for online sales, the online merchant may want to send a regular weekly newsletter to subscribers with the latest hot offers on Sunday (or even on Friday), trying to make the customers interested in buying products in the beginning of the next week (i.e. on Monday). Or if the customers tend to buy more products on Tuesday, Wednesday, and Thursday, the newsletter can be sent on Monday to inform existing subscribers about hot offers and new products, and also advertising budgets could be increased on Tuesday, Wednesday, and Thursday so that more and more visitors are converted into customers — as obviously the conversion rates are likely to be better those days.

For some osCommerce online stores, the time of the year or the day of the month mean a lot. If an online store sells seasonal products (like sunglasses, swim suits, and other products for summer holidays), it obviously makes sense to increase advertising budgets just before the holiday season hits, as more customers will be buying such products during that time.

Or if the online store sells quite expensive products, it may make sense to increase advertising budgets and send newsletters during those days of the month when the target audience are likely to get paid at work, and have money to spend on quite an expensive purchase.

Of course, using such a report requires a very good understanding of prospective customer behavior.

Sales Forecast Reports

There is no built-in default sales forecasting solution for osCommerce, but there are certain third-party solutions that osCommerce merchants could have integrated with their online stores.

One such solution is available at www.lokad.com.

Based on the number of visitors, customers, and the amount of sales during a certain time period, a prediction could be made of future sales volumes.

Bestselling Products

osCommerce features a report by bestselling products as a part of its default installation.

Standard report allows for seeing the bestselling products, but at the same time, it doesn't allow for applying filters (at least by time, category, the number of sales, etc.) and seeing summary by category and brand/manufacturer.

Therefore, an additional report like the one described below would be convenient for online merchants to be able to manage their online store effectively. It could be based on a copy of the existing bestselling products report, or created as a new module of the Reports section of the osCommerce back end.

The report can have a number of columns, filters by start and end date may be applied, and the following information can be made available to the online merchant or e-commerce manager:

- Product name
- Product code
- Manufacturer
- Category
- Number of products ordered
- Total turnover
- Total profit
- Minimum cost (based on sales)
- Maximum cost (based on sales)
- Free stock
- Current cost
- Current sale price
- Average margin (in %)
- Date when the stock is likely to run out (based on previous sales)

Being able to sort data on the report by each of the above columns would be beneficial for whoever works with the report. Besides the time filter, it should be also possible to set the filter by:

- Minimum number of sales for period
- Brand/manufacturer
- Category

- Free stock
- Region where the customer lives
- Average margin

Based on the report by bestselling products, the online merchant can make an educated decision as to how the product catalog should be re-arranged, if at all.

For example, by comparing the bestselling products for different time periods and seeing a product with a good margin dropping from the leading positions, the online merchant may want to check if the price is still competitive and possibly lower it a bit to bring the product back to the top of the list.

On the other hand, the price of a product with a lower margin that always dominates in the list of bestselling products can be altered and its margin made higher, so that even by making less sales, the online store will still be making approximately the same amount of profits.

Also, it's possible to check using the report whether all bestselling products are available in free stock, as such products are very likely to be running out of stock very often. And, having calculated the approximate date when the stock of a certain product is likely to run out, it's possible to see if the supplier or the manufacturer of the product offers better rates if more products are ordered together, and add that product (which probably still has certain amount left in free stock) to the purchase order knowing that should the sales go same way as before, the stock of that product will run out by approximately the calculated date.

By changing the region filter, it's possible to find out what are the preferred products for customers who live in different regions and to adjust local advertising campaigns, accordingly.

Finally, if an online store also has a warehouse, it may make sense to lower price on products that are still in free stock but are not very likely to be sold soon to free up the space to buy other products with a good margin that are more likely to be sold to customers.

Bestselling Brands and Categories

These two reports can be run against an osCommerce database similar to the Bestselling Products report. Columns in both reports will be similar, with only the exception of the Bestselling Categories report having one more column — parent category, where the Bestselling Manufacturers report won't have one — as there is no support for multilevel brands/manufacturers in the default installation of osCommerce.

Information in both reports may help the online merchant to rearrange the product catalog in the most efficient way. Only, instead of having statistics on each individual product, those two reports will have sales statistics on groups of products.

Like the Bestselling Products report, Bestselling Categories and Bestselling Brands reports could be used to:

- Check if the average sale price of products that belong to a particular category or are produced by a particular manufacturer is competitive, or, on the contrary should be increased.

- Check if there's enough free stock in bestselling categories, and when that free stock is likely to run out, so that the online merchant could plan further purchase orders from suppliers wisely.

- Find out customers of which region prefer products of which category or brand, and how this tendency changes in time—hence advertising campaigns could be improved in particular regions by concentrating on promotion of certain categories or brands.

- Find out which categories or brands do not sell well, and where there's still free stock—so that whole categories or brands could be discounted to get free space for products that sell better. Later on the online merchant may decide to discontinue certain categories and brands on the site to make it (the site) more competitive by being focused on a niche market.

Most Profitable Products

The report by the most profitable products is actually a part of the Bestselling Products report. It allows seeing the products that bring the most profits to the online store, whether it's a relative profit (profitability, actually the margin the online store can get when it sells a product at a certain sale price) or the absolute gross profit (where the result depends not only on the margin, but also on the number of sales).

The profitability of a product is very important, but if the product doesn't sell well, its gross profits could be lower than the gross profits of some less profitable products.

In either case, the most profitable products can be marked as "featured" products, i.e. the products that are most likely to be noticed by customers of an online store and bought by them.

The Product Listing routine of osCommerce could be changed, so that once a product gets marked as featured, it starts to appear at the very top of each product listing page. Hence, there are more chances for a featured product to be noticed and purchased by customers.

The most profitable brands/manufacturers and categories can be found out in the same way as the bestselling brands/manufacturers and categories, except this time the report will concentrate on profits (as with most profitable products, it's about relative and gross profit).

Report on Sales by Region

A special report displaying sales by region of one country, or by countries if the online store trades internationally can help the online merchant to see differences in how customers from different regions or countries buy products, and adjust advertising campaigns in the corresponding regions or countries to ensure the best sale figures.

Alternatively, if customers living in a certain region or country do not buy enough products to even pay for the advertising budget dedicated to that region or country, it may make sense to cease pushing products in that particular region or country, and use the spare budget in other areas where customers are more willing to buy products offered by that particular online store.

There could be multiple reasons why sales by region may differ. But of course, the main one is that some regions would have more prospective customers who are members of the target customer group, and some less. It may also depend on if the online store sells products that most customers would prefer to buy from a more local supplier, or if it doesn't matter if the product comes from another region or even from another country—it's only the product itself and/or its price that matters.

It's important to be able to apply time filters to see how statistics of purchases change.

When looking at the report of sales by region, it also make sense to apply a filter by distance from a certain point, like from a certain post code. Online merchants in many countries can get data that helps to calculate a rough distance between the two post codes. Therefore, it's possible to see how the sale figures change along with the distance from a certain post code.

This could be from the post code of where the online store is located, or where the warehouse is located, or where the most of the target audience is supposed to live.

The report can provide the following information:

- Region name (or post code)
- Country name (if the online store trades internationally)
- Total number of sales

- Total number of visitors
- Total number of customers
- Total amount of sales
- Total amount of profits
- Average spend by visitor
- Average spend by customer (i.e. average order amount)
- What part of the online store's profits the region is responsible for (in %)

Report on Best-Buying Customers

Some online stores reward their best-buying customers with certain special offers, discount coupons, and so on. Also, if the online store has several customer groups, it's important to be able to see how each customer group performs (i.e. orders online).

The report may contain the following information:

- Customer name
- Customer email address
- Customer group (if there are several customer groups in the online store)
- Address (country, region, city/town, and post code is usually enough)
- Number of orders placed
- Number of products purchased
- Total amount of purchases
- Total profit
- What part of the online store's profits the customer is responsible for (in %)

The summary by customer group can be run as a separate report with similar columns.

It's important to be able to apply filters by:

- Customer name
- Total amount of purchases
- Number of orders placed
- Number of products purchased

- Address (country, region, city/town, and post code)
- Customer group (if there are several customer groups in the online store)
- Referring source
- And of course, time period

Best-buying customers could be rewarded by a discount coupon. Or their customer group could be changed to reward them with better prices on products should they choose to buy from the same online store in the future.

Report by Net Profit

One of the most important reports for an online merchant is the report by net profit. It's the report that actually shows how the online store performs and how efficient the business is, and what should be changed or improved to help the online store perform better and achieve certain targets.

This report could be run as a relatively simple MS Excel spreadsheet. Before it can be compiled, it requires the online merchant to already know certain parameters of the business, such as:

- Average number of orders per day
- Average order amount
- Average margin (in %)
- Average order processing cost (P & P)
- General conversion rate from visitors into customers
- Average cost per paid visit
- How many paid visitors does the online store have compared to the total number of visitors (in %)
- Non-operational expenses (such as rent, website support, bank monthly fees, etc.)

Once those business parameters are known, it's possible to compile a report that would show:

- Required number of visitors to achieve a desired number of orders per day
- Turnover based on the desired number of orders per day
- Gross and net profits, again based on the desired number of orders per day

Variables:		Orders daily	Avg order amount	Avg Margin (%)
		20	$50.00	40.00%
		P & P cost	Conversion rate	Cost per visit
		$7.00	2.00%	$0.40
		Paid visitors		
		50.00%		
Daily:				
Rqrd. number of visitors	1000			
Costs of Paid Adv.	$200.00			
Gross profits	$400.00			
Monthly:				
Misc Expenses:			**Operation:**	
PR		$500.00	Advertisement	$6,000.00
Bookkeeper		$75.00	Order processing	$4,200.00
Site support		$500.00		
Bank fees		$50.00		
Monthly totals:				
	Misc Exp.		Operations	
	$1,125.00		$10,200.00	
Totals:				
Turnover	Gross Profits	Net Profits	Profitability	
$30,000.00	$12,000.00	$675.00	2.25%	

Here, the required number of visitors per day is calculated by dividing the desired number of daily orders by general conversion rate.

Cost of paid advertising (pay-per-click advertising here) is calculated as a multiplication of the required number of daily visitors, average cost per visit (click), and average percent of visitors referred by the pay-per-click means of advertising.

Gross Profits is a multiplication of the desired number of daily orders, average order amount, and average margin.

Net Profits is the difference between the turnover (which, in its turn is the multiplication of the average order amount, the desired number of daily orders, and the number of days in a month—30 in this example) and operational expenses (order processing and pay-per-click advertising), and miscellaneous expenses (such as PR costs, bookkeeper services, support of the website, and bank monthly fees in this particular example).

This sample report shows that having 20 orders per day, with average order about of $50, and average margin of 40%, order processing cost $7, conversion rate from visitors to customers 2%, average cost per paid visit $0.40, and at least 50% of visitors referred to the online store by the pay-per-click advertisement, also having certain non-operational monthly expenses $1,125 in total, the online store can actually make only $675 net profit per month, despite having a turnover of approximately $30,000! The profitability of such business is only 2.25%.

This clearly shows us that the business is not very profitable after all, and the online merchant should work hard on improving the situation in order to make enough money.

For example, the online merchant may want to put 30 orders per day as a goal.

Variables:		Orders daily		Avg order amount	Avg Margin (%)
			30	$50.00	40.00%
		P & P cost		Conversion rate	Cost per visit
			$7.00	2.00%	$0.40
		Paid visitors			
			50.00%		
Daily:					
Rqrd. number of visitors		1500			
Costs of Paid Adv.		$300.00			
Gross profits		$600.00			
Monthly:					
Misc Expenses:			**Operation:**		
PR		$500.00	Advertisement		$9,000.00
Bookkeeper		$75.00	Order processing		$6,300.00
Site support		$500.00			
Bank fees		$50.00			
Monthly totals:					
	Misc Exp.			Operations	
	$1,125.00			$15,300.00	
Totals:					
Turnover	**Gross Profits**	**Net Profits**		**Profitability**	
$45,000.00	**$18,000.00**	**$1,575.00**		**3.50%**	

If that goal is achieved, with all other parameters left intact, net profits of the business will be approximately $1,575 per month with monthly turnover of $45,000. It's already a bit better, as the profitability of the business will grow to 3.5% then.

By increasing the number of orders placed by visitors to the website, the online merchant reduces the effect of order processing costs and cost per paid visit on net profit figures. Note that in order to achieve the required 30 orders per day the online store would have to attract at least 1,500 visitors daily.

The good news is that this report doesn't take into account orders placed by repeat customers—such orders are more profitable as there's no expenditure on advertising involved there, and cost per customer acquisition is spread across several orders placed by the customer.

We will continue learning how different parameters affect the efficiency of the business.

If the online merchant manages to increase the average order amount to $60, leaving the number of daily orders equal to 20, it will make a significant impact on the profitability of the business keeping all other costs the same.

Variables:		Orders daily	Avg order amount	Avg Margin (%)
		20	$60.00	40.00%
		P & P cost	Conversion rate	Cost per visit
		$7.00	2.00%	$0.40
		Paid visitors		
		50.00%		
Daily:				
Rqrd. number of visitors		1000		
Costs of Paid Adv.		$200.00		
Gross profits		$480.00		
Monthly:				
Misc Expenses:			**Operation:**	
PR		$500.00	Advertisement	$6,000.00
Bookkeeper		$75.00	Order processing	$4,200.00
Site support		$500.00		
Bank fees		$50.00		
Monthly totals:				
	Misc Exp.		Operations	
	$1,125.00		$10,200.00	
Totals:				
Turnover	Gross Profits	Net Profits	Profitability	
$36,000.00	$14,400.00	$3,075.00	8.54%	

With a turnover of $36,000, the online store would produce $3,075 worth of net profits per month, and the profitability of the business would then grow to to 8.54%!

If the online merchant could negotiate better terms with suppliers, and the average margin grew to 50%, it would make an even more dramatic affect on the profitability of the business, because with the same turnover of $30,000, the online store would be now making $3,675 net profits each month—it's a 12.75% profitability.

Variables:		Orders daily	Avg order amount	Avg Margin (%)
		20	$50.00	50.00%
		P & P cost	Conversion rate	Cost per visit
		$7.00	2.00%	$0.40
		Paid visitors		
		50.00%		
Daily:				
Rqrd. number of visitors		1000		
Costs of Paid Adv.		$200.00		
Gross profits		$500.00		
Monthly:				
Misc Expenses:			**Operation:**	
PR		$500.00	Advertisement	$6,000.00
Bookkeeper		$75.00	Order processing	$4,200.00
Site support		$500.00		
Bank fees		$50.00		
Monthly totals:				
		Misc Exp.		Operations
		$1,125.00		$10,200.00
Totals:				
Turnover		**Gross Profits**	**Net Profits**	**Profitability**
$30,000.00		$15,000.00	$3,675.00	12.25%

If the online merchant could improve the order handling process and the order processing fee dropped to $5, making the same turnover of $30,000, the online store would be now making $1,875 at 6.25% profitability level.

Variables:		Orders daily	Avg order amount	Avg Margin (%)
		20	$50.00	40.00%
		P & P cost	Conversion rate	Cost per visit
		$5.00	2.00%	$0.40
		Paid visitors		
		50.00%		
Daily:				
Rqrd. number of visitors		1000		
Costs of Paid Adv.		$200.00		
Gross profits		$400.00		
Monthly:				
Misc Expenses:			**Operation:**	
PR		$500.00	Advertisement	$6,000.00
Bookkeeper		$75.00	Order processing	$3,000.00
Site support		$500.00		
Bank fees		$50.00		
Monthly totals:				
	Misc Exp.		Operations	
	$1,125.00		$9,000.00	
Totals:				
Turnover	Gross Profits	Net Profits	Profitability	
$30,000.00	**$12,000.00**	$1,875.00	6.25%	

This shows that changes in order handling and processing fee affect profitability of the business, but not as much as changes in the average order amount, and average margin.

Looking into how the conversion rate affects the business profitability, we can see that changing the conversion rate to 3% from 2% changes business profitability from 2.25% to 8.92%, leaving the turnover intact.

Variables:		Orders daily	Avg order amount	Avg Margin (%)
		20	$50.00	40.00%
		P & P cost	Conversion rate	Cost per visit
		$7.00	3.00%	$0.40
		Paid visitors		
		50.00%		
Daily:				
Rqrd. number of visitors		666.67		
Costs of Paid Adv.		$133.33		
Gross profits		$400.00		
Monthly:				
Misc Expenses:			**Operation:**	
PR		$500.00	Advertisement	$4,000.00
Bookkeeper		$75.00	Order processing	$4,200.00
Site support		$500.00		
Bank fees		$50.00		
Monthly totals:				
	Misc Exp.		Operations	
	$1,125.00		$8,200.00	
Totals:				
Turnover	Gross Profits	Net Profits	Profitability	
$30,000.00	**$12,000.00**	**$2,675.00**	**8.92%**	

Of course, it's not very easy to improve the general conversion rate of an online store; this requires a lot of work and sometimes serious investments in improvements of usability of the website.

How does the cost per paid visit affect the business's profitability? If the online merchant can negotiate better costs per click with other websites, say to $0.30 per click instead of $0.40 per click, or find other websites ready to provide the same amount of traffic for lower pay, it will affect the profitability of the online store too, in fact, it will improve to 7.25%, giving $2,175 net profit with the same turnover of $30,000.

Variables:		Orders daily	Avg order amount	Avg Margin (%)
		20	$50.00	40.00%
		P & P cost	Conversion rate	Cost per visit
		$7.00	2.00%	$0.30
		Paid visitors		
		50.00%		
Daily:				
Rqrd. number of visitors	1000			
Costs of Paid Adv.	$150.00			
Gross profits	$400.00			
Monthly:				
Misc Expenses:		**Operation:**		
PR	$500.00	Advertisement		$4,500.00
Bookkeeper	$75.00	Order processing		$4,200.00
Site support	$500.00			
Bank fees	$50.00			
Monthly totals:				
	Misc Exp.		Operations	
	$1,125.00		$8,700.00	
Totals:				
Turnover	Gross Profits	Net Profits	Profitability	
$30,000.00	$12,000.00	$2,175.00	7.25%	

By working hard on search engine optimization of an online store, by making it more search engine friendly, the online merchant can also achieve better profitability of the business. If the number of users referred either by other means of advertising than pay-per-click, or simply by search engines grows to 60%, leaving the number of users referred by pay-per-click advertising at 40%, it will change the profitability of the business to 6.25%, which with the same turnover of $30,000 gives the online merchant $1,875.

Variables:		Orders daily	Avg order amount	Avg Margin (%)
		20	$50.00	40.00%
		P & P cost	Conversion rate	Cost per visit
		$7.00	2.00%	$0.40
		Paid visitors		
		40.00%		
Daily:				
Rqrd. number of visitors		1000		
Costs of Paid Adv.		$160.00		
Gross profits		$400.00		
Monthly:				
Misc Expenses:			**Operation:**	
PR		$500.00	Advertisement	$4,800.00
Bookkeeper		$75.00	Order processing	$4,200.00
Site support		$500.00		
Bank fees		$50.00		
Monthly totals:				
		Misc Exp.		Operations
		$1,125.00		$9,000.00
Totals:				
Turnover		**Gross Profits**	**Net Profits**	**Profitability**
$30,000.00		$12,000.00	$1,875.00	6.25%

In an ideal situation, which may never be achievable but is still something the online merchant needs to try to achieve, all those parameters would be improved as in the following table. Priftability would have changed to a fantastic 32.92% then, making the online merchant $17,775 each month with the turnover being $54,000.

Variables:	Orders daily	Avg order amount	Avg Margin (%)
	30	$60.00	50.00%
	P & P cost	Conversion rate	Cost per visit
	$5.00	3.00%	$0.30
	Paid visitors		
	40.00%		
Daily:			
Rqrd. number of visitors	1000		
Costs of Paid Adv.	$120.00		
Gross profits	$900.00		
Monthly:			
Misc Expenses:		**Operation:**	
PR	$500.00	Advertisement	$3,600.00
Bookkeeper	$75.00	Order processing	$4,500.00
Site support	$500.00		
Bank fees	$50.00		
Monthly totals:			
	Misc Exp.		Operations
	$1,125.00		$8,100.00
Totals:			
Turnover	**Gross Profits**	**Net Profits**	**Profitability**
$54,000.00	$27,000.00	$17,775.00	32.92%

As a conclusion, the online merchant should constantly work on increasing the average order amount, average margin, general conversion rate, and the number of visitors referred by search engines and by means of advertising other than pay-per-click. The online merchant should also work hard on reducing order processing costs, and cost per visit in pay-per-click advertising to ensure the constant growth of profitability of the business and amount of net profits.

Depending on the number of orders the online store receives daily, parameters like order processing costs and cost per visit/click may have a stronger or weaker affect on the profitability of the online store.

Tracking Stock

If the business setup of an online store includes warehouse and stock management, it becomes essential to know which products are in stock, which products are likely to be out of stock soon, and when products ordered from suppliers are to come back to stock.

There is no built-in report for stock management in osCommerce, therefore new reports should be created.

Report by Stock

This report can be the basic and most important for stock management in osCommerce. It should list all products with their stock figures, allow for applying various filters, and display summary by category and manufacturer/brand.

The report may include the following columns:

- Product name
- Product model
- Product category
- Product manufacturer
- Product cost
- Free stock quantity
- Free stock amount (multiplication of product cost and free stock quantity)
- Allocated stock quantity (i.e. product's stock allocated to all orders with status different from "dispatched")
- Calculated "run out" date (based on the previous sale history for a particular product)
- Back to stock date

Filters by the following parameters could be applied:

- Product name
- Product code
- Category
- Manufacturer
- Free stock
- Allocated stock
- Run out date

Finding products belonging to the same manufacturer that have the same or very similar calculated "run out date" allows the online merchant to place larger purchase orders with suppliers of products. This usually allows for buying the products more cheaply and eventually, increasing business profitability.

Further similar reports could be created for categories and manufacturers/brands. The following columns could be included into such reports:

- Name (of either category or manufacturer/brand)
- Average product cost
- Total free stock quantity
- Total free stock amount (sum of all products' free stock amounts)
- Total allocated stock quantity

The report by product stock could be used for stock take. It should be printed by the online merchant or the warehouse manager and then all stock could be checked against figures on that printout.

Turnaround Report

The turnaround report (which can be created either for manufacturers/brands or categories) is a report that displays how fast the orders are processed from the moment the customer places an order to the moment the order is sent to the customer.

Turnaround depends on whether the online store has enough products in stock, and of course on how fast the order is processed by the Administration or the warehouse team of the online store. If the online store doesn't use its own warehouse and doesn't have any stock, the turnaround report will not play an important role in determining efficiency of the online store because turnaround on all or most of the orders will always be immediate.

The report can be run on either manufacturers or categories; the following columns could be made available on that report:

- Name (category or manufacturer/brand)
- Allocated stock (i.e. stock assigned on orders with status other than dispatched)
- Average turnaround

The turnaround report can help the online merchant to determine manufacturers/ brands or categories that are usually dispatched to customers very promptly, and those manufacturers/brands or categories that usually delay dispatches.

Corresponding measures could be taken to improve the situation, and reduce the order processing time. The faster the orders are processed, the sooner the space in the warehouse will be free again to put new products there, and the sooner the online store gets paid, as many online stores do not charge the customer the full order amount until the goods are dispatched. Also, the sooner the order is dispatched, the sooner the customer gets the order. This affects the customer's satisfaction with the delivery service, and with the online store overall.

Tracking Customers

Knowing your customers, being able to communicate with different customers and accordingly to address their needs and stimulate to them to order is one of the most important tasks of an online merchant.

The standard installation of osCommerce doesn't provide reports that could help the online merchant to see how customers buy online; also there are no built-in facilities for getting the lists of customers who bought certain products but didn't buy other products, or created an account with the online store but never placed an order, etc.

Report by Customers Who ...

This report can help an online merchant or marketing manager of an online store to split customers into target groups by their previous order history.

As soon as customers belonging to this or that group are identified, the list of customers could be used to send a special newsletter, discount coupons, etc.

Columns on the report would not be very much different from those of the report on best-buying customers, and would include:

- Customer name
- Customer email address
- Customer group (if there are several customer groups in the online store)
- Number of orders placed
- Address (country, region, city/town, and post code is usually enough)
- Number of products purchased
- Total amount of purchases
- Total profit
- What part of online store's profits the customer is responsible for (in %)

It's the filters that would make that report different and especially useful for marketing purposes:

- Customers who bought a certain product (by name and model)
- Customers who bought products of a certain manufacturer/brand
- Customers who bought products belonging to a certain category
- Customers who first created an account during a certain period of time
- Customers who placed orders during a certain period of time
- Customers who live in a certain area
- Customers who didn't buy certain products, or products of a certain manufacturer/brand, or products belonging to certain categories
- Customers who didn't buy during a certain period of time
- Customers who do not live in a certain area
- Customers who placed not less than a certain number of orders
- Customers who placed not more than a certain number of orders

By implementing those filters and making them work together when required, it becomes possible to easily split customers into target groups for marketing purposes.

The list of customers brought up by such a report could be exported into CSV or XML format for further use.

Using Reports when Sending Newsletters

Having multiple lists of customers who placed orders with the online store or, on the contrary, never did buy from the online store allows for very flexible marketing approaches.

For example, customers who bought product A and didn't buy product B from the online store could be offered product B with a discount as product B is related to product A (like customers who bought a digital camera, product A, may be interested in a tripod, product B, and vice versa). To get the list of such customers, the online merchant or marketing manager of the online store would specify a filter—customers who ever bought product A, and never bought product B—then get the list of customers, and contact them with special offers on product B (or on the category of products that product B belongs to).

Another example would be to get a list of customers who used to buy from the online store, but didn't order for the last couple of months. Filtering by the total number of orders placed by the customer, by customer account registration date, and by the date when the last order had been placed will help to get the desired customer list.

A brief reminder letter could be sent to such customers, with the newest product catalog entries advertised there and possibly with a question asking why the customer has stopped ordering products from the online store.

It makes sense to announce new products of certain brand to customers who bought products of either that brand or the same category before. It also makes sense to send the latest industry news and news received from manufacturers to such customers.

Those customers who registered their account with the online store but never placed any online orders could be sent an email reminder, and again, the newest products and special offers could be a part of that email.

Customers on the lists could be sent a newsletter to, using either the standard osCommerce newsletter feature, or some third-party solution.

Technical aspects of sending newsletters to customers have been covered in Chapter 2 of this book.

It makes sense to use osCommerce when the hosting company where the online store is located allows for sending newsletters to a reasonable number of recipients, and the number of customers in the list complies with those requirements. It makes sense to use third-party services otherwise, when there are too many customers on the list, or when the online merchant would like to get some better tracking of customer responses, bounced back emails, unsubscribe requests, etc.

Time of the day, day of the week, and day of the month may be important when sending a newsletter to customers. Ideally, the newsletter should arrive to the customer's mail box when the customer has free time to read it, and also is likely to be ready to buy products.

If it's known that most of the prospective customers get paid by their employers on the 20th of each month, it makes sense to send a newsletter on the 19th of the month, to ensure the customers have seen it a day before or on the very day when they get paid. Or if it's known that a large number of prospective customers would use the Internet at home during the weekend, it makes sense to send a newsletter on Friday lunch time, so that the customers would be able to see it and think over the announced special offers over the weekend.

Summary

The standard installation of osCommerce doesn't provide the online merchant with enough reporting facilities that could help the online merchant to improve the product catalog, improve communication with the customers, and make the online business more efficient.

Fortunately, as always with osCommerce, it's a very flexible solution and can be improved. A number of additional reports can be created to assist the online merchant when making business decisions. Each report should be sortable by its columns, it should be possible to apply filters, totals or average value for each column should be calculated, and it should be possible to export the report into either CSV or XML, or print it out.

Obviously, it's very important not only to be able to create those reports, but to read and understand them.

Reports can help an online merchant to plan the advertising budget, re-arrange advertising campaigns, track and to some degree forecast sale figures, find bestselling and most profitable products, manufacturers, and categories and highlight certain products by marking them as featured, locate best-buying customers and reward them, track stock and ease re-ordering of the most popular products from suppliers, track customers and use previous order history for marketing purposes, send targeted newsletters to customers, and even plan the online store's net profit figures and its profitability.

In the next chapter, we will consider how the online store can benefit from having repeat customers, and how to convert customers into repeat customers.

12

Repeat Customers

Repeat customers are those customers who come back to the online store to place another order, and, sometimes, would keep coming back repeatedly if the online store:

- Provides products the customer requires periodically or on certain repeated occasions
- Ensures that the customer is satisfied with the high-quality service provided on all stages of the purchase process, from browsing the product catalog to timely delivery of ordered goods
- Is reasonably active in communications with the customer, so that the customer never forgets about the very existence of that particular online store, and is always informed about all updates and improvements of the product catalog

Apparently those may be not the only requirements for a customer to become a repeat customer, but they are some of the most important criteria that affect whether a customer will or will not become a repeat customer.

Why Repeat Customers?

Why should an online store be bothered if its customers are eventually becoming repeat customers? What is it all about with repeat customers and why not just concentrate on product sales and not think about whether customers come back and become repeat customers?

The answer to that question is very simple. It's all about money.

There are two reasons why doing business with a repeat customer is cheaper (and more profitable!) than doing business with a new customer.

First of all, there is the so called "cost per acquisition". Usually, to "acquire" a customer the online store would have to spend a certain amount of money on advertising, PR, marketing, etc. Dividing the costs of certain advertising campaigns by the number of customers referred by those advertising campaigns to the online store will give the actual cost of each new customer's registration. Depending on general conversion rates and on advertisement costs in the selected media, cost per acquisition may vary and be hundreds of times different for different online stores.

As we demonstrated in Chapter 11 of this book, the cost per each visit (no matter if the visitor has placed an order or not), and the number of paid visitors compared to the total number of visits both play a serious role in defining the profitability of an online store and should be constantly improved to keep profitability growing or at least staying at the same level.

The more customers of an online store become its repeat customers, the less paid visitors the online store has to attract and convert into customers to produce the desired amount of turnover and profits. The more repeat customers the online store has, the more profitable is the business as there are no costs involved in motivating repeat customers to come to the online store and place an order (or at least it is considerably less expensive than motivating new visitors to come to the online store and place an order).

The second reason why repeat customers are profitable for an online store is that they refer other new customers to the online store. Recommendation from an existing customer is sometimes one of the most important and valuable factors that affect a prospective new customer's decision to place an order with one or another online store.

As we have mentioned above, attracting a repeat customer to come back to the online store can be almost free or cost considerably less than attracting a new customer. Since there's sometimes quite a valuable difference in costs, some online stores keep constantly rewarding their repeat customers with certain discounts and special offers available to the repeat customers only. That is why attracting a repeat customer to the online store may in fact cost the online store a certain amount (which is spent on discounts and special offers), even though it will still be cheaper than attracting completely new customers.

Customers and Repeat Customers

Having said all that, we now need to look more deeply into the difference between customers and repeat customers.

A customer is obviously an individual or a company that has placed at least one order with an online store. A repeat customer is ... but here definitions usually vary.

Some online merchants would consider a repeat customer an individual or a company that has placed at least two orders. So after the first order, at some moment of time, the customer decided to buy another product or several, went to the same online store and ordered them online. In fact this definition is right—as soon as the customer has placed the second order, the online merchant has received an additional profit as there were no customer acquisition costs involved into the whole second transaction.

But there are online merchants who would consider a repeat customer to be an individual or a company that has placed at least about eight to ten online orders! Of course it all depends on the nature of the product that is being sold online, on the target customer audience, and on the average margin the online store operates on. As to the margin in the previous phrase, it's quite obvious. The tighter is the average margin the online store operates on, the more the repeat visits by customers it will need to ensure the business profitability, because customer acquisition cost will be spread across all orders placed by the same customer.

If prospective customers may require products that are offered by the online store periodically (for example, consumables such as coffee, tea, wine, or printer cartridges, or spare computer parts, or collectibles such as stamps and coins, etc.) or from time to time on certain occasions (such as birthdays, anniversaries, etc.) converting customers into repeat customers and maintaining long term relationships with repeat customers becomes an opportunity for an online store to increase the profitability of the business.

Online stores may use different approaches to keep the customer interested in returning, and not starting shopping around on the Internet instead. Special business strategy can be developed to maintain relationships with the customer from the first order up until when the customer has become a definite repeat customer.

One of the possible strategies is as follows:

- After the customer has placed the first order, the online store tries to cross-sell the customer certain products or services that may be complementary to the one(s) already purchased.

- After the customer has placed the second order, and up to the moment the customer has placed the sixth or seventh order, the online store ensures the customer is always aware not only of all new products and special offers available to regular (new) customers, but, more importantly, of all new products and special offers available to repeat customers only!

- Finally, after placing several orders with the online store, repeat customers become like member of an exclusive club, where members are given certain privileges, such as: additional features (for example a Personal Calendar), special prices, discounts, and exclusive products. Some online stores may open access to certain product ranges only to repeat customers not only because of the marketing strategy, but also because new customers may not have as much trust in that particular online store as repeat customers have, so new customers may not be ready to buy certain more expensive products online. Repeat customers can also be rewarded by special delivery options (like free next-day delivery, or free Saturday delivery), or special payment options (like pay on delivery, or a credit account) that are not usually available to regular customers.

Another possible strategy could be called "recurring subscriptions". It works perfectly well for businesses that sell consumables or products that customers are likely to require periodically.

Businesses like wine stores, food stores, some clothes stores, and printer stores can benefit a lot from selling their customers not individual orders, but rather recurring subscriptions. The customer chooses the desired product type, the number of products of each type to be delivered, and the frequency—it can be anything from, for example, once a week for coffee to once in a month for wine or several times in a year for socks.

Then the online store sends the first order, and the remaining deliveries follow according to the selected frequency of the subscription.

The margins of some online businesses can be tight, and customer acquisition costs very significant, and without repeat customers their business model may not work at all.

It becomes essential that such businesses develop their strategy on how to convert customers into repeat customers, and have a clear definition of when a customer becomes a repeat customer in their particular circumstances.

How to Keep in Touch with Customers

Keeping in touch with the customers is just one of many required activities that an online merchant should undertake to see more customers converting into repeat customers.

The database of customers should be supported and updated with the latest information about the customers and their orders.

Customers who placed an order with an online store, and have received some positive experience dealing with that online store, may just not remember its name afterwards. So when they require a similar product again, they would start a new search for such products in the Internet and this time may choose a competitor's online store.

The online store should constantly remind its customers about its very existence, about improvements that take place in the business (lowered product prices, new additions to the product catalog, improvements related to delivery options and customer support, and any business achievements — like local, regional, and nationwide business awards, etc.).

The online store should motivate its customers to be active in communications.

The online store should ask customers about their experience with the website and ordered products. Repeat customer feedback, reviews, comments, and suggestions are very important. Customers should know their opinion and comments have been heard, and, if they are experiencing any problem, it will be dealt with promptly, professionally, and to the customer's utmost satisfaction.

A repeat customer has received positive experience with the online store and/or with the products purchased online — with the customer's permission the online store should use such positive feedback on the website, in printed materials, advertising campaigns, etc.

Gathering and Using Personal Information

Online merchants should be interested in getting more personal information about their customers. In osCommerce, a customer enters address and contact information during the registration process. The customer may also be invited to enter date of birth (which should never be a required field, but rather optional, unless certain age restrictions are applied to some products offered by the online store — DVD movies, printed materials, cutlery, weapons, products of undoubtedly adult nature, etc.).

To motivate a customer to order online, and create stronger relationships with the customer, having the date of birth stored in the database, the online store can automatically send the customer a special birthday discount voucher. Or for any other occasion, like national holidays, Christmas, Easter, etc. When sending a discount voucher it may make sense to highlight the fact that the vouchers are only sent to repeat customers. The feeling of exclusivity is important.

If an online store offers products that could be used as presents for people or companies on certain occasions, the idea of a Personal Calendar can be implemented in an osCommerce online store.

A Personal Calendar acts as a personal reminder to prevent customers forgetting about the birthdays, anniversaries, and other special occasions of their relatives, friends, colleagues at work, and business partners. Customers will have a facility to put any number of events into their Personal Calendars.

A number of event types and special occasions can be configured by the Administration of the online store. The online merchant can link products from the product catalog to various event types and occasions.

An automatic newsletter featuring specially selected products could be sent to a customer a week or two before each special event or occasion date from the customer's Personal Calendar. The newsletter will contain products recommended by the online merchant especially for that event type or occasion.

Of course, a text giving the customer a warm personal feeling will improve the look and feel of the newsletter.

There is no contribution available for osCommerce to implement support for a customer's Personal Calendar, but it is of course possible to hire a qualified developer to have that feature added to the online store.

Using Order History Information— Cross-Selling

A customer's order history can be of a great help to the online store, as it allows for finding out what the customer is usually interested in, and proposing to the customer other products that may also be of interest.

Even if the customer has placed only one order, it's still possible to assume the customer would be interested in this or that product based on the order history of other customers.

This conception is called cross-selling, and is used by many osCommerce online stores while the customer is browsing through the product catalog. We will consider how the cross-selling could be used to motivate customers to place more online orders.

After the order has been dispatched to the customer, the online store can send an automated email asking the customer to confirm whether the order has been delivered on time, or if the customer has any comments or suggestions on how the ordering or delivery processes could be improved. And along with that more or less standard text the email may also contain links to products that are complementary or related to the products recently purchased by the customer. If the email is sent in HTML format, links and even product images can be included.

The relations between the products could be set up either manually by the Administration of the online store, or be discovered based on analysis of orders placed by other customers.

Using Order History Information— Re-Ordering and Subscriptions

Customers could be also offered discounts on products of certain categories they have ordered several times in the past. Then the customer will be more likely to order products belonging to those particular categories again in the future, and along with those products the online store could suggest to the customer some other related products.

Re-ordering functionality can make the whole order placement process very easy and quick for customers. So if the customers of an online store are likely to order the same combinations of products periodically, the online merchant may want to consider implementing the re-order facilities in customers' accounts and making the customers well aware of such facilities.

It is even possible to offer customers a special re-ordering discount if they order exactly the same configuration or combination of products as was on one of their previously placed orders. Some customers will then get used sooner to ordering such products from only that particular online store, and will not be tempted to start shopping around when they need the same products again in the future.

Technically, the re-ordering feature would simply add a predefined set of products to the Shopping Cart of an osCommerce-based online store. If some products are not available in stock or have been removed from the product catalog, a corresponding message should inform the customer and alternative products (at least from the same category) would be offered them.

Subscription is yet another way to convert a customer into a repeat customer. Of course it very much depends on the product range that the online store has to offer. There are quite a number of products that could be sold on subscription, such as CDs and DVDs, coffee, wine, collectibles—all things that the customer may have certain preferences about, and where the customer can choose between various categories of products to subscribe to.

Subscription is convenient to customers as there's no need to place new orders every time the customer needs some of the products—instead the products are sent by the online store at the desired time intervals. Subscription is of course very convenient to online merchants, as every subscriber automatically becomes a repeat customer—if the quality of the products and service meets customer's expectations.

Implementation of the subscription feature requires advanced osCommerce development skills, and it's better to allow a professional developer to implement this feature.

Online merchants should be aware of possible issues related to storing credit card information in their osCommerce database. The best solution to avoid any security issues would be to not store credit card information in osCommerce, but rather process subscription payments outside the osCommerce-based online store, and import the results of transactions afterwards.

Unfinished Orders

Often a visitor starts the order placement process, but then either changes his or her mind or gets distracted, and as the result the order never gets completed.

Looking into conversion rates, it may be noticed that the number of customers who placed their online order is equal to or even less than the number of customers who went through the customer registration/login process, filled in their billing and delivery address details, and other information, but never actually completed their order! Some online stores lose up to 50% of prospective customers who have reached the very final step but never pressed the "Complete" button.

Good news for osCommerce online merchants! osCommerce creates a customer account during the checkout process, before the order is created. Therefore when using osCommerce, it is possible to extract information about those customers who added some products to their shopping carts, created their account or logged into an existing one, but never completed the order.

It is possible to create a special report in the Administration panel of osCommerce on unfinished orders. In fact, there's a contribution available for osCommerce called Recover Cart Sales that already does this. It can be downloaded from `http://addons.oscommerce.com/info/1688`.

Such reports provides the sales team of the online store with a facility to contact customers who abandoned the checkout process and their shopping carts. An automated email could be sent from the website to such customers, just to remind each customer about an unfinished order. There's always a possibility the customer did want to place an order but either the credit card didn't go through the payment processing gateway (but the customer would not mind paying using another card or another payment method) or the customer simply got distracted and never completed the order (but would not mind completing it now), and so on.

If the customer was going to buy some expensive goods, but abandoned the shopping cart, it may be indicating that the total order amount seemed too high for that customer. In that case, it may make sense to send an automated email to the customer several days or even weeks after the unfinished order was created and inform the customer about changes in price of those products, or about a special discount that could be only used by that customer and only by a certain date in the near future.

Since some product prices change quite often, the difference between the price the customer was quoted and the current price can be quite significant. For example, if the customer was going to buy products for total amount of $2,000, the total price of the same shopping cart can be 5% cheaper a month later, i.e. the customer would have had to pay only $1,900 — it's a $100 cheaper deal! The customer could be informed about that fact via email, especially if the nature of products the online store has to offer suggests prospective customers do not usually require them urgently.

Or, if the sale price doesn't change, but the online store would still make a good profit on the content of the shopping cart if it was sold at a price 5% or even 10% cheaper than quoted to the customer earlier — a special email with an individual discount coupon (one usage by that particular customer only) could be issued by the online store in an automated email to the customer.

Taking into account that the number of unfinished orders could be approximately the same as or even larger than the number of finished orders — motivating customers to complete their unfinished orders can significantly increase the turnover figures, and also help convert more customers into repeat customers.

Loyal Customers

Loyal customers are what ensures success of an online store. Loyal customers are repeat customers; they would always come back to the website to place an order if they required products offered by the online store in the future.

The main principle an online store should follow to gain loyal customers is very simple and straightforward—it is to be loyal to its customers! Being loyal for an online store means, first of all, providing customers with products and service of the highest quality, and also trying to provide customers with the best price. Though as a matter of fact some customers are prepared to pay a bit more for the same product if they have total trust in their supplier. The combination of the highest quality of products, service, and the best price is unbeatable, and will guarantee customers becoming loyal customers.

There are certain methods that could make more customers loyal customers, such as for example the loyalty points program.

Each product can be given its bonus value and price in Loyalty Bonus Points. Each time a customer buys a product, its bonus points value is added to the customer's Loyalty Bonus Points account.

During the checkout process, the customer is given an opportunity to use the Loyalty Bonus Points account as a payment method either for some of the goods or for the whole order (often excluding the shipping fee). If the customer's Loyalty Bonus Points account doesn't have enough bonus points to pay for the selected goods, the rest of the order amount could be paid using regular payment methods.

A special automated email could be sent to customers motivating them to use their bonus points to buy certain products. That email could list the bonus points price of products the customer can afford to buy using the Loyalty Bonus Points account.

There are several solutions for osCommerce that implement the functionality of loyalty program. One is called Points and Rewards Module and is available for download from `http://addons.oscommerce.com/info/3220`.

This solution is a Points and Rewards system, (more or like a cash back or discount system) aimed to improve online sales and get new users to sign up. The system awards shopping points to customers for the amount they spend.

According to its description, features for online merchants include:

- Enable/disable the Points System
- Enable/disable the Redemptions System — maybe you would like to offer a gift and not money back
- Set the number of points awarded for every $1.00 spent (or based on the currency system)
- Set the value of each point (based on the currency system)
- Snable/disable points awarded for shipping fees
- Enable/disable Products Restriction
- Enable/disable Points Limitation and set the number of points needed before they can be redeemed
- Enable/disable Welcome Points, and set the Points amount to be auto-credited to newly signed up customers

Features for end customers are:

- Newly registered customers can be awarded welcome points.
- Customers can earn points for every item purchased at the store.
- Customers can choose the amount of points they would like to spend to pay for some products offered by the online store.
- Customers can view their shopping points account status.

Earned reward points cannot be spent without an approval given by the Administration of the online store. Once pending points are approved by the Administration, they become available to customers. Redeemed points stay recorded in customer's order history.

Another available solution is a bit simpler, and allows for giving customers certain discounts based on the amount they have spent with the online store in the past. It's called Customer Loyalty Discount Scheme and can be downloaded from `http://addons.oscommerce.com/info/1286`.

It is possible to set different discounts depending on if the customer has spent a certain amount during certain time period. The time period can be also configured in the back end of the online store.

The discount is implemented as an order total module for osCommerce. Customers can see their discounts applicable to newly placed orders during the checkout process.

It's not only the products the customers could get Loyalty Bonus Points for; customers could refer other customers to the online store. If a referred customer places an order, the full order amount of Loyalty Bonus Points could be put in the new customer's account, but also, in addition to that, a certain amount of the order's Loyalty Bonus Points could be put in the account of the referrer. To refer other prospective customers to the online store existing customers could use the Tell a Friend-like feature to send an inviting email to their friends, relatives, colleagues, etc.

Yet another idea for an online merchant to explorer to get more loyal customers and at the same time attract more new customers, is to give customers a discount coupon that could be used either by the customers themselves, or maybe by their friends, relatives, colleagues, neighbors, and so on.

Such discount coupons should be delivered to the customer in a way that will not allow them to be missed. A discount coupon code could be issued for each customer automatically, and then printed on the invoice and dispatch note that are sent to the customer along with the ordered products. This approach will ensure the customer gets the discount coupon code.

Also, if the customer orders a present for someone else (i.e. billing and delivery addresses are different), putting a discount coupon code on both the invoice and dispatch note will ensure both the customer and the recipient of the present will get a discount coupon and may order again. The amount of the discount should be always less than the average cost per acquisition. As no or almost no expenses are involved if either the customer or the recipient of the order places another order with the online store — the deal will be always profitable for the online merchant.

Loyal customers become such when they have constant positive experience with the online store, throughout the whole pre-sale, sale, and after-sale process. Everything matters, and everything can make a difference. Simple navigation on the website, complete product description and clean and crisp images, secure and simple, straightforward checkout process, understandable confirmation emails, facility to track order status and status of the delivery, immediate availability of the customer support team, surprise gifts from the online store sent along with the order, even the way the products are packaged, all these can affect the customer's decision whether or not to place another order with the online store.

Creating positive customer experience and maintaining it on a proper level is an important duty of an online merchant.

Summary

Repeat or loyal customers are what make many online stores really successful in business. For an online store having repeat customers is profitable, first of all because if the customer places several online orders—cost per customer acquisition is spread equally between all those several transactions. Secondly, it's profitable because repeat customers will more likely recommend their favorite online stores to friends, relatives, colleagues, business partners, etc.

An osCommerce-based solution can be used to convert more customers into repeat customers. There are many approaches that an online merchant could use to increase that conversion rate, like for example motivating customers to purchase products complementary to products they have already ordered, or constantly informing repeat customers about new additions to the product catalog, and special prices only available to repeat customers, or making certain special features of the online store, special delivery and payment methods, or specific product ranges available to repeat customers only.

Customers should be motivated to become loyal customers. An online store should provide loyal customers with additional benefits, like for example Loyalty Bonus Points that could be used to pay for online orders along with other payment methods. Depending on the implementation, repeat customers can log into their osCommerce accounts and see their Loyalty Bonus Points balance and also the list of products that could be bought for those points. Or instead they could get a discount each time they place new online orders depending on how much they have already spent during the previous month or any other time period. Repeat customers could also get rewarded for referring other customers to the online store.

Online merchants should keep in constant contact with the customers, listen to their comments and suggestions, instantly and professionally deal with any issues and ensure positive repeat customer feedback is made available to as many visitors and new customers as possible.

Afterword

That chapter was the last in the book, but of course your journey with osCommerce is not finished!

Ideas and solutions described earlier in the book may or may not be applicable to certain online stores based on osCommerce or its variations.

Every business should make its own decisions and experiment a lot to find the best solution. But the best solution today, may already not be such tomorrow!

Making the most of any e-commerce website is a never-ending process of evolution, modification, and perfection. With osCommerce, online merchants receive a reliable, featured, and flexible solution to satisfy their current needs and grow further along with the business.

Index

Thank you for buying

osCommerce Webmaster's Guide to Selling Online

Packt Open Source Project Royalties

When we sell a book written on an Open Source project, we pay a royalty directly to that project. Therefore by purchasing osCommerce Webmaster's Guide to Selling Online, Packt will have given some of the money received to the osCommerce project.

In the long term, we see ourselves and you—customers and readers of our books—as part of the Open Source ecosystem, providing sustainable revenue for the projects we publish on. Our aim at Packt is to establish publishing royalties as an essential part of the service and support a business model that sustains Open Source.

If you're working with an Open Source project that you would like us to publish on, and subsequently pay royalties to, please get in touch with us.

Writing for Packt

We welcome all inquiries from people who are interested in authoring. Book proposals should be sent to authors@packtpub.com. If your book idea is still at an early stage and you would like to discuss it first before writing a formal book proposal, contact us; one of our commissioning editors will get in touch with you.

We're not just looking for published authors; if you have strong technical skills but no writing experience, our experienced editors can help you develop a writing career, or simply get some additional reward for your expertise.

About Packt Publishing

Packt, pronounced 'packed', published its first book "Mastering phpMyAdmin for Effective MySQL Management" in April 2004 and subsequently continued to specialize in publishing highly focused books on specific technologies and solutions.

Our books and publications share the experiences of your fellow IT professionals in adapting and customizing today's systems, applications, and frameworks. Our solution-based books give you the knowledge and power to customize the software and technologies you're using to get the job done. Packt books are more specific and less general than the IT books you have seen in the past. Our unique business model allows us to bring you more focused information, giving you more of what you need to know, and less of what you don't.

Packt is a modern, yet unique publishing company, which focuses on producing quality, cutting-edge books for communities of developers, administrators, and newbies alike. For more information, please visit our website: www.PacktPub.com.

www.ingramcontent.com/pod-product-compliance
Lightning Source LLC
Chambersburg PA
CBHW081501050326
40690CB00015B/2884